Montreal: 375 Tales
Drinking, Living and Loving

MONTREAL: 375 TALES OF EATING, DRINKING, LIVING AND LOVING

Kristian Gravenor

Megaforcemedia
Montreal

CONTENTS

ACKNOWLEDGMENTS

Exploring Montreal's magical past is a quest best done by lifting and strapping the heavy yarns to a flatbed and flooring it past a forest of nostalgia jammed with ancient wood huts, discotheques, vaudeville clubs, drive-serve diners and horse taxis driven by pious drivers who stop at crosses to pray. Assembling and writing this has been a brain-melting blur involving countless treks deep into obscure texts and marathon conversations with old timers.

Thanks to the following for encouragement, support and inspiration: David Ahara, John Allore, Stephen Arkilanian, Claude Aubin, Chris Barry, Chris Bashatly, Gordon Beck, Darren Becker, Nick Dagan Best, Dave Bist, Bob Blackburn, Marlene Blanshay, Steven Bodzin, Alfred Bohns, Mike Boone, Sam Boskey, William Bumbray, Justin Bur, Dan Burke, Tom Burke, Richard Burnett, Brian Busby, Velma Cabriole, Carlo Calvi, Neil Cameron, Byron Chichester, Rony Chidiac, Chimples, Kevin Cohalan, Juergen Dankwort, Graeme Decarie, Christopher DeWolf, Ann Diamond, Robbie Dillon, Denis Delaney, Jo Disensi, Michael Em, Paul Etch, David Farrell, Michael Fish, Howard Fox, Raymond Fraser, Gerry Fyfe, Holly Gauthier, Cliff Gazee, Patrick Gelinas, Billy Georgette, Jamie Gilcig, Joseph Glazner, Charles Gurd, Terry Haig, Kenny Hamilton, Marc Haumont, John Faithful Hamer, Ron Harris, Davy Hilton Jr., Alex Hilton, Peter Anthony Holder, Ian Huggins, Alan Hustak, Patrick Hutchinson, Heather Christine Irving, Jo Ann Lachance, Stephen Lack, Martin Lamontagne, Mike Lynes, Robert Lozoff, Pamela Marchant, Valerie Marchant, Liam Maloney, Anne Marie Marko, Lucas Markov, David McCall, Christy McCormick, Darcy MacDonald, Don MacDonald, Karen Mcdonald, Kate McDonnell, John McFeteridge, Mike McManus, Connie Messina, Carmen Miller,

Cathy Moore, Lori Morrison, Marc de Mouy, Brian Nation, Bernard de Neeve, Colin Niven, Taylor Noakes, Miranda O'Connor, Mike Paterson, Debbie Pierson-Maligno, Mario Pompetti, Paul Robert, Harold Rosenberg, Pat Shearing, Ilmi Siiman, Jen Solley, Stratton Stevens, Mutsumi Takahashi, Rick Trembles, Dennis Trudeau, Eric Tschaeppeler, Rob Van Hell, Kevin Vahey, Rod Vienneau, Alfie Wade Jr., Mike Wyman and Jimmy Zoubris.

Thanks to the writers and reporters whose stories have made this book possible, including Al Palmer, Edgar Andrew Collard, Alain Stanké, Tommy Schnurmacher, Norman Olson, Mary Anne Poutanen and many others.

And thanks to all of those Montrealers who have routinely shown kindness at every turn year after year, people who make Montreal the epic place it is.

INTRODUCTION

Montrealers have come and gone like snowflakes floating down onto Mount Royal, then melting and flowing into the mighty St. Lawrence. Those countless lives are only sometimes recalled by headstones and fancy-dress photos inadequately noting lifetimes full of passions, dreams and appetites.

This book aims to get to know those forgotten Montrealers by flipping the rock up on where they ate, slept, danced and created some crazy messes.

The Paris of North America, The Queen of River Cities, Vegas with Icicles, The City with 100 Steeples, Sin City and The City of Saints: Montreal has been all of those things and has uneasily withstood the chaos involved in reconciling its contradictory tendencies and competing ambitions.

This book is a time machine that transports you to wonderlands of the past. These words aim to slam you like a John Kordic uppercut and bring you on a runaway bus ride down the bald face of Mount Royal.

1

Bars

Drinkers started hanging hats and bending elbows at Montreal's first bar in 1693—Jean-François Charron's joint on Youville near St. Pierre—and Montreal's taverns, nightclubs, tiki bars, strip clubs, saloons and brasseries have, ever since, offered a bubbly liquid reflection of the soul of the city. Check your coat for this ride through Montreal's saucy past.

Neptune Tavern *121 De la Commune W. (1832-1976)* Hefty waiters in spotless white shirts served strong brown ales, bowls of pea soup and meat pies at this cozy 70-seat waterfront bar

where fights were frequent and brutal, according to resident drinking historian Charlie Swallow, who visited daily for 50 years from 1897, an era which saw his wife and two sons die of pneumonia. Newspapers alternately complained of the bar's decadence and then of its post-crackdown dreariness. Police officer Louis Cyr ended Neptune fights by locking the door, grabbing one combatant per hand and crashing their heads together. The fighters often required hospitalization and police brass asked the legendary strongman for his resignation in 1898 after six months on the waterfront beat. Female staffers were "smooth-tongued, sly-eyed sirens," who would "squeeze the hands of susceptible sailors in the upper halls of song," according to a 1909 description. But they were replaced by men "who constitute no temptation" and music was banned from the Neptune and other *café chantants,* sparking complaints of boredom. "If drinks be taken at all, they are swiftly swallowed and the drinker departs. The saloons have grown

Louis Cyr

dull and the lounges have grown comparatively few," read one lament. The Neptune gained infamy after escaped convict James Earl Ray made it his watering hole while on the lam in Montreal in 1967.

Whelan & Ray

He claimed a mysterious stranger named Raoul approached him and offered him $12,000 to commit petty acts of smuggling and to eventually assassinate Martin Luther King. James Patrick Whelan, who shot and killed Father of Canadian Confederation Thomas D'Arcy-McGee in 1868, was also a Neptune regular.

Joe Beef's Tavern *207 De la Commune W. (1870-1962)*

Bears, wolves, foxes and monkeys lived under the floor of the bar owned by gruff-but-softhearted Charles "Joe Beef" McKiernan, who ran his legendary saloon for 19 years before dying in 1889, aged 54. McKiernan—who claimed a skeleton he kept on display was his father—was a "strange, contrary, mocking man," who'd taunt anti-alcohol preachers that would drop into Canada's largest tavern to denounce drinking. McKiernan was an accomplished food scavenger for the British in the Crimean War  and used his army buyout to open a place across from the Bonsecours Market but was forced to relocate when the road was widened. One *New York Times* writer described his waterfront locale as a "den of filth," and "near what the Revised Version calls Hades." The *Daily Witness* called it a

McKiernan

"low rum hole" and denounced regulars as "poor dupes who frequent his place laugh at his vulgar wit and think him a smart man." McKiernan—who called himself "Son of the People"— sued after the paper claimed he broke a customer's arm for not paying. Friendly witnesses included a cop who claimed no fights had ever occurred at Joe Beef's. Others noted that McKiernan gave them free food, bed and medicine. McKiernan—who once fought off a bear after his son fell into its pit—ridiculed religion. "Joe trusts to the almighty dollar," he said of himself. But he donated meals to Lachine Canal strikers in 1877, without whiskey, urging them—in a rhyming speech—to avoid provoking police retaliation. McKiernan fathered four children with wife Margaret, who died young in 1871. He then married her friend Mary. The Salvation Army took it over after McKiernan died but served no liquor, resulting in swift closure. It returned as Joe Beef tavern and lasted until 1962. Other establishments, including a leather bar, filled the space for two decades following.

French Mary's *De la Commune E. & St Gabriel (c. 1879-1906)* Sailors emptied glasses aplenty at French Mary's waterfront music hall, named for owner Thomas Burdette's wife,

Sorel-born Elisabeth "Mary" Langevin, who stood six-feet and sported a corn-coloured mane. "For years she has presided over this den and last night was in one of her happiest moods; business was good and the coin kept rolling in as her customers gradually grew drunker," read a disapproving 1894 description denouncing illegal Sunday drinking at the establishment. "Seventy-five human beings were pouring down their throats the vilest of drinks, here they sat and cursed and laughed; here the busy waiters rushed from table to table and here French Mary stood with demoniacal smile, as the wealth poured into her coffers." Actors from the nearby Theatre Royal re-enacted performances, John George Arless covertly propelled beans from his trombone at unsuspecting customers, English-born Tommy Tatlock danced in clogs on a marble surface, Pit "The Frogman" Chaput did his

contortions and musicians banged out Ta-ra-ra Boom-de-ay! Mary hired only women staffers, poured beer from pumps of German silver and had no bouncer, as she simply allowed the frequent bloody fistfights—often between Irish and French customers—to continue for five minutes before ending them with a sonorous bang on the bar. A drunk slashed a father-of-seven with a knife after being expelled in 1897 and officer Émile Bujold once disarmed four "revolver-flourishing toughs." Mary remarried and died soon after in March 1896, although an alternate version has her moving to San Francisco. City officials eventually forced the bar to close.

Maples Inn *121 Lakeshore Rd., Pointe Claire (1902-1985)* A stately West Island coastal manor and boarding house was a relaxing place where "distinguished gentlemen" played cards until it picked up the pace after a ballroom was added in 1910

and new owner A.J. Verity transformed it into a hotel four years later, adding Canada's first mini-putt golf course in 1930. Willie Constant bought the joint in 1948 and made Charlie Legault's big band a magnet for live music, which peaked in the 1970s when The Mapes, as it became known, became the place where waitresses hauled trays of irresistibly fragrant pepperoni slices to underagers with fake IDs on the Caboose side. Rockers who pounded out tunes on the other side included Brian Adams, Loverboy, Michel Pagliaro, Ian Thomas, April Wine, Offenbach and Corey Hart who promised to "kick Boy George's ass" when opening for him at the Forum a few nights later (he didn't). Brian Newman became owner in 1983, a time when neighbours increasingly objected to the noise and inebriated youth venturing into backyards to smooch or pass out drunk. Newman threatened to knock the building down if he lost his liquor license but it burned down two years later.

Bagdad Café *186 Peel (c. 1923-28)* Prohibition-fleeing Americans and other swizzle stick-seeking revelers could head to Peel and St. Catherine for their gin fix, at a spot described in one American magazine as "one of the most notorious night resorts in the city." Rules be damned, booze was served until 7:30 a.m. and management could supply customers with a wide selection of female companionship on 15-minutes notice. The venue two doors south of St. Catherine was also home to "the battle of continuous dancing," overseen by Broadway producer Elmer Floyd. Previous tenant Ciro's Restaurant was once denounced for refusing Jewish patrons.

Café St Jacques *415 St. Catherine E. (1928-1974)* Co-owner François Pilon, who started as a busboy at the age of 14, had a massive place to fill. So he invited students to do their homework within the ancient stone walls of the old Bishop's Palace section

of the 1860-built Eglise St. Jacques (aka the St. James Presbytery.) Those students grew up and became regulars and their names were engraved on plaques honouring their loyalty. Police, plumbers, taxi drivers, shoe workers, longshoremen, textile workers, landlords, typists and meat packers came for meetings that routinely turned nasty, as rival fur unions feuded at the premises, as did the Canadian Alliance for Women's Vote in Quebec, while hecklers drowned out Abbé Aimé Boileau when he denounced Communism in 1930. Pilon pushed to extend opening hours to 4 a.m. in 1961 and tried to settle persistent musician labour squabbles, as a rare owner who contributed to their pension fund. Gimmick marathons were also frequent: a woman rocked on a rocking chair for 60 hours, a man danced for 36 hours straight in 1957 and radio host Frenchie Jarraud held a 100-hour marathon DJ-versus-pianist duel in which he smashed 225 Elvis Presley 45s. Its six rooms included a singalong saloon with a pianist in a straw boater, a *yé-yé* room (where 30

Francois Pilon

underagers were busted in 1965) and a bar with telephones on tables to allow customers to dial other hotties, a crowd-pleaser that helped fill the place even in the daytime. It even housed a 250-seat movie theatre. Performers included Tex Lecor, Joël Denis, Claude Valade and Willie Lamothe. The building was vacated, torched and demolished in 1974. A UQAM campus now fills the site.

Rockhead's Paradise *1082 St. Antoine (1928-1981)* A

charismatic bossman, flashy neon marquee, an upstairs with a giant round hole in the floor, all helped make Rockhead's a must-

visit spot, run by rum-running Jamaican immigrant Rufus Rockhead. The vibe was so central to Montreal's blacks that its location at Mountain and St. Antoine was simply dubbed The Corner. Musical royalty like Louis Armstrong, Pearl Bailey, Cab Calloway and Sarah Vaughan both performed at Rockhead's and also dropped in to enjoy the merriment.

Rockhead would bus to work sporting his trademark red tie and cardboard collar, handing flowers to all female patrons. He balked at shakedowns and paid the price for his stubbornness, as his liquor license was rescinded in 1952 following his refusal to pay provincial officials a $40,000 bribe. Authorities cited closing-time violations for the ruling, although Rockhead's was just one of many clubs that ignored official closing times after

Rufus Rockhead

World War II. Attempts to reverse the verdict proved futile and a

forlorn Rockhead could often be seen sitting alone amid the cobwebs of his shuttered establishment until 1961 when the Liberals returned to power and allowed him to reopen. Rockhead neither smoked nor drank but he just adored fleshy women and was quick to fire employees for tardiness or send an inadequate band packing with a full-week's salary. Rockhead suffered a stroke in

1978 and died two years later. His son sold to Doudou Boicel who moved his six-year-old Rising Sun jazz club down from St. Catherine near Bleury in 1980 but that only lasted 18 months. A forlorn parking lot filled the space until until 2016.

Venus de Milo Room *970 St. Catherine W. (1922-1981)*

The VD Room started as restaurant where you could get your

future read by Madame Hungary, a clairvoyant who sat in the lobby all afternoon in the 1930s. Calypso acts like Lord Caresser and King Dave "Bandit" De Castro hosted four-month stands in the 1950s, drawing a mixed crowd. Folk musicians serenaded beatniks in the 1960s at the sit-down, no-dance floor venue across from Simpson's department store. Groups like The Courriers and The Chanteclairs played for the longhairs while late-arriving mobster knuckle-draggers swallowed steaks until new Go-Go dancing clubs stole its business.

Café Cleopatra *1230   St. Lawrence*

(1930—) Montreal's quintessential throwback peeler joint was not always home to unpretentious strippers lit by 17 blood-red light bulbs. Needletrade reigned at the building

before Prohibition inspired the arrival of The Colorado Café (1930-35), Albion Cafeteria (1937-39), Riviera Grill (1940-45) and then the Sierra Café (1946-51), deemed so disreputable that The Sacred Heart League begged authorities to revoke its liquor license. The Café Canasta opened in 1951, with a shootout there in 1960, while a bathroom bomb claimed the personal parts of tourist Werner Prillwitz two years later. Greeks took over in 1977 and renamed it after the Elizabeth Taylor film playing at the Midway across the street. Transgender Marcelle Godbout persuaded ownership to devote its vacant second floor to gender benders, making it a pioneering haven. Owner Johnny Zoumboulakis became a folk hero to nostalgiaphiles by fending off pressure to sell out as the city aimed to sanitize the Lower Main.

Chez Maurice *1244 St. Catherine W. (1930-1949)* Phil

Maurice aimed to create the swankiest place in Canada at his Empire Building venue and that formula included singing waiters. Maurice also spent big on top acts from New York, as

Cab Calloway at Chez Maurice 1943

well as a line of 16 leggy showgirls. One typical night in 1933 featured Haskell the Magician, Barbara and Barry Leslie's Ultra Modern Dance, Wes Warren and Mildred Bodee's "beautifully blended voices and infectious good humor," as well as "eye-filling dance routines" and Jack Bain's "appropriate orchestral background." Heavyweight champ Jack Sharkey barked *Singing in the Rain* through a megaphone after a prizefight win that same year and Cab Calloway, Marlene Dietrich, Charles Laughton, Charles Boyer and Olivia de Haviland also headlined. Others were hyped with no shortage of enthusiasm: "whimsical entertainer" Sammy Walsh," Helen Wehrie "dancing star of two continents," and Frances McCoy the "pert blonde from Hollywood." Maurice sold out in 1939, citing health issues and it became

Chez Maurice Danceland, a dime-a-dance place. "There's always a hepcat session on; the girls have lost none of their pep. It is a common sight to see a poor fellow staggering around in the last stages of exhaustion while his woman is still rarin' to go," a newspaper reported. Draft dodgers were occasionally rounded up at the Danceland and military goons beat on Zoot Suiters there in 1944. Jazz legend Sarah Vaughan hit its stage in 1949, as did Brooklyn Dodgers pitcher Ralph Branca, who earned off-season bucks as a crooner. It's now a retail outlet.

Samovar / PJ's *1424 Peel (1930-1989)* Sam Cleaver's Russian-themed Samovar sat upstairs from the McCuaig & Bros financial firm near the signature intersection of Peel and St. Catherine and battled larger rivals with casts-of-dozens shows, including the pantomime stylings of Judy Magee and the sweet-singing sounds of Melton Moore.

Ballerina performer Marta "Queen of the Desert" Becket described The Samovar in her memoirs as "exquisite, a remnant of old Russia. Paintings lined the walls and pillars surrounding the dance floor. " Things soured after a horrific gay scandal at the Crescent Street apartment of the club's manager, hulking Carol Grauer in 1946. Comedian William Acorn, 22, who was staying at Grauer's, stabbed and killed boxer Lester Velez and then slashed his own throat. He survived to stand trial. It became the Caroussel for a year in 1949, then the Belmar Club for three years, where business was hurt when the King Cole Trio simply didn't show up, leading to threatened litigation. Female impersonator Armand Monroe became a groundbreaking gender-bending emcee at the club in 1957, which by now was Solly Silver's Down Beat, where gays danced together and were served by brethren for the first time in Montreal. Arsonists hit in 1965 and bookie Peter Skylar and loan shark Johnny McGuire (P & J) opened it as PJ's. It closed for 18 months in January 1981 and a returned as a dark and wild place where everything was for sale and

Armand Monroe

under-aged hustlers stood cheek-to-jowl with male dancers dangling their manhood. The gay fun disappeared when the man's-man crowd migrated east. Carlos and Pepe's restaurant has filled the space since 1989.

The Frolics / Au Faisan Doré et al *(1417 St Lawrence (1930—)* Montreal's first big stab at nightclub greatness came when gangster owners hired New York's wildest nightclub

character to push $15-a-bottle champagne. Underground speakeasy owner Texas "Hello Suckers!" Guinan, a brassy Mae West prototype, lured alcohol-deprived Americans north to legal drink. Guinan

Texas Guinan

once danced the Jelly Roll with a customer and was so impressed by his moves that she deemed him the king of the dance. All knew him as Jeli-Rol King until the day he died decades later. The Frolics was so posh that many ranked it as Montreal's greatest-ever nightclub but its bubble burst when Prohibition ended. It then plodded along as Connie's Inn after 1933, complete with highly-flammable wall treatments that offered predictably fiery results. The Casino de Parée carried the ball for four years, followed by the mob-owned Val D'Or Café whose manager Sammy Lipson playfully booked dwarf performers to dazzle alongside the Beef Trust Revue, which featured women weighing over 350 pounds. The Au Faisan Doré

(Golden Pheasant) settled in and offered French-speakers a chance at nightclub shows in their own language. The Café Montmartre also served up French song and entertainment from 1952 to 1970. Tuouynh

Au Faisan Doré artists

Restaurant (1982), The Black Lite (1987), the African-themed Coconut (1990), The Manhattan and then rap-flavoured Colors later filled the space, which has been occupied by the Kingdom strip club since 2006.

Chez Paree *1256-1258 Stanley (1932–)* Montreal's most time-honoured booze pursuit starts with a 65-step stumble down from St. Catherine to a spot now known for bikini-clad

sirens leveraging their pulchritude to distract dreams of victory from visiting hockey teams. The Chez Paree has served up more besotted indulgence than any local other show bar, dazzling yokels, wrecking families and breaking hearts and wallets through generations. Its biggest magic came in 1953

Chez Paree staff 1951

when it hosted both jazz legend Charlie Parker and a mopey Frank Sinatra, who was paid $300 for a week of comeback mojo crooning to a crowd that included gangsters like Louis Greco and Frankie Petrula lining up to kiss his ring. Chez Paree started as the Lido in 1932 and became Jeremy Taylor's Air Conditioned Tic Toc Club five years later, featuring two-orchestras (so someone would be brushing that drum kit at all times), comedians, torch singers, maybe a juggler, ventriloquist, animal or bicycle act and emcees, all for no cover charge. The Solly Silver-owned Chez Paree kicked off the 1950s with the upstairs Fontaine Bleu connected by elevator. Veteran nightclub czar Phil Maurice hired local heartthrob emcee Dino Vale, while Boston-born bar brawler Albert Lean managed the joint in 1956 until busted for dealing drugs. The club was "one of North America's leading tourist attractions," wrote blind syndicated columnist Victor Riesel after Frank Cotroni and 30 Mafia henchmen wrecked a grand piano, stole fancy mirrors and smashed a drum kit in a wanton attack in

November 1960, sending owner Solly Silver—and all clubs across North America—the message that the mob wants to see fat envelopes every week. Cops Joseph Horvath and Harry Fisk

turned a blind eye to the attack, earning them two week suspensions. The club closed but returned only to be pestered into extinction by Morality Squad cops. The Chez Paree reopened in 1982 as a posh strip club with a free lunch buffet. Dancer Christina Mitriou, 23, was shot dead driving home from work, tough guy David Joseph, 28, was shot dead outside in 2002 and fraudster Vincent Lacroix ran up a $39,000 bill at the place, money wisely spent no doubt. Chez Paree seductresses included Gerda Munsinger, who bedded two federal cabinet ministers she met at the club in 1955, and decades later Swedish Susann Branco met her future husband baseball slugger Barry Bonds there.

Magnan's Tavern *2602 St Patrick (1932-2014)* During its glory years, Magnan's was the place to name-drop at the water cooler when boasting of your everyman roots. Father-of-seven

Armand Magnan launched a humble beer hall after getting laid off from Dominion Glass, only to find workers had a prodigious thirst for his suds. Sons Yves and Hubert took over 25 years later and quadrupled its seats to 250 in 1976, with many filled by old-timers spending pension cheques on chilly Molson products. Tough-guy and unlikely Verdun mayoral candidate Roddy Diamond was barred after delivering a speech bemoaning the oppression of English in 1983 and some Irish regulars from the Point later defected to the Capri after management banned singing. Owner Yves Magnan, who served on city council, was slammed in the mid-1980s for pushing a zoning change to prevent other bars from opening nearby, at a time when crowds (men only until 1988) were lining up to get a table. Magnan's became known as a police hangout, leading to an exodus of a certain colourful element that didn't want to rub shoulders with lawmen. Employees unionized and went on strike

in 2005, with labour friction returning eight years later when a cancer-stricken manager was laid off, leading some to urge a boycott. Magnan's reputation as a working-class joint was betrayed by high-priced fare served by staffers that couldn't serve lunch fast enough to get diners back to work in time. Owners pulled the plug in 2014.

Terminal Club *1144 St Antoine (1932-1941)* Talented black Montrealers stuck in railway porter employment purgatory found sweet solace in divine melodies and rhythms at

Mastins & Davis Jr.

Mountain and St. Antoine, a spot that sat between the Bonaventure and Windsor train stations, where world-class musicians healed all wounds brought on by the working life. Billie Holiday, Dizzy Gillespie, Duke Ellington, Dot Dash, house band Mynee Sutton Orchestra (aka Myron Sutton's Swingsters), Lloyd Bacon, Johnny Hodges and Billy Wade lit up at this plain place known for its fried chicken and pot bellied stove. Bands played to packed houses until dawn, belting out jazzy Broadway tunes with piano, two saxophones and fiddle "If you ordered a bottle of champagne, the first bottle was champagne, maybe the next few bottles was watered. The odd time maybe a girl would take a trick out, but that was her business, eh?" Sutton told author John Gilmore. The Will Mastin Trio later took over as house band and a young Sammy Davis Jr.—Mastin's nephew—performed with them while living in Montreal. The spot previously hosted the Standard Café from 1915 on a strip that included the Nemderoloc ("colored men" backwards) and Utopia where manager Levi Spencer was shot in 1916.

Ma Heller's *5617 Sherbrooke W. (1934–)* Platinum-blonde, Romanian-born Jennifer Heller scooped plenty of ice cream for kids at her cigar shop near NDG Park only to see the tykes grow

Ma Heller

up and fight in World War II. Heller kept in touch, sending letters full of maternal advice to 300 soldiers a week, many of whom died in battle. Hollywood mogul Darryl Zanuck mused of making a movie of her relationship with the servicemen in 1945 and Ma promised to donate all profits to wounded soldiers but the film never materialized. Her war vets wanted beer, not ice cream and Heller snagged a license with a convoluted argument that taverns are permitted near bus stations and there was a provincial bus stop nearby. It helped that Heller was friendly with politicians and was even encouraged to run for office in 1956. She later bucked puritans by supporting a

burlesque cabaret at the nearby Empress Theatre, reasoning that veterans had earned all the girly entertainment they wanted. Heller sold in the mid-1970s and died a decade later. It briefly became the Festival Restaurant before Rosalinda Comitini and husband, West End Gang notable Peter White, rechristened it MAZ to confound language inspectors, as Peter Jr. laced up for over 200 NHL games. Mega-owner Peter Sergakis bought it and made it the Jersey Saloon in 2015.

Sextuple et al *5777 St Lawrence (1938-2010)* Sextuple owner Maurice Lemieux, who claimed half his 105 dancers were lesbians and all were bisexual, played a role in legalizing fully-nude performers in Montreal after funding dancer Stella Quinn's fight against obscenity charges, a battle that ended when courts okayed full nudity in 1975, although performer Susan Lee Bunce

was still busted four years later for "making a knot" with her intimate parts. Babette Bardot, Renée de Bec, Moon Maid and Trixie Delight all impressed but none left a mark like media-friendly Lindalee Tracey, who used the stage name Fonda Peters (fond of peters, get it?). Tracey organized an annual Tits for Tots fundraiser for sick kids before blasting the skin trade in the documentary *Not a Love Story* before dying of breast cancer at 49 in 2006. The building previously housed the Frontenac Café (1938), Café du Coin (1939-44), Café Democrate (1945-54) and El Dorado Café (1955-66) whose owner Antonio Moquin was forced to fight to keep his liquor licence. It became Au Petit Baril Café, where Mafioso felled two friends of gangster Richard Blass in May 1968 and a bomb was set off three months later, sparking a gang war. The St. Tropez Discotheque lasted four years before the Sextuple started its 16 year run in 1974, its darkest moment

Tracey

coming in September 1988 when dancers and customers were forced onto the floor while armed robbers shot bartender Denis Bedard dead. Dance club Eugène Patin was followed by Bain Douche, blown up during the biker war in May 1997. Bar Belle Gueule was replaced by Cream Underground, homeland of porn performer Carol Cox. The Syndrome was its last nightclub, with rock blasting ears for six years from 2004.

Café St. Michel *770 Mountain (1940-1955)* Wild saxophone,

frantic piano and thumping bass wowed those who ventured into Montreal's greatest-ever jazz club. Soulful virtuosos would hop

off trains, stride to Mountain Street, flip open instrument cases and blow minds with jazz sounds considered among the finest the city has heard. The magic began when the Monte Carlo Grill joined the tradition of black-themed bars near Mountain and Craig (later St. Antoine) in 1934, along with the nearby Terminal Club and Ideal Garden. It became the Café St. Michel in 1940, with music courtesy bebop trumpeter Louis Metcalf, who thrilled for a decade until returning to the States following a narcotics bust. A typical night's fare included former Duke Ellington

band singer Madeline Green, comedian Duke "Baby I'm Sick of You" Jenkins, an emcee, tap and house dancers, while future Hollywood star Percy Rodrigues manned the door. The club was remodeled in 1948 and five years later a manager and a customer were nailed for robbing a patron of $192, resulting in a pair of two year jail

Louis Metcalf

terms. Cops shuttered it and seized its alcohol in 1955, weeks after doing the same to Rockhead's Paradise across the street. (Closures which surely helped the mob-owned Montmartre, which had just launched a short-lived black entertainment policy.) The Harlem Paradise opened at the spot in 1962, boasting "everything that the show-seeker could possibly want." Otis Redding performed for free with The Hot Tamales after a show at Expo 67. Jazz greats Grant Green, Stanley Turrintine and "Fat Head" Newman also hit its stage. Outlaw owner Adrien Dubois shot rival upstart Bryce Richardson in the club in April 1967, leaving Richardson in bad shape.

Algiers/Aldo's *1061 Mountain (c. 1940-1973)* Gunslingers, judges, jazz musicians, pugilists and outlaws fraternized at what was previously a four-woman bordello run by Madam Blanche

BORED?

Join the Fun at Aldo's . . .
and see
The Top Stars of . .
BURLESQUE
Continuous Shows Nightly

NO COVER, MINIMUM, ADMISSION

ALDO'S
1061 MOUNTAIN ST.
866-9072

until authorities tired of the high toll of venereal disease among soldiers aiming to take down Hitler, so they had it shut down. It became the short-lived but much-referenced Algiers Club, considered one of the most extravagant on the continent, under Albert "The Syrian" Lean and co-owner Joe Delicato, whose wife was another famous Montreal madam. Shisha pipes and waiters wearing fez hats were on tap in what was "one of the roughest and readiest joints around," according to columnist Bruce Taylor. It became Aldo's under ownership that included mobster Frank Scanzano, his brother Leo (whose house was bombed in 1961), wrestling promoter Eddie Quinn and former ex-NHL defenceman Jimmy Orlando, who managed it with brothers Johnny, Joe and Frank.

Orlando

The food was good, dance-oriented stage shows adequate and there was no dance floor, so no chance of your sweetheart dragging you up to do The Twist. Jimmy Orlando, known in his NHL days for staying on ice after sustaining a gaping head wound, ran the club in the same fearless spirit. Gangster Charles Wagner brawled with Aaron Marks at Aldo's and then killed him at his rooming house hours later, setting off a string of murders in 1951. Orlando split in 1960 but Aldo's kept rolling with "10 exotic beautiful dancers," including Colette Chabot, 19, busted for stealing a ring from an American tourist in 1966, while four young toughs beat up a Morality Squad cop at the bar the next year. The area south of Dorchester had, by that time, lost its charm. Aldo's lost its liquor license in 1973 and was razed soon after, remaining a parking lot for decades following.

Esquire Show Bar *1224 Stanley (1940-1972)* Sam

Cleaver's club downstairs from the proper Palais D'Or Ballroom (aka Stanley Hall) was a run-of-the-mill show bar until the

landlord hiked the rent in 1948. Cleaver dealt an interest to Norm Silver who rolled the dice on rock'n'roll after overhearing teens at his Miss Montreal restaurant raving about the new sound. Emcees, $35-a-week showgirls (paid also to mingle with customers), torch singers, acrobats and comedians were sent packing and skeptics waited for it to flop. But the Esquire thrived thanks to week-long visits from acts like Bo Diddley, Wilson Pickett, Little Richard, Fats Domino, Bill Haley and Chubby Checker and even Jerry Lewis and Dean Martin. Drummer Rudolph White barely survived a 1958 stabbing, American tourist Joseph Cohen, 19, suffered a savage 1963 beating, armed robbers surprised manager Alfred Vallée to grab a $8,000 weekend-take later that year. Others beat a sailor in in 1965. Silver had teen musicians

Kenny Hamilton and Trevor Payne come in after school and flip through Billboard magazines to recommend affordable bands to booking agent Roy Cooper.The Manhattans, Edwin Starr, Jimmy Ruffin played, as did locally-grown Robert Charlebois, who was a hot 1969 ticket. Provincial authorities claimed that the place was

King Curtis at the Esquire

crawling with prostitutes in 1972—same as any other downtown bar—and yanked its liquor license, its subsequent closure breaking hearts of many music fans. The venue was born as the 1930s Kit Kat Cabaret and Chesty Morgan performed when it became Les Filles d'Eve strip club in the 1970s, with the old "Esquire Showbar" mosaic still tiled into the floor.

Swiss Hut *394 Sherbrooke W. (1942–1972)* Young boozers came of age exchanging views in this cosmopolitan place where constrictive booth seating prevented drinkers from engaging in spontaneous, ideologically-inspired fistfights. Swiss Lena Haefliger launched the Swiss Hut Restaurant in the old Stadium Café space during WWII with celebrated waiter Bill Miller hauling chickens-in-a-basket in a homey log cabin atmosphere that included hand-shaped wooden coat racks affixed to booths. Serious

Auf der Maur

dining happening in front while out back 20 booths of thirsty souls guzzled affordable quart bottles. *Refus Global* art rebel reformists, LSD dealers, students from McGill and the *École des Beaux-Arts* rolled in, as did journalist Nick Auf der Maur, a boulevardier and chronic bum-pincher, who barman Nick temporarily barred after Auf der Maur's female friend covered the bathroom with anti-Canada *"100 ans d'injustice,"* stickers. Auf der Maur brought friends ranging from dancer Rudolph Nureyev to young mogul Conrad Black.

Sportsmen's Tavern *1486 Mansfield (1944-1971)* This basement alehouse featured lengthy tables where a mix of gays, students, war veterans and CN train employees shared views on nuclear disarmament, Freud, Marx and hockey goaltenders. The tavern scored a license that permitted it to stay open until 1 a.m., one hour later than competitors and regulars would come down the stairs and see waiter Gaetan placing a brew at their table even before they sat down. Regulars included Walt Huston, a stand-up bass player who told war stories and of his lineage as a descendant of composer Anton Dvořák. Beer was cold and cheap at just 40 cents a quart in the 1960s, a price that rivaled The Lodeo as Montreal's most affordable. What started as the Mansfield Tavern in 1944 became the Sportsman in 1957 but the Simpson's department store, which owned the building, opted to demolish the structures in 1971 because they were "uneconomic to maintain." A parking lot then occupied the site for decades.

Café de l'Est *4558 Notre Dame E. (1944-1997)*

A remote booze barn first tried its luck in the 1930s as the Democrat Club, and wrestler Yvon Robert had it named after him for a brief time

before the 600-seat Café de l'Est began its reign near the waterfront at Bennett, a 15-minute drive from Peel and St Catherine. Actor and emcee Armand Marion offered bilingual introductions of interpretative dancer Germaine Giroux, war veteran Eddie Sanborn's Black Cat Orchestra, singers Patrick Norman and Muriel Millard. So impressive was 14-year-old Ginette Reno's 1960 debut that talent show organizer Jean Simon leaped to become her manager and she became his meal ticket. Toga-clad yé-yé pop band *César et Les Romains* took the club by storm when

Ginette Reno

they came from Noranda in 1966, while mentally deficient and mentally ill performers took to its stage in 1969 to bumble through song and dance performances in front of up to 400 jeering and mocking viewers. Promoters defended the spectacle, which saw the winner take a prize of $5 or $10, but

César et Les Romains

authorities ordered it stopped after three years because the performers "had no contact with reality." The biker-friendly Xanadu Club took over in 1981 and a 23-year-old lost his legs to a bomb outside in 1986 (a 20-year-old waiter was also shot dead driving home in 1965). Club l'Énergie took over in 1986 with DJs MC Al and Rick trying to make famous their Double Funk Sound. Hells Angels settled in and biker bombings led authorities to revoke its liquor permit in 1997. The building burned down a year later and now forms part of a vacant streetscape.

Slitkin & Slotkin's et al *1235 Dorchester W. (1946-1983)*

Boxing promoters Lou "Slitkin" Wyman and Jack "Slotkin" Rogers punched above their mythological weight, thanks to their Runyonesque patter between 1946 and 1951. "Listen to what I have to saying yet and maybe you wouldn't feel so good either,

"Slotkin" Rogers

after you return me my change what the waiter left for me, not for you, my fine friend of a partner," said Slotkin. "It's like this, enyhoo. As you know I do not go for 'rassling myself, even though I am about to go into the Forum and get a laugh at the antiques of Quinn's actors," said Slitkin. Former hearse driver Joe "Meat Wagon" Brown slung drinks for boxer-turned-tailor Maxie Berger, who inspired Morley Callaghan's *The Many Colored Coat* about an editor mocking a tailor for a poorly-sewn jacket, while Al Palmer immortalized it as the Breakers Bar in *Sugar Puss on Dorchester Street*. Louis Bercowitz came on July 25, 1946 after killing mob boss Harry Davis on Stanley Street. Palmer brought him to *The Herald* where Ted McCormick typed up a big scoop confession. Scribes Elmer Ferguson, Harold McNamara, Jim Coleman, Dink Carroll were regulars, as was Alfred de Marigny, acquitted in the murder of millionaire Harry Oakes. The duo, whose nicknames came from a Cohan and Watson comedy skit popular at the Gayete in the 1920s, also welcomed boxer Johnny Greco and baseball star Roy Campanella, ads boasted. The All American Bar and Grill lured tourists after 1951 with singing pianists, dancer Marlene Hall and a "certain intimate style of entertainment which has become a Montreal hallmark." Gangster Frank Pretula hired boxer Charlie Chase and friends to shoot up the joint in

Where Everyone Goes Before and After Every
Big Sports or Theatrical Event
Slitkin & Slotkin
CAFE & RESTAURANT
The Place for
Good Food
COCKTAIL LOUNGE & BAR
1235 DORCHESTER ST. WEST
For Reservations—Platau 8906 - 6273

July 1955. Former wrestler Denise Cassidy said English and French women didn't mingle much when she ran is as the city's first lesbian bar Baby Face from 1975 to 1983. It was demolished soon after.

Café André *2077 Victoria (1946-1981)* Slightly beyond chuckle range of McGill University's Roddick Gates on Sherbrooke sat "The Shrine," a three-storey Victorian greystone

that attracted ambitious comedians and folk musicians. Cut-up comics included Dave Broadfoot, Dan Ackroyd and Tom Kneebone, who quipped that his endless on-stage practice taught him "how to dodge plates and get out a back door real fast." The venue started as The Good Luck Tea Room in 1936, with proprietor Mrs. Lazar offering 25 cent lunches for students. Café André took over a decade later and was where you needed only "45 cents for a quart of beer and a voice loud enough to be heard in the sing-song," wrote Al Palmer. Hard-drinking Welsh poet Dylan Thomas, according to legend, got his booze-on after a McGill appearance in 1952, about 500 days before drinking himself to death in New York City. The Up Tempo Revue troupe regularly served up what columnist Nick Auf der Maur described as "the best comedy I've ever seen" after launching in 1957 with a cast that included

Montrealer Wally Martin (who later died of cirrhosis of the liver at age 57) while cast member Joan Stuart struck up a near-marriage romance with Sammy Davis Jr. after meeting him in Montreal. Folk music became a staple after 1961, with 21-year-old Penny Lang packing them in for 36 sets a week until sidelined by bipolar disorder. Business dipped after McGill's Student

Union moved uphill to the McTavish Building in the mid-1960s. By the early 1970s its doors were occasionally padlocked by creditors and management severed ties with the Montreal Folk Workshop in 1973 because "people just don't like folk music anymore," as manager Jimmy Arvanitakis bluntly put it. The building was demolished in the early 1980s.

Bellevue Casino 375 *President Kennedy W.* *(1948-1961)*

Harry Holmok made enough loot at his Vienna Grill across from what's now the Papineau metro to launch a 700-seat budget

show bar at Bleury, just east of the downtown core. By his logic, if he could keep prices down—beer and a show for less than $2—he'd pack the joint. And so he did, as the 1,400 nightly customers, 2,000 on a Saturday, earned him enough to hire 100 staffers and $10,000-per-

Holmok, left, & The Boulevardiers

week acts from New York. Success was not assured, as 15 clubs offered similar floor shows, while 25 others had smaller shows. Holmok banked on acts like Trixie's *Watch it Bounce* and the Wong Sisters' *Chinese Dancing Dolls* to fill Canada's largest nightclub. Chorus line legs flew high, house singer Charles Danforth howled his tunes and Bill Deegan emceed, while patrons craned necks waiting for tables. Singer Pearl Fields tired

of hearing management complain about cigarette sales, so she piled packs on a tray and made the rounds, becoming the first cigarette girl to push cancer sticks in the already-smoky air. Martha Adams, the high-profiled 1960s madam,

started out as a Bellevue Casino dancer, while performers included Sammy Davis Jr. and Alan Mowbray, who brought his surely-electrifying English butler routine in its late days. Holmok died in 1961, the nightclub closed a few months later and a few months after that, Holmok's co-owner and brother-in-law Jack Suz died at age 33. Costly chandeliers and carpets were rescued before the building was expropriated and demolished in September 1962.

Skyways Lounge *1080 University (c. 1949-1968)* Postwar

Montreal got a shot in the arm when the United Nations implanted its International Civil Aviation Organization in a

shiny new building in what had been the Dorchester pit at Central Station. The newly-arrived diplomats complained bitterly about chilly Montreal winters and conspired to move the organization to somewhere warmer, sharing frostbite gripes over martinis at the

Skyways. Aviation diplomats enjoyed lofty liquid lunches over easy-listening tunes provided by early-1960s Hammond organist Connie Marson. The ladies bathroom offered an automated perfume dispenser, slam a dime down the slot and *s-s-spritz!* you're scented for the evening. Ralph attended to all appetites at the building, which offered a good view of Mount Royal until the upstart Place Ville Marie arrived to obscure the view.

Blue Angel Café *1228 Drummond (1949-1992)*

Drummond Street was a teetotaler compared to its Golden Square Mile neighbours but an exception came with fiddles,

cowbells and six-string guitars accompanying tales of dogs dying and lovers leaving. The country music began

Bob Fuller

when the Blue Angel took over from the Palace Provisions grocery store and held its own against country music competitors the Country Palace on Sherbrooke and the Wagon Wheel on Union. The Blue Angel attracted purists with the highest of standards, a club best-known for Bob Fuller's Monday evening Hillbilly Night, a sacred event for old time fans of live country music where no music written after 1965 was permitted and instruments remained unplugged.

French Casino *1224 St Lawrence (1951-1969)* No dice were tossed at this so-called casino, which borrowed its monicker from a New York nightspot and found an identity as a place where uniformed sailors would strut and fights were plentiful. The French Casino—one door south of the Café Canasta (now Cleopatra's)—offered live jazz and comedians but was mostly celebrated for its exquisite and pulchritudinous dancers. Chaos often reigned, such as the night in 1955 when patron Roger Lévesque fired at cops, hitting an officer in the arm. He was given a vigorous 10 hour police interrogation that required two weeks of hospitalization. Such Lower Main mayhem prompted authorities to order area bars shut at midnight, a bylaw that lasted for three years until Pal's Café owner Vic Cotroni had it overturned in 1958. French Casino shake dancing attraction Tangerine Hopson made news that year when she married Philadelphia lightweight champ Bob Montgomery over the phone. Their telephone union didn't last, alas as they divorced soon after.

Alonso

Dancers Rita Delmar, Kitty Karr and Sayed Samal pleaded guilty to indecent dancing the next year but the police attention didn't hurt the bottom line, as the next year the club signed rising Cuban temptress Chelo Alonso to a six-month contract. She sought to wriggle out of it though, noting that the commitment kept her away from her Italy-based film career, which included a role in *The Good, the Bad and the Ugly*. Fire damaged the building in October 1964 and it closed five years later. The Katacombes punk bar called the venue home for a short time around 2007 before the building went vacant.

Casa Loma *94 St. Catherine E. (1951-1971) Chanteurs,* slick-haired emcees and hardened Mafioso filled Andy Cobetto's multi-level club, where *Shooo-ootime!* as he called it, entailed acts

like Pierre Lalonde, Ginette Reno and Alys Roby. The club launched after such show bars had started a slow decline, but Miles Davis, Duke Ellington and John Coltrane filled its Jazz Hot Bar and it found a hit with the *New Nude Musical Revue* starring Marilyn Apollo, which was held over in 1970. The bar

included a strip club, a disco and the Jacques Antonin Bar, described by some as the Mafia's motherhouse, during a time when the Dubois Brothers gang was attempting to muscle in on the area. Thugs were drinking after hours on March 12, 1971 when Jean-Marc Morin, 32, shot a customer and a bartender dead before fleeing. Bar staff—including Mafioso Joe Di Maulo—ushered Morin's companion Jean-Claude Rioux to a back room and killed him. Stripper-eyewitness Paulette Gingras switched her story so many times in the ensuing marathon trial that all were acquitted. Male strippers took over the venue in 2002 with the arrival of Club 281.

Toe Blake Tavern *1618 St. Catherine W (1952-1983)* Imagine the Habs' coach managing the tavern where you quaff your post-game suds and then picture that coach quitting the

team after winning his 11th Stanley Cup so he could devote his efforts to his beer hall. It really happened in 1968, as Toe Blake left the Canadiens because he had "no more worlds to conquer." Blake ran his place like a hockey team, banning bearded men and keeping females out, even after laws made it easier to welcome both genders. Blake berated an Ontarian who brought his girlfriend inside. "Ever heard of Rocket Richard? I taught him everything he knows and now I'm going to teach you a lesson!" Waiters Vic, Gaetan, Frank, Lucien, Roland and Cliff hauled steak and fries to solid wood tables which sometimes hosted heads slumped in

Blake & fan on final night

beer-fueled daze, while a cop cruiser sat permanently out front and the sound of bowling balls hitting pins from the upstairs alley rattled nerves of those unaccustomed. Blake's final years at his tavern were as hard as the years he spent working as a miner, he told a reporter. A female TV news reporter was not allowed inside on its final night, as Blake shook every customer's hand on their way out. He coped with dementia before his death a dozen years later.

The Edgewater *228 Lakeshore (1953-1985)* A 12-year-old boy gazed at the Edgewater Hotel and was infected with a dream of one day owning the place. "I almost fell over," said a grown-up

Tony De Vito when he realized his dream as part-owner. But faulty wiring led to a devastating blaze in 1964 and De Vito set up a makeshift restaurant tent while construction crews buzzed all around. De Vito's family construction firm unveiled the new establishment in 1970, which now had a hotel, restaurant, pub, the Marina Disco, The Vista Lounge and a sizable 300-seat terrace. De Vito laid faith in calypso musician Earl Haywood to bring music lovers, while other acts included doomed crooner Guido Pucci, the Perry Carmen Trio, King Eric and the Knights and aging belly dancer Fawzia Amir, who did her farewell hip thrusts in 1970. Visiting violinist Florian Zabach left a priceless 18th century

Guarnerium violin lying around in 1976 with predicable results. It was later recovered in the hotel trash. A rowdy buck-a-beer atmosphere reigned in later years and workers attempted to unionize, complaining that they were forced to buy their own uniforms. Pointe Claire purchased the property—which was originally opened by W.P. Harlow way back in 1932 as the Pointe Claire Hotel—for $1.8 million, putting an end to the entertainment. It became green space in 1996.

The Palomino *1691 Wellington (1953-1987)* Point St. Charles had no shortage of bars, including the 1 & 2 on Butler, the Wellington Pool Room, The Olympic Tavern across the street The Fiesta on Centre, the Westlake Tavern, The Capri and

Magnan's which all offered a well-oiled brotherhood of blarney. White's became the Paddock Tavern and then the Sports Tavern, operated by Ambrose the Ukrainian who'd serve suds to night-shift workers from Northern Electric and CNR at 7 a.m. Ambrose scooped much free ice cream for kids before marrying and moving away. The Palomino took over as a country-themed bar run by Richie Matticks and Dougie Nimo, a killer known to move large quantities of cocaine. One regular toted a bum-pinching ventriloquist's dummy and shot a gun into the ceiling while singing an Irish tune, a display that impressed visiting gangster Adrien Dubois. "Tabarnac! You guys are crazy like us!" he screamed. Patrons tossed bottles in the dark during one power outage while Vance the Greek and a doorman ducked and giggled at the madness. Customers were difficult to dislodge at closing time, so management turned off the heat an hour before closing. Tough-as-nails doorman Mike McManus was shot six times inside the bar in an incident in 1987 but he miraculously survived. Flames, however, killed the bar a month later. The building later became a rooming house.

El Morocco / Your Father's Mustache *1443 Closse*

(1954 – 1987) Elvis impersonators and hard-working rock quartets attracted mullet-haired rockers inside this red stone

structure in the 1970s, in a venue that began as the El Morocco, which was previously on Mansfield, then Metcalfe, both also above St. Catherine. Monique "The Girl in the Champagne Glass" Monet was arrested at the El Morocco and charged with obscenity in 1960 but a judge blasted police instead, declaring the show an entirely non-shocking underwater-ballet routine. Esquire Show Bar's Norm Silver purchased the struggling club in 1966 and used it as a venue for small-scale Broadway shows before settling on a retro theme, calling it Norm

Silver's Mustache Club with staff clad in straw boaters and seersucker suits. Al Jolson tunes, silent films and singalongs made the place a hit during Expo 67. Bands like the Wackers sweated it out for eight sets a night over nine weeks in

front of a 1970s Camaro-driving crowd sometimes inclined to indulge in epic fistic battles between jocks and bikers. Silver got too old to motor to work in his 1978 Lincoln Continental to collect $2-a-head profits for Ozzy Osbourne and Anvil shows. It closed to become offices for rock promoter Donald K. Donald.

Lodeo Café *1050 St Lawrence (c 1955-1987)* Country acts

like Slim Rogers and the cheapest beer in town attracted unpretentious drinkers to the Greek-owned Rodeo Café, where a gun battle between pimps broke out in November 1961, leading to an attempted murder charge. "There's bound to be more trouble," manager Billy Bactis unreassuringly promised. Hippies ventured in but barely watched lowbrow shows starring budget magicians sawing women in half. Tiger, a tall blonde lesbian junkie hooker who worked at a nearby hot dog joint, was one of many dead-end regulars who inspired playwright Michel Tremblay's *Sainte-Carmen of the Main* (1976), set at the bar. The Chans owned the building and took over the bar in 1972,

renaming it to what everybody had been calling it for years, the Lodeo—out of respect, or disrespect—for the Chinese pronunciation. Degenerates recall its later years as a strip club managed by tough guy Mike Stemkowski who was always wary of ejected patrons returning with violence. "It's the guys that don't say anything that you got to watch," he said. It became a strip venue that cops closed for 18 months in 1985, with an undercover officer describing sex for sale as the most flagrant he had seen. A Chinese grocery replaced it in 1987 and burned down 20 years later.

The Mocambo *2591 Notre Dame E. (1956-1965)* Good looking man-about-town and pro wrestler Johnnie Rougeau was the face of this well-east-of-downtown riverside club, which

enjoyed its greatest moment when an unknown 14-year-old Stevie Wonder tickled its piano in 1964. Mild-mannered Quebec City nightclub king and French language teacher Pierre Thibault owned it at the outset but Rougeau stepped up with a hefty $800,000 in 1958. Manager Hyppolite Ross brought it to life with help from Nat King Cole, Chubby Checker, Frank Lymon and Fats Domino. But most often on stage were female contortionists, comedians, acrobats and singers such as Joe Valnil, The Field Sisters, a trained dog show and the aggressively-promoted Carmen Deziel. Rougeau hired pro wrestling friends, including Gerard "Gerry Bright" Duchesne. Police questioned them both over vote-rigging for fledgling Liberal MNA René Lévesque in 1960 but the affair was quickly forgotten. The club

attained immortality when it was featured as a comfy refuge for a snow clearing duo in the feel-good film *La vie heureuse de Léopold Z.*, which attracted big audiences in 1965. Authorities suspended its liquor license and Rougeau sold in 1965. The strip was demolished for a highway that never got built.

Champs Sho Bar *1220 Crescent (1960-1970)* This va-va-voom skin joint was once the lone watering hole on the Crescent strip, offering 20 pastie-clad dancers overseen by owner Jimmy Orlando who was forced into early NHL retirement due to war enlistment-type legal troubles in Detroit. Dancers Santana, Kelly Barton and Mary "Irish Colleen of Burlesque"

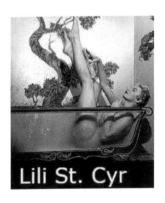

Lili St. Cyr

Kelley headlined at the 250-seat club, which had taken over the premises from the much-sleepier Danube Restaurant. Naughty, well-fed, stand-up comedian Tubby Boots was a frequent attraction, while a 47-year-old Lily St. Cyr stripped fully naked for the first time in Montreal at the jam-packed bar in 1965. Police arrested the aging temptress two years later, deeming her on-stage bubble bath routine unacceptably obscene. Emceee Kevin Hunter enforced audience participation by vigorously ensuring customers competed in the Twist dance-off. Police kept raiding the club and busting manager Fred Loyello until it closed in 1969. The building later housed various restaurants and bars, including the Mad Hatter, before being replaced by a condo tower in 2013.

The Sahara Club *374 Sherbrooke W. (1960-1968)* Arab custom proved far sexier than Montreal's sexually-repressed Catholic ways, as proven nightly at Fawzia Amir's Sahara belly

dancing nightclub, which showcased female flesh for cultural enrichment. PR hustler Norman Olson raised Amir's profile by writing her a serious-sounding speech entitled "The Role of the United Nations in Peacekeeping and its Relationship to Belly Dancing," and he had her ride a Granby Zoo camel to a car dealership to swap for an Austin Mini. Gambling boss Harry Ship persuaded Amir to relocate to Montreal in 1957 and supplied her with a basement venue that became Canada's only Arabian-themed nightclub.

An oversized postcard from admirer King Farouk of Egypt welcomed guests who could expect to be pulled onstage to sway alongside the low-belted temptresses. Amir battled to keep those tummies rotating after Mayor Jean Drapeau invoked an obscure zoning bylaw in an attempt to revoke its booze license. Amir beat an obscenity rap by dancing for a judge in court in 1961, averting a deportation bid in the process.

A gunman pumped a pair of bullets into Harry Ship's legs at the club the next July, sidelining him from the gambling scene. In later years Amir would skip work to hit the racetrack with her squeeze, the movie star Omar Sharif. The Sahara fused rock bands with Go-Go and belly dancing when it moved to 1177 Mountain in 1966. Fires and cop raids made that stay brief.

The Seven Steps / Rainbow *1430 Stanley (1960-1984)*

Robert "Bicycle Bob" Silverman was a self-described "bum" when he hosted a Seven Steps bookstore opening bash attended by

literary stars Irvin Layton and Louis Dudek. He allowed shoppers to read for hours without buying. "My friends thought I was nuts but I don't care," said Silverman, whose goal was "not to make money." He succeeded. Morris Feinberg's The Pot Pourri moved in with acts like Bob Dylan, who played four nights for $125 in June, 1962 (and one show at The Finjan on Victoria). Young Gary Eisenkraft briefly oversaw a folk venue, as did Jacques Labrecque with his basement Blue Lantern. Caged Go-Go dancers shook miniskirts at The Sans Souci and Jerry's Go Go Club after 1966 before La Lune Rousse came in 1968, managed by ill-fated killer Bryce Richardson. Short-lived Seven Steps Pub closed after a biker shot at police. Sir Winston Churchill staffers Don Woodward and Judy Ponting opened The Rainbow as a laid-back place but staff was ready. "Violence upsets me but if it has to be, I'll tear the guy's head off," promised bouncer Gord Ruland. Sociologist Taylor Buckner paid $8,000 for a one-ninth share in 1972, with its "clouds of tobacco smoke shimmering in the 25-watt gloom. Heavy conversations. Beards drooping onto chessboards." He concluded that "bars provide a synthetic primacy group where within a week someone could have a circle of friends." Actor Michael Pollard settled a tab with a Bible illustrated by Salvador Dali. W.C. Fields III limoed there while searching for grandpa's scattered bank accounts. David Wittman, from Toledo, Ohio, became doorman, then bartender after blowing his European travel cash on beer. He and wife Nancy Nelson, who sold $1 roses in bars, drained clientele after opening Darwin's on Bishop Street in 1976. Schlomo Prizant purchased the Rainbow for $3,000 and started requiring respectable attire. It died soon after.

Peppermint   Lounge *1182   St   Lawrence*

(1962-65) Solomon Schapps, aka Solly Silver, had a higher purpose for his club located in the magnificent *Monument National* on the crime-riddled Lower

Main, Montreal's most-hardened artery. Silver promoted peace by inviting youngsters to dance Chubby Checker's The Twist instead of popping goofballs and shanking each other in alleyways. "How can anyone plan crimes while they're doing the Twist?" Silver noted that dancing also promotes fitness. "It reduces the waistline and gets get rid of the blubber." The club later embraced "low down funk," "Sound a Go-Go" or "Deep South Music," as performed by Jay Jay and the GoGos, whose leader Charles Izeard was "steeped in the traditions of his race." Silver was irritated when co-owner Colin Gravenor purchased the *Monument National* but the deal collapsed after many objected to an Englishman owning the symbol of French Quebec. The club closed after brass snubbed bribe-thirsty cops who then came nightly to card patrons. Similar cop shenanigans toppled its successor. The club borrowed a name from a Manhattan hotspot but had no connection to an eponymous topless club at 5777 St. Lawrence.

Casa Del Sol *2025 Drummond (1962-1969)* Jammed
between the old figure skating rink and the hollowed-out Drummond Court sat a bar that—like so many of us—started out with the noblest of intentions before turning wicked. Julio Peidra, said to be the world's greatest flamenco dancer, headlined in the heady summer of 1962 and the next year Eartha Kitt and her grown-up daughter Kitt McDonald hit its stage together. It gained further traction when its Chef Navarro taught TV host Pierre Berton how to cook paella. But the dignity would not last. Willie Cohen's joint, which included the upstairs Kismet Room, was soon devoting itself to semi-clad women, who practiced

something called "tummy tossing," an unexplained trend that one columnist insisted "was catching on." The club became a clip joint, scamming tourists visiting for Expo 67. One Japanese visitor called police after he was charged $600 on a $150 tab. A

liquor board hearing exposed the club's watered-down drinks scam in which 10 waitresses and dancers supposedly consumed a mind-numbing 2,340 drinks in 17 working days but still managed to perform their duties. The owner said he was oblivious to such offences and only wanted the business to stay alive. It did not. Police hammered it shut with the newly-contrived bylaw banning mingling between customers and staff but not before management trapped Morality Squad Chief Paul Boisvert into an undisclosed act that led to his resignation.

Brasserie Iberville *5195 Iberville (1963-1975)* "To the head! To the head!" was the blood-chilling chant heard in what was by far Montreal's most dangerous bar. Trouble started in

Ellefsen & Forget

1975 when Devil's Disciples bikers Gilles Forget and Claude Ellefesen disagreed over who should pay for a newly-built meth lab. Forget soldier Philippe Beerens, 19, threatened Ellefsen inside the bar and was soon after found dead at his apartment. Gaetan Poulin was kidnapped from the place in May and the same fate befell five Ellfesen soldiers kidnapped from the bar on June 11 and never seen again. The next day a busboy and another hood were shot dead in the club as onlookers chanted their encouragement. Police made some swift arrests. But that didn't end the chaos. Three men locked seven customers and four employees in a bathroom and set off an explosion on June 25. All fled to safety just in time. The place opened as *Taverne des Sportifs* in 1963 and is no longer a bar.

Spanish Association / Casa Pedro 485 *Sherbrooke*

W., 1471 Crescent (1964-1986) Andalusian *tavernero* Don Pedro
Rubio-Dumont's love of poetry and art helped create a bar so

lively that Montreal's most discerning
booze hounds pronounced him the
city's real minister of culture. Rubio-
Dumont opened the humble Spanish
Association above Johnny's Hideaway
snack bar on the north side of
Sherbrooke near City Councillors on
what was then a buzzing nightlife strip.

The place was meant to close at midnight but
Rubio-Dumont persuaded police that Spaniards
sleep in the afternoon and thus require extended
nocturnal revelry. Bearded chinwags full of lofty
impractical notions were conferred legitimacy in
liquor-fueled *filosófico discusión* attended by such
frequent visitors as politicians Pierre Trudeau and

Don Pedro

Jacques Parizeau, sculptor Armand Vaillancourt and journalist-
boulevardier Nick Auf der Maur, who discouraged FLQ terrorist
regulars from blowing things up, to the benefit of all. The
Spanish Association carried on without Rubio-Dumont until
1980, as Pedro moved to Crescent and De Maisonneuve with
help from landlord Johnny Vago. The Casa Pedro lured drinkers
away from Mountain to Crescent, wiping out high-flying Pierre
Bourgetel who was forced sell his eponymous nightclub and
become a prison cook. The Casa Pedro poured sangria for artists
who mingled with receptionists, preps and jocks, many enjoying
a top-notch window view onto students, office workers and
steno clerks. Giant Jean Ferré , aka André the Giant, undertook
epic feats of drinking at the bar, which was once attacked by a
crazed arsonist and also targeted by kidnappers who briefly took
off with Pedro's nephew in 1983. Pedro also served as president
of a mediocre Supra pro soccer team in the late 1980s and
attempted to bring bullfighting to town. He retired in 1986 and
died nine years later.

Chez Mado Cabaret *10181 Pie IX (1965-2015)* The seeds of the second-floor peeler joint on Pie IX were planted after a mother sold her home for $11,000 and opened a snack bar in order to support her two daughters. Madeleine "Mado" Groulx soon added a mini-putt golf course and a swimming pool out back and the place became a magnet for families on summertime ice cream-seeking missions and splashfest quests. Mama raised her young ones upstairs from the shack-like structure. The snack bar eventually graduated to social dancing and live music in 1967, when Mado sold

Mado Giroux

her 1962 Pontiac in order to purchase the club's first liquor inventory. It switched to daytime-only nude dancers in 1972 and the strippers proved to be a lucrative draw, so the apartments were ripped out and the strip club expanded upstairs two years later. Groulx sold to former Montreal

police Morality Squad officers Maurice Lacroix and Normand Beauchamps in 1976. Mado's daughter Lison remained an employee until it closed in 2014, while doorman Gilles Lacroix, who had worked at the red-lit skin shack for four decades, was also still toiling there on closing night. Its closure was accelerated by the condo craze and pressure from local politicos.

Playboy Club *2081 Aylmer, 2015 Mountain (1967-1976)* Waitresses trained in the proper usage of bunny ears, fluffy tails and colourful corsets starred at Montreal's Playboy Club when it opened as a franchise of the Chicago-based operation. The 565-seat club was a smash, taking in over $1,000 a day for its first three months during Expo 67 as Tony Bennett and Engelbert Humperdinck played shows in the Penthouse Room and groovy bunnies became instant scenesters, hitting the post-work party trail, supposedly always accompanied by chaperone. Bunnies could earn $500 a week plus tips, about 10 times what a secretary took home at the time. Many were called but only 70 chosen, as bow-legged or pigeon-toed applicants were rejected. "You aren't a waitress, you're a bunny," management told winners. Bunny Patsy Gallant later became a pop music celeb while Ginette Pelissier married Expos shortstop Tim Foli. Bunnies who drank on duty or dated members (yes, membership was mandatory) were immediately dismissed and Chicago headquarters sent hunky undercover inspectors to narc out bunnies who agreed to meet them. Bunnies were measured for bulge and could be suspended until they slimmed down. "Most girls failed the bunny test

because they are not bilingual, lack the personality, have deadpan voices and are never able to exude the bubble of youth," a supervisor noted. The club was defaced at least once with feminist slogans in 1970 and stayed closed for three months in September 1972 when it shifted to a venue further west. Customers became frustrated as busy bunnies hopped from table to table and had no time to field their pick up line icebreakers. It closed in August 1976 with the chain folding a decade later. Chef Arnold Morton found a backer to help him launch what became the 75-restaurant Morton's burger chain.

Hunter's Horn *1214 Peel (1968-1987)* Four Irish-Montreal radio ad salesmen launched Canada's first Irish bar after Expo 67 by imitating Manhattan's legendary McSorely's Old Ale House. Co-owners Martin Conroy and Dany Dooner's place was favoured by downtown office workers and notables like sports columnist Tim Burke, hockey announcer Danny Gallivan, baseball umpire Tommy Gorman and Chicago Cubs radio legend

Harry Carey who dined there daily while in town. On St. Patrick's Day bartender Mike Jetté poured Irish coffees, house poet Allan Mack read his verses, The Black Velvet Band played tunes like "Farewell to Nova Scotia" and moonlighting high school teacher Walter Evans worked the door, tsk-tsking students he knew to be underaged. Dooner, who had made a small fortune launching and selling CFOX radio, traveled to and from his second home in Florida to oversee an oft-jammed club. He and Conroy bought out their partners in the early 1980s and purchased the building. Boxing patriarch Davey Hilton Sr. seriously injured Conroy after he intervened in a brawl but the two remained friends. Dance clubs stole its younger drinking demographic, so the duo sold the building at a nice profit. "We didn't love it but we were making so much money we had to love it. We made a fortune. I beat the government," said Dooner in 2016.

Café Campus *3315 Queen Mary (1967-1992)* The *Université de Montréal* student union's co-operative bar was launched after a labour strike closed the school cafeteria and the new place fast became an oasis for intellectual yammerfests and attracted performers like Charles Mingus. the McGarrigle Sisters and nationalist *chanteurs* Félix Leclerc and Gilles Vigneault. Table hockey tournaments and brainy chess competitions were held and bartenders Serge Cantin and Robert Paquette raced a boblsed at the Lake Placid Olympics. Residents near Decelles started complaining about broken bottles, vandalism and public urination and fought to rescind its liquor license in a legal battle that cost both sides massive legal fees. It was finally ordered out at the end of its lease on December 10, 1992. The Café Campus name was revived in 1994 at 57 Prince Arthur E.

Mousse Spacthèque / Sexe Machine 1467-1469

Crescent (1966-1979) Artist Jean-Paul Mousseau, best known for creating the bright-coloured circular tile murals in Montreal's metro stations, decorated a wall at the Chez son Père restaurant

that caught the eyes of the cutting-edge owners of the La Licorne discotheque. They handed Mousseau a blank cheque to design their new bar on Crescent and the result was the Warhol-inspired Mousse Spacthèque, which aimed to turn nightclubbing into a sensual, surrealistic, artistic experience where clubgoers would bathe in light bouncing around wooden ceiling mobiles and over various scattered female mannequin parts. Ties and dresses were mandatory at the club which housed the Cybèle, Pluton and Orphée rooms, seen later by an art critic as, "a manifestation of the 1960s cultural utopia with its pursuit of emotional liberation and self-fulfillment." Mousseau designed similar bars

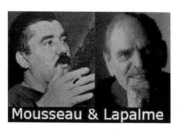

Mousseau & Lapalme

in Alma, Ottawa, Quebec City, the car-themed Crash at 1073 Dorchester W., and the Metrothèque at Berri metro, the first Montreal nightclub to be connected by metro and where Liberace watched on with DJ Alfie Wade as police busted underagers. The Spacthèque was replaced in 1971 by the Sexe Machine, where cartoonist Robert Lapalme, 60, created a part-Clockwork Orange, part-Fellini fantasy with topless waitresses and plastic breasts festooned on walls and penises for seat handles. "It's just funny sex, what's more harmless than that?" asked Lapalme. Fire struck and it became part of an expanded Casa Pedro.

Smitty's *6610 Sherbrooke W. (c. 1968-1975)* Middle-aged Dorothy Strange would spontaneously strip naked on the pub dance floor and fights were routine at what's now a commercial space on the ground floor of the high-rise at Sherbrooke and Cavendish. Norman Smith, a former doorman at the 1 & 2 Salon

on Butler in the Point, took over with other investors and pushed the Monday Rock Out Night, as the Wackers and other rock heroes lured stubby-toting beer drinkers from pool table to dance floor. Regulars included Tommy Sullivan who started and ended fights swiftly before being shot dead at home by a teenage son sick of seeing mom get beaten. The Dudes, whose drummer Eddie Crevier was among the 37 killed in the Wagon Wheel Fire of 1972, played Smitty's often, as did Pete & The Country Gentlemen who sported red dinner jackets while playing Freddie Fender and Charlie Rich tunes. Their drummer also died tragically. Bar stools were filled by longhaired next-generation West End Gang recruits who favoured selling drugs over knocking over banks. They spoke on a bar telephone bugged for two years by police wiretap. In its dotage, a jukebox offered a half-dozen songs from McCartney's Band on the Run album. Mellowed-out former tough guy Smith, who had a metal plate in his skull from a barroom conflict, closed it up after neighbours complained of noise. Previous owner Bill Bickerdike was repeatedly sidelined by drug convictions.

George's / Biddle's et al *2060 Aylmer (1968—)* Early fans of the discotheque experience boogied to tunes by house band Still-Life at George's, a compact 150-capacity hot-spot with red and black décor and low ceilings, considered the city's hottest club in 1970. Owner Georges Durst, a French Algerian War draft dodger, rechristened it Maxwell's Comedy Club in 1973 but the bar enjoyed its golden era after 1981 after Charlie Biddle lent his name, charm and stand up bass to the club. The jazz-and-ribs concept was Durst's biggest winner yet and stars like Wynton Marsalis, Eddie Murphy and Sarah Vaughan enjoyed the vibe while Bruce Willis was so charmed that he shot a long scene of his *The Whole Nine Yards* inside. Biddle died in 2003 and Durst has kept it going as House of Jazz. Durst had previously launched such nightclubs as Dominique's, Annabelle's and Tiffany's along with partner Dominique Tordion but he made his best money launching the publicly-traded *Cage aux Sports* sports bar chain.

Biddle

Robert Bar Salon *5090 Notre Dame W. (1969-1975)*

Robert Nantel saved for years to purchase his own bar, which never lived up to its boastful "Steak House" sign, as stage-side

food offerings consisted of mystery cold cuts jammed between white bread. The strip club was progressive, once awarding Stripper of the Year to Carole "Saria" Jean, a 21-year-old transsexual who was subsequently murdered with her friend on the Plateau. The Dubois brothers gang made Nantel an offer he could not refuse: hand over $100 a week plus 12 percent of earnings to Marcel Martel or sell to Tony Bartuccio for $60,000. Nantel declined and in May 1969 Martel kidnapped Nantel and a female employee and left them in a field in a mock execution. Dubois thugs bullied employees, who stopped showing up for their shifts, forcing Nantel to sell for a mere $25,000. New owner Bartuccio added insult to injury by suing Nantel for $21,000. Bartuccio and 25 patrons were uninjured by 32 bullets in a January 1976 drive-by. Martel was later found dead with a bullet in his head. Successor Cabaret Erotika lasted until the mid-1980s in what is now a long-vacant building.

The Old Munich *1170 St. Denis (1969-1994)* Armies of beer-influenced patrons—including a sea of American tourists—joined in chicken dance polka lines led by *lederhosen*-clad oom-pah bands at this expansive downtown *Bierhalle*, launched to continue the success of the popular Bavarian Beer Garden at Expo 67. Owner Georg Reiss, who owned bars in Germany and Austria, transformed the former Desjardins Furs ("devoted to the origination of fur masterpieces" from 1910 to 1994) into the *volksy* 1,200-seater and his son Jochen oversaw annual sales of 30,000

litres of beer and 10,000 kilograms of sauerkraut. Hand-picked musicians were flown in from Germany, Yugoslavia and Austria and lodged at a nearby apartments, their salaries constituting the club's biggest expense. Jochen blamed the club for his hearing loss and praised local police for their efforts keeping the peace when he sold to Swiss Alain Bolay in 1984 and moved back to Europe. The building kept deteriorating after Robert Lemay became owner and cash got tight. Lemay was unable to pay workers for three months and locks were changed in 1994 after he failed to make his

mortgage payments. The massive venue became 1,800-seat The Medley in 1999 and held 180 shows annually, including a memorable 2003 George Clinton event. Fans of the Scottish punk act The Exploited rioted outside after their show was canceled that same year. Co-owner and noted pop-star Garou opted not to inject the $8 million in needed repairs. It was replaced by condos in 2009.

Limelight *1254 Stanley (1973-1982)* Gas masks, fishing waders, six-inch platforms, kimonos and fishnet stockings were regular attire at this club known for its worship of disco beats and every form of associated excess. A chrome dance floor, bottle-juggling bartender and world-class DJ Robert Ouimet were features of Yvon Lafrance's three-story club, which included the first floor *Le Jardin*, which catered to a gay clientele. Hippies would swiftly convert to disco after hearing the

throbbing beats of Robert Kelly, Grace Jones and Georgio Moroder. The club became an intentional attraction, inspiring out-of-towners to to make all-night-drives over the border to party. Some even moved to Montreal to be closer to the club where massive speakers and amps shook walls and ceilings. The sonic explosion combined with a swirling, no-expenses-spared light show to create an otherworldly atmosphere that impressed visiting stars such as Elton John, David Bowie, Freddie Mercury and Cat Stevens. Devoted regulars, a group that included many underagers, perpetuated Montreal's reputation as a primo nightclub city, keeping the disco flame lit bright until 1980, after the trend was forgotten elsewhere. But crowds dwindled and costly renovation failed to revive interest, as once-unstoppable disco became passé. Late

days DJs cautiously spun five percent new wave tunes and punk legends The Dickies played a memorable show in 1980. But just as cocaine and disco hammered a nail into peace-and-love, so too did the punk-new wave scene doom the Limelight. Gays had already started partying in their newly-created village and disco faithful snipped their feathery locks, slapped on the hair gel and moved elsewhere.

Alfie's Le Strip *6510 Decarie (1975-1996)* "Howya fuggen doing?" was brash-talking Alfie Segal's greeting to guests at his embattled club at Decarie and Kenmore. Warren the Dwarf watched the door and dancers included sisters Charmaine and Kelly, Latinas Carolina and Cassandra, loudmouth Bobbie with slicked back hair and bodybuilding Amber. Manager Brian bedded many dancers, including Brandy who did $5 table dances to throwback tunes like Age of Aquarius. Boys aged 14 would be served without hesitation, as staffers didn't bother checking fake IDs and customers were occasionally mugged in the parking lot. Police sought to shut it down in 1982 after gangster Maurice Dubois was seen exiting with $1,500 hidden in a rag. The fun ended after arsonists torched the building in Dec., 1996.

Night Magic *22 St. Paul W. (1975 – 1996)* Bobby Di Salvio was sick of his dumb job—and who isn't?—so he twisted five friendly arms to pony up for his own spot on ancient St. Paul Street in Old Montreal, a venue vacated by the second iteration of the Black Bottom jazz club. Di Salvio aimed to conjure up a place that artsy icon Leonard Cohen would enjoy. Lenny became a regular, frequently strumming his morose tunes in the club's Beautiful Losers Room. Margaret Trudeau and Parisian disco queen Régine made the scene and Mick Jagger was friendly enough to bring the newly-pressed *Black and Blue* album for its first public spins. Filmmaker Robert Lantos saluted the saloon in the 1985 rock opera dud *Night Magic*, with Cohen and Lewis Furey co-penning tunes. Bob Marley visited and Guy Laliberté juggled on the cobblestones outside before he became a billionaire Cirque du Soleil owner. Rocker Michel Pagliaro, who lived across the street, was a regular at this place full of ferns and comfy-couches, a style that became popular all over. Back when cocaine was considered a fun pick-me-up, patrons—including a uniformed police officer—would brazenly snort lines off tables. Nuit Magique became a members-only key club in 1982 and briefly boasted a reggae theme before being replaced by a succession of less-celebrated establishments.

1234 *1234 Mountain (1978-1985)* Decades of mourning over corpses in caskets were swept clean overnight by The Hustle and The Bump, as bell-bottomed gyrations took over this old-time funeral home after Bishop's College grad Michael Bookalam and Outremont High class-of-'57 grad Saul Zuckerman (who also

owned the Jockey Club and Polo Lounge) transformed it into the city's glitziest disco on August 8, 1978. The stately mansion originally housed Father of Confederation Alexander Galt in 1859 and became the Wray-Walton-Wray funeral home in 1902. The owners injected $1 million into the disco-ball reno and soon all the *gliterrati* were driving a path to their dance floor, including hockey star Guy Lafleur and PM Pierre Trudeau. Co-owner Bookalam later told a reporter that he sniffed $1 million of cocaine during his disco ownership tenure. It led him to crime, culminating in a nine-year manslaughter conviction for a drug deal gone wrong. Montrealers embraced disco with a passion, as it allowed them to swap seated anonymity for a crack at dance floor stardom and nowhere was Montreal's love for disco

expressed more exuberantly than at the 1234, as funky bass plucks repelled ghosts reputed to haunt the building. The Gatien brothers of Cornwall opened the Club L'Esprit at the spot in 1986, with disco diva Grace Jones appearing on opening night. It survived until the early 1990s and a 2004 reboot entailed a $1.5 million reno. Other clubs have since inhabited the building sometimes mentioned as a candidate for demolition.

Blues *1186 Crescent (1979-81)* A pimply mix of New Romantics, mods and assorted underground heroes of the punk revolution found a short-lived refuge in the basement of a mobbed-up Italian restaurant in the early 1980s, an adventure that ended with the murder of a celebrity chef. Ill-fated Angelo Mirra, considered Montreal's top Italian chef, sought a tenant for the empty unit beneath his restaurant at 1184 Crescent. Management sought to open a mainstream rock bar in the space but a funny thing happened on the way to becoming a haven for Fleetwood Mac and The Eagles. Manager Gaétan Proulx hired record-importing Marc Du Mouy of Records 2000+ on Metcalfe to spin tunes and the new DJ happened to possess a never-ending supply of freshly-imported vinyl. He shunned rock in favour of new bands, as songs like U2's *I Will Follow* got their first-ever Montreal listens at the place. Subsequent turntable doctors Bill Varvaris and Will Baird kept up the tradition and mods and

De Mouy

punks crowded in to nurse warm beers, all waiting for the evening crescendo when *Dancing With Myself, Antmusic* or *Public Image* would kick off the slam dance as colourful lights flashed in synch underfoot. Tightwad owners failed to retain the DJ talent, who were lured to spin elsewhere. The punks and mods found new places to visit, while paranoid gun-toting doormen did little to encourage continued custom. Mirra was shot dead at his home in Laval at age 44 in 1984. His money was untouched.

Club 281 *281 St. Catherine E., 94 St. Catherine E. (1980—)* When hunky Leonard Lalumière stripped down on stage at the former Club Abitibi in April 1980, he became the first man to dance for women at a male strip club in Montreal, pioneering a tradition that thrives at the same club decades later. Owner France Delisle, a former construction worker from Abitibi, had operated a Latin-themed bar for a decade when he caught wind of a wildly popular male strip club in Miami. Delisle sought to adapt the concept to his Latin-themed bar but was clueless on how to recruit male strippers in a city which had none. Delisle took to the streets and spotted the hunky Lalumière, 40, strutting down St. Catherine and followed him in his white Cadillac, eventually persuading him to become the first Montreal beefcake stage star. Andrea Puzo, who played for Canada's soccer team, became another early attraction for wide-eyed women who routinely giggled and screamed while watching the muscular entertainers flex abs and biceps and drop trou.

The club was a smash, as busloads of transfixed women came to ogle and shower money and gifts on the 45 dancers showing off their manly charms on all three floors for 13 hours a day in the first five years. Stars included Randy "Johnny Banana" Thomas who invited women to pull bananas off of his belt, until only his own remained. James The Rocker was a top heartthrob, as was Andrew, now 47, whose soapy shower show is still an attraction after his 28 years at the 281. Fake cops, firefighters and businessmen, as well as acrobats, fire-breathers and a classical

violinist also remain popular. The club relocated from its original home after UQAM purchased and demolished the building in 2002. France's daughter Annie took over just as the club moved a little west to the former Casa Loma, a spot where it still thrives. Early-era clientele took great pleasure in turning the tables on chauvinism, according to current owner Annie, but she says current audiences have no such political axe to grind.

Checkers *4514 Park (1981-1993)* Funk reigned supreme at this second-floor venue on Park Ave. but only after revelers persuaded a DJ to de-turntable his Velvet Underground LP and play *Superfreak* by Rick James, giving birth to a new funk vocation at this upstairs place. Owner Peter Lymbariou, who also owned Dusty's restaurant downstairs, initially called it The Acropolis Café, a place that that aimed to please nearby-residing Springsteen-loving blue collar Greeks and Portuguese. New York City funk band Kinky Foxx, Freddie James and Naughty by Nature attracted long lineups while DJs Everton, Carlos, Spec II, Mike Williams, Don Smooth and Butcher T cultivated loyal followings. The cozy club was ruined by spoilsports, as a patron was shot in the foot while enjoying the 1989 vibes, a doorman shot and badly hurt three years later and a 28-year-old man was gunned down in the bathroom that same year.

K.O.X. *1182 Montcalm, 1450 St. Catherine E. (1982-1994)* Picture a cigar-smoking, leather-clad biker riding his growling hawg past oil barrels, then rising aloft on a hydraulic lift while *Black Velvet* by Alannah Miles blares from giant speakers. This leather bar was filled with tough guys who'd weep openly when *That's What Friends are For* played, as survivors of the AIDS epidemic created family-like bonds amid the sexually-charged atmosphere. Owner Bruce Horlin's New York-style place sported metal-and-black décor, leather-clad clientele and lots of man-on-man passion in the unsupervised bathrooms. Horlin credited its success with the profound care that people felt about the club, which offered an essential coming-of-age experience for gays. It moved to a more prominent spot in the 1911-built Station C post office building on St. Catherine in 1988, where police arrested 165 in February, 1994, leading 200 to protest later. K.O.X. closed in March 1998. Condos replaced the original building in 2012.

Foufounes Electriques *87 St. Catherine E. (1983—)*

Montreal was once awash with scruffy punks, students, drag queens, bolero hat-wearing subversives in ripped jeans, all desperately seeking a place to be accepted. They found their home at Foufounes Electriques, which offered a non-judgmental carnival of noise, music, art and style, where rowdies, goths,

misfits, vagrants and hookers stood cheek-to-sweaty-jowl in a style-off for best hair and biker jacket. West Island rockers beware: this was a place where the unusual became the normal, where nobody batted an eye at the bizarre where performance artist Renetsens stood still, pointing fingers meaningfully at lights overhanging the dance floor, and chubby bouncer and cocaine fan Michel would police the affair (they both died young) while eccentric Neoist artist Monty Cantsin played to a chorus of boos. Police raids could only temporarily slow the bedlam, as cops would order lights on, exposing punk lovers swiftly decoupling from dark corners, while the DJ would spin the Clash's *Police on My Back* as cops

departed. Barmaid Ava Rave would watch over punks known to climb the outside ledge to steal booze bottles. Bands on the cusp of success—from Nirvana to Green Day, Shonen Knife, Jesus Lizard —performed shows that everybody later claimed to have attended. Foufs previously housed underground gambling with the Metropole Club, which saw dice first launched in 1955. Party Dance Club, Eddy Toussaint's Ballet Jazz and *Eglise du Christ* and Zoobar used the space in the 1970s.

Garage / Backstreet et al *382 Mayor (1928-1997)*

Gangsters, hippies, gays and headbangers have all populated this basement space in the downtown fur district, which some might best as The Garage gay nightclub (not to be confused with the Sex Garage after hours club busted in July 1990). Garage opened in 1985 with a vehicular theme featuring car seats and a DJ booth made of a truck cab, complete with a sonorous air horn. Women flowed in to the monthly ladies night, followed by their heterosexual beaus. The space was rechristened Backstreet Underground in 1991, a 900-capacity metal-loving home for hair bands, where part-owner Nick Kandola and well-loved manager Louis Adams (later tragically killed) hosted Aldo Nova, Winger, Helix, Gene Simmons and Slaughter, as well as inexplicably popular tribute bands who did their best to imitate acts ranging from Pearl Jam and The Doors. The rose wilted on the metal vanue, with shows by obscure bands like Wacky Pack of Lobster Men from Mars foreshadowing its demise. Other operations occupying variations of the same basement space (but with an entrance at 1459 Alexander) include The Old Heidelberg Café "Montreal's Largest Restaurant" (1928), Chez Maurice (1930), Maxime Cabaret (1932), The Piccadilly (1935), Olympia Restaurant (1938), The Savoy Café (1939), a show bar at the centre of the action during Louis Greco and Frank Pretula's gang war in 1952. It housed La Cave (1957) where thieves once hid out until after closing to take off with $800. It was also The Rathskeller (1964), Café de la Place (1965) and Le Tarot (1970) where trippy artists dripped food dye onto slides to project colourful blobs onto walls and spinning mirror balls, while couples necked to rock music as management stayed open illegally until 6 a.m. It was also home to the Little Munich Restaurant (1977) and The Broadway Live (1980).

Louis Adams, left

Business *3500 St. Lawrence (1986 –1991)* The Wax, as

regulars called the Holder brothers' black-painted, half-million dollar imitation of Manhattan's Area Club, became an instant landmark as it blasted open a cultural gateway to the Plateau at Sherbrooke and the Main. Plateau nightspots like Chez Swann, Belmont, Le Set, Passeport and Taxi (where striptastic Kama Sutra now sits) all welcomed revelers but none rivaled Business' savvy art-punk allure that attracted a crowd that could appreciate tunes ranging from *Three Days Later* (a rap about a STI contracted after a late night pickup) to ethereal Gene Loves Jezebel, favoured by timid DJ Robbie Jackson. Everything from rockabilly coiffs to sleeveless industrial heroic sweatshirts were on the fashion palette while others aimed for a nattier Bryan Ferry-like respectability. Within the steel and sprayed concrete confines sat white airport runway-style spotlights that lit the house music worship on Sunday nights, while anniversary parties saw body-painted topless waitresses offering free shooters from booze-filled jetpacks. The legendary good times came to an end after a new clientele moved in and a violent closing-time fracas outside pitted police against 250 exiting clubgoers in July 1991.

Le Lézard *4177 St. Denis (1997– 1998)* Bodypainting, outrageous transvestites, walls painted by art legend Zilon, costumed lip-sync contests, and electronic live acts were enjoyed

 by uninhibited vedettes and gay activists at the only LGBT place on the Plateau, a place so focused that it even published its own rebel zine. Star regulars included female impersonator Mado Lamotte who later opened her still-thriving joint on St. Catherine, and Worst-Stars champ Georgette du Ruisseau-Joly,

who cut a sweater to expose his or her breasts to promote the *Analbum* album launch. Later incarnations of the loft-like venue included The Dogue and The Jungle where four young women partied in August 1997 before scrapping with rocker Serge Fiori and friends.

Di Salvio's *3519 St. Lawrence (1987-1998)* The Main above

Sherbrooke became a fashionable spot after the Scandale fashion boutique and the fabled Business nightclub launched open doors, turning the strip into something other than a place to buy skinned rabbits, sausage sandwiches and to get a wristwatch re-springed. The re-invigorated road provided fertile ground for forty-something nightclub orphan Bob Di Salvio, who sought to revive his Night Magic bar success. Di Salvio opened the second-floor dance lounge in November 1987, hoping not to repeat the failure of his short-lived Pepsee club further up the Main. He added a fireplace and skylight and considered naming it Second Night, in tribute to the old club, or Various Positions, in honour of Leonard Cohen before humbly naming the club after himself.

Soon after launching, filmmaker Wim Wenders handed his top prize trophy for *Wings of Desire* to Canadian filmmaker Atom Egoyan at the bar, deeming him more worthy. Would-be clubbers waited endlessly behind the velvet rope, offering a *schadenfreude* people-watching opp for diners at the downstairs Shed Café. Its compact dance floor and pink leather sofas welcomed regulars who included a homeless vagrant who needed to seduce a woman nightly to avoid sleeping on a park bench, and a dreadlocked Trustafarian who left a tiger in his Jeep. Di Salvio frequently intervened in his DJs musical selection and once vigorously smashed a James Brown disc after a DJ ignored the James Brown ban. Longtime Di Salvio's DJ Marc "Don't Look Any Further" Du Mouy eventually protested Di Salvio's musical micromanagement by storming out, leaving a Pavarotti CD playing on repeat mode. Di Salvio sold out in the early 1990s recession but he still considered it his masterpiece until it closed. The long-divorced father of two (Bran Van 3000 star James and serial entrepreneur David) died of cancer at age 66 in 2010. A variety of bars have filled the venue since, including the Upper Club, the scene of a 2006 double murder.

Brique /Dome / Opera *32 St. Catherine E. (1991-2010)*

The Main and St. Catherine was blessed with junkies, hookers, perverts and fur-clad pimps when La Brique opened in the

former hotel between Burger King and a supersized corner sex boutique. Owners invested $1 million into renovations and hosted Joan Jett, Bad Brains, Extreme, David Bowie's Tin Machine, Ice-T, Bo Diddley, The Ramones, Alice in Chains and Ron Wood. Co-owner Nick Kandola said that he sought to attract a headbanging rocker clientele because "they drink their weight's worth." The glorious metal mania proved short-lived and after two years new ownership turned the joint into The Dome, a buzzing techno and house dance

venue with a hefty cover charge and top notch acts like Nas and local hero Bad News Brown (later the victim of an unsolved murder). The Dome was a larger-than-life spot, sometimes compared to the Limelight of the 1970s but its 20 bouncers proved unable to stop street gangs from turning it into an occasional battleground with constant skirmishes that cost the club its liquor license for a month in 2007. Opera Club took over the 15,000 foot, 1,200 capacity venue one year later and made a splash by reportedly handing aging bikini starlet Pamela Anderson $100,000 to host an event during Grand Prix weekend, one-upping club rival Tribe Hyperclub, which had P. Diddy on tap. The fun and games ended in January 2010 when Opera closed. No more would feet fall on the forlorn dance floor, leaving only echoes of terpsichore nostalgia in a frayed building that sat abandoned until its 2017 demolition.

Café Sarajevo *2080 Clark (1993-2006)* Gypsy dances from the Balkans filled this joyous space after 52-year-old Bosnian immigrant Osman Koulenovitch became an unlikely impresario

by purchasing a stubby box of a building on hilly Clark Street for $100,000. Nobody wanted to rent the space, so he moved in upstairs and launched a bar downstairs that attracted former Yugoslavians, who flowed into at an eye-popping regularity. He welcomed spoken-word artists, musicians and gypsy dancers while its most famous regular performer, Rufus Wainwright, tickled the upright piano in frequent shows before being signed to a big record contract in 1996. But as real estate values rose, so too did noise-averse

neighbours who complained frequently. Koulenovitch disputed the noise allegations, pointing out that he raised three children upstairs who never lacked sleep. The city also sought to make Clark strictly residential, so Koulenovitch gave in and sold his property for $715,000 in

2006. The owner's tears were somewhat abated by his hefty resale profit. Koulenovitch opened another version of the Café Sarajevo at 6548 St. Lawrence that lasted a few years.

Other notables The Silver Dollar Saloon *174 Notre Dame E. (c. 1896-1918)* Customers strode over 350 silver dollars embedded into a wood floor that aimed to prove a sense of affluence. Courthouse lawyers, clerks and judges were regulars and posterity notes that Big Joe Mufferaw beat the British army boxing champion with a mighty kick at the bar. It's now a tourist information centre. **Midway** *1219 St. Lawrence (1927—)* Dufferin Tavern was rechristened for a neighbouring theatre (later The Pussycat) in 1960 when purchased by the Auclair family. Muggings, stabbings and shakedowns helped it onto the police blotter for many years and in 1989 a man with a grudge lit a fire that killed three. The Auclairs retired in 2014 and

millennial patrons now tote smartphones rather than brass knuckles. **Peel Tavern** *1452 Peel (1933-1961)* Englishman Billy Allen's beer-and-oyster joint across from the Mount Royal Hotel grew so popular that it fetched the then highest-ever price for a Montreal tavern when he sold it after World War II. Allen started at the St. Lawrence Hall Hotel, then launched his Cosy Corner in Point St. Charles before graduating to his downtown madhouse, where he doted on thirsty servicemen who gobbled pickled eggs alongside a discreet contingent of Peel Street gays. Allen sold and died of a heart attack on his return from the Montreal Royals spring training in 1948. Excessive exercise was the culprit, ventured a sports columnist. The space is now retail. **York Tavern** *2301 St. Catherine W. (1936-c.1998)* This became an

infamous landmark for racial discrimination after two black Montrealers were refused service soon after it opened inside The Forum in July 1936. Chauffeur Fred Christie sued and won $25 but the Supreme Court, regrettably, ruled that establishments were permitted to refuse to serve blacks. **Copacabana** *1260 McGill College (1947-1960)* Montreal's first South American-themed club kicked off with Quebecois singers doing Latin-flavoured songs. Thieves stole a safe full of $3,000 in cash by hiding inside after closing the next year but the club survived at the southwest corner of McGill College until 1960. Another bar with the same name operated from 1112 St. Catherine from 1963 to 1979, featuring one awkward period in which reluctantly-topless waitresses did the rounds. It was the scene of a brutal murder-robbery and was succeeded by Rendez Vous, T.C. and 6/49. A third Copacabana opened in 1990 at 3910 St. Lawrence and became a haven for students, musicians and underpaid alternative weekly newspaper staffers. **Kit Kat Dining Room** *1469 Bleury (1949-1975)* Singer/

bouncer Art "Little Elvis" Smith and a supply of cheap beer attracted budget drinkers in the 1960s. Regulars Sonny and Roy were known to drug, kidnap and sexually assault females who ventured in. The Blue Danube Dining Room opened at the spot in 1938 before Nick Di Sciullo transformed into the Kit Kat fried chicken restaurant a decade later. **Diana Bar** *1825 St. Catherine W. (1954-2013)* Hard-drinking downtowners and visitors from Northern Canada spent welfare cheques in this and similar dives just east of Atwater. A man was murdered outside in 1973 and a steady stream of violence occurred within. **Times Square Café** *1434 Bleury (1962-1970)* An Irish flavoured country music place near the Imperial movie theatre once saw a

Art "Little Elvis" Smith

disgruntled client stab the owner and a staffer after being refused entry in the mid-1960s. In another clash, a Bonanno-clan tough guy was beaten to death with a pipe by Dubois gang toughs after he attempted to shake the joint down. **Peel Pub** *1107 Ste. Catherine W. (1962-2001)* Auctioneer Ben Weshler's sprawling basement place attracted beer-sipping gays among others until the joint exploded in popularity with trivia quizzes and sometimes-recycled pitchers of beer, leading to a variety of franchises beset by issues like murder outside (St. James in NDG) and staff brutality (de Maisonneuve near Stanley closed in 1996). Heir Frank Weshler sold half to Sterios Mimidakis and moved to Toronto where he pushed franchises. Its current iteration is at 1196 Peel. **La Licorne** *1430 Mackay (1963-1968)* North America's first discotheque, ie: a recorded music dancehall, was an imitation of a Parisian progenitor. It closed after Expo 67 and the building was replaced by an apartment highrise in 1973. Owners André de Carufel and Gilles Archambuault later opened other clubs. **Cock and Bull Pub** *1946 St. Catherine W. (1965—)* Piano singalongs, darts, amateur nights, four-ounce martinis and British coins embedded into the bar were trademarks of this place founded by Peter Barry, Montreal's best-known freelance musician. Atwater Al Jolson wept on stage during his open microphone version of Mamie weekly for three years straight. **Country Palace** *400 Sherbrooke W. (1966-1969)* Thirsty folksies wandered over from the liquorless New Penelope for cold brew at this country music drinking hole. Richard Mertick was irritated when co-owner Peter Demascos demanded that he pay a $17 drink debt in October 1967 so he and armed robber Brian Melvin, both 22, returned with guns. Undercover cops killed Mertick and injured Melvin (who was killed in a robbery three years later). **The Maidenhead Inn** *Alexis Nihon Plaza (1967-c. 1980)* Medieval-style wenches in low-cut skirts served off-duty Mounties cold beers, as Irish bands played seven nights a week. **The Bali Hi** *Alexis Nihon Plaza* Plaza The Hill brothers owned this Pacific-flavoured experience, complete with an elaborate aquarium. George Seivwright, 39, was beaten to death in the bathroom on Sept 15, 1977. Friends covered up for the killer. **Boiler Room** *1459 Crescent (1968-1974)* So many bright academics were on staff that management considered a lowly undergrad

dishwasher under-qualified. It was also "the best place in town for chicks," according to one male patron. Drug-dealing bikers overran the place, leading owner Johnny Vago to incorporate it into his neighbouring Sir Winston Churchill Pub. **Le Vieux Rafiot** *406 St. Sulpice St. (1970)* Alfie Wade's frequent visits to New York taught him the magic of loudspeakers. He returned home and installed sound systems in many sleepy Montreal spots, converting them into wildly-popular dance clubs. Wade's final club before moving back to New York was a short-lived, nautically-decorated basement dance club at the home of Pierre Lemoyne d'Iberville just down the street from Place D'Armes.

Dice Club *6530 Papineau (1972-2015)* A hair salon became the Flip Café that ended after biker Salvatore Brunetti earned his psycho stripes by shooting the doorman dead. Successor C-Plus disco lost the right to serve booze for two years after 58 of 99 customers were charged with partaking of indecent acts in 1986. The Dice Club then came in after 1994 and lost its liquor license for 45 days in 1998 and 2007 for allowing underaged girls to strip. Owner Giovanni Cotroni, who often told dancers that he won the club in a poker game, shut it down when more license trouble hit in 2015. The orgy-friendly Hotel Lust upstairs closed also. **Darwin's** *1187 Bishop (1976-1994)* Rainbow barkeep Dan Wittman up saved tips and wife Nancy pitched in cash earned by

David Wittman

selling $1 roses in bars and became half-owners of a new fern-filled place that opened on the last day of the 1976 Olympics. Darwin's was as bright as the Rainbow was dark and staffers and drinkers migrated over. Night Squad cops happily accepted freebies and last call rushes were routine, while Irish mobster Ricky McGurnaghan tossed stools in rage when told it was closing time. Retail heir Tommy Caplan bought the Wittmans out in 1980 while co-owner Aftab Khan (owner of the Pakistan House Restaurant on Mackay) stayed on. Dawin's closed after a fire Jan. 3, 1994. **Glace/Metal** *1426 Stanley (c. 1980-1985)* Headbangers hung out upstairs while the downstairs Glace experience had non-dancing poseurs looking down over a dance floor full of

people shaking to bands like A Flock of Seagulls and Rational Youth. Wayne Gretzky dropped in whenever in town as did Tones on Tail who were surprised that their B-side *Yeah!* was the hottest song at the club, forcing the band to quickly relearn the notes for the show the next night. **Secrets** *40 Pine W. (1980-1992)* Herman Alves and Andy Mitchell transformed this Cheers-style neighbourhood bar into a live music venue with acts like Three O'Clock Train, Jerry Jerry,

Weather Permitting, Kali and Dub and an "international" reggae festival in 1988. Singalongs reigned one troubled night after bailiffs seized the DJ equipment, leaving turntable jock David Ahara with nothing to spin. Mitchell quarreled with a customer who returned with his Colombian crew and vandalized the bar while the bouncer hid in the bathroom. Noise complaints hastened its demise. **The Beat** *968 St. Catherine W. (1983-1988)* Scenesters looked intense while leaning on black walls watching dancers move to New Order and The Cult. Regulars included Outremont private school kids, downtown fashion clerks, lesbian introverts and enough gays to inspire at least one man to sport a Not Gay badge on his shirt. **Thunderdome** *1252 Stanley (1987-1991)* This two-story alternative club was known for its wet T-shirt contests starring ringers from Chez Paree and its long staircase, handy for bouncers who pushed people down for little cause. It closed after cops shot patron Presley Leslie, 26, dead after he fired a celebratory gunshot at the ceiling while dancing in April 1990. **Bobards** *4328 St Lawrence (1989-2015)* This 300-capacity hub of cultures overlooking Portugal Park was where to catch live music while munching on peanuts from plastic containers on tables over unswept floor strewn with crunchy discarded shells. Owners blamed road repairs, bad parking and noise complaints for its closure. **Solid Gold** *8820 St. Lawrence (1995—)* Management beat early anti-lap dance crackdowns to help make stripping a contact sport in a building that previously housed the Rivieria theatre from 1954, which falsely advertised itself as a drive-in because it had a parking lot out back. Capo Vic Cotroni's sister owned the building and was forced to manage the theatre after the Supreme Court allowed Greeks to back out of a lease due to insufficient bathrooms. The Violi-Rizzuto mob war began in its parking lot where a mobster was shot after attending Godfather II in 1976.

Strip club excess Montreal island was home to 72

strip clubs in 1977, almost four times as many as today's rapidly-diminishing total. Many tried outlandish gimmicks designed to attract clientele. **The Shack** *1200 St. Catherine W.* For years a shadowy silhouette attracted sidewalk eyes by dancing in a second storey window at the place later known as the Downtown Club. **Nick's Palace** *9600 St Lawrence (1984-2002)* A small malodorous "sexaquarium" was where dancers would swim like mermaids. A customer once saved a drowning dancer whose hair got stuck in a drain but a bouncer beat him up, believing his mouth-to-mouth resuscitation constituted an unsolicited advance. Another time a stripper banged her head badly after slipping in the adjacent shower. **Calèche du Sexe** *328 St. Catherine E.* came with a perilous contraption which allowed dancers

Nick's Sexaquarium

to sit naked on a platform, which was transported overhead inside the club. **Tango Vert** *4919 Jarry E.* Extra large booths, like mini hotel rooms, allowed clients (including one overly-intense young mob boss) and dancers to get intimate until authorities put an end to it. **Castel Tina** *4885 Jean Talon E.* A rotating bed emerged from the stage at this club where male strippers reigned on one floor, women on another. The father and son owners were both later murdered and the building demolished.

2

Restaurants

For centuries Montreal restaurants have fed a city that marches on its stomach. Pull up a chair, tuck in a bib and feast from Montreal's past.

Dolly's Chop House *45 Great St. James (c.1845-1867)*

Englishman Robert Philip Isaacson attracted glances with his old-style John Bull suit, knee breeches and bushy sideburns, as sun beams sparkled off his silver boot buckles while he

Dolly's Tavern by Cornelius Krieghoff 1845

lounged on a bench in front of his steak house. Isaacson's establishment emulated a well-known London namesake when he opened near the bottom of François Xavier before soon shifting to where the courthouse now stands. Lawyers, judges, soldiers and sportsmen appreciated hearty meals and stiff drinks from a bar advertised as "the most select in Canada." Montreal Snowshoe Club members would trample nearby fields and then drop in for meals, as would hunters who blasted woodcock in the nearby swampland and curlers from the Thistle Curling Club, who slid their stones on outdoor ice. Isaacson boycotted Montreal-grown beef, calling it "wretched stuff," and once penned an emphatic note praising Eastern Townships cattle. When a diner described his steak as "tough" Isaacson cursed him, poured ketchup on it and ate it in front of him, while apologizing for his verbal blasphemy. Regulars included colonial administrator Benjamin D'Urban who once reversed his decision to

"Dolly" Isaacson

declare martial law after a satisfying meal. When Colonel Ermatinger tossed merchant Alfred Perry into prison on suspicion of participating in the burning of Parliament, Dolly—as Isaacson was known—showed up to jail with toast and treats for the prisoner. Confederates, including Lincoln-assassin John Wilkes Booth, also favoured Dolly's, which closed in 1867. Dolly went on to run the less-celebrated Isaacson Hotel on nearby St. Gabriel Street.

Mother Martin's *915 Peel, 990 St. Antoine (1861-1987)*

James Martin soothed bellies on Notre Dame just east of McGill before hauling griddle to the New Carlton Hotel—Montreal's

first skyscraper—at Peel and St. Antoine in 1887. Soldiers added "Mother" to its name in honour of Martin's daughter Rebecca and ate pig's knuckles, corned beef, steak and kidney pie and onion soup, although

many came just to drink. R. A. Patterson changed nothing when he took over from the family in 1958. Five dozen regulars were so loyal that their names were engraved onto chairs as part of the 33 Club, so-named for the number of the telephone at their table. Veteran staffers like manager Bill Watt, bartender Mike Jupzca, organist Ronnie Matthew and comedian Dave Broadfoot, who cracked wise

nightly for two years, kept the ship steady. Over 1,600 sentimental diners attended its final meal in 1964 as the Canadian Pacific Railway demolished the hotel for the dreary Place du Canada office building. But the restaurant

relocated east near the Montreal Gazette where regulars included sporty scribe Brodie Snyder and colleague Chris Haney who invited patrons to invest in his Trivial Pursuit board game, an offer that proved massively profitable for the few who made the leap of faith. Owner

Jacques Lemyure shut it down after a fire and auctioned the furniture off. The restaurant's familiar "what a man's really thinking" painting, which featured a discreetly-drawn nude woman on a man's forehead, sold for $3,200.

Drury's *1082 Osborne (1868-1959)* Montrealers yawned as authorities razed all measure of gorgeous architecture but they were livid when this old-style, slow-eating chop house was

earmarked for demolition. Drury's was housed in a Victorian mansion souped up with iron grills and canopy, stained glass windows, old-fashioned lamps and a massive wooden door, all creating a mellow downtown oasis from a bygone world.   Diners,   who included Anthony Eden, Mary Pickford, Maurice Chevalier and Eleanor Roosevelt,

sat in the warm seclusion of small rooms with dark paneled walls jammed with high-backed, brass-tacked leather upholstered chairs and feasted on lamb chops, steak, chicken pot pie and jumbo finnan haddie. John Drury's original 1868 location had been forced out to make room for Windsor Station, so it shifted to nearby Osborne Street where his son Jimmy Drury—an accomplished multi-sport athlete—took over. He sold to Montreal Canadiens owner Leo Dandurand in 1938, who hosted many Stanley Cup celebrations within its walls. A road redevelopment scheme called for the block to be razed but Mayor Jean Drapeau vowed that Drury's would stay while everything else went. But he was voted out and successor Sarto Fournier gave the restaurant 30 days to evacuate, insufficient time to fight the expulsion or organize a new location. Pleas proved futile. "In its closing, something has gone out of the city's life," an editorial lamented. However unlike other fallen institutions, the editorial noted, Drury's "never knew a decline."

Desjardins *1518   Dorchester   W.,   1175   Mackay*

(1892-2003) Eugène Desjardins cashed in on Montreal's love for oysters at Peel and St. Antoine before moving to Guy and St. Catherine in 1902, then to the southeast corner of Dorchester and Guy nine years later. Late-night passersby could ignore his CLOSED sign and

SE corner Guy & Dorchester

he'd fill their ears with chatter and their bellies with oysters until 5 a.m. The nocturnal hospitality led to a half-dozen robberies and Desjardins vowed to start handing over the cash after getting slugged in the head with a pipe and dodging a bullet that long remained lodged in the ceiling. Desjardins, 77, was run over by a car and killed outside of his restaurant on a rainy day in May 1947. The building was claimed by road widening so his kids built the only downtown building designed specifically as a restaurant behind the old Ford Hotel. Its crab crêpes and free parking helped it thrive but Albert Desjardins died and no new generations of family could be found to take over operations. Barry Kauffman purchased it in the 1980s and filled it with armchairs patrolled by waiters in red

Eton jackets. Negative reviews hurt. A long succession of other attempts fared no better and the longstanding Quebec Catholic custom of eating fish on Fridays also faded. The once-hopping place closed and was left abandoned as a graffiti-covered eyesore until it was finally razed in 2017.

Au Lutin Qui Bouffe *753 St. Gregoire (1897-1972)*

Booming baritones serenaded diners feasting away at "Canada's only opera restaurant," while a photographer toured the room

with a piglet ready for a souvenir photo-op. Bertram McAbbie's place, named after a hungry pixie ghost from France, relied on convoluted gimmicks to get people off-the-beaten-downtown-track to the Plateau-area landmark. Visits became culinary culturefests, as diners soaked up the artwork-lined walls and appreciated aria-intensive opera performances. The pig-feeding souvenir photos have since permitted countless grandchildren to know their ancestors as

smiling folk charmed by swine, animals which the restaurant claimed were saved from slaughter. The elderly McAbbie was killed late one night in 1953 by thieves hoping to get their mitts on the $10,000 he reputedly kept in his safe. The

thieves fled with less than half that total and crafty police tracked phone records and fingerprints to locate a suspect who ratted out his gang, who included Gerry McKuhen, by then a newly-married car salesman in Texas. His ex, cold-hearted gangster moll Gertrude Servant was also slapped with 10 years in prison for her involvement. The restaurant survived and Canadiens anthem singer Roger Doucet and his talented wife Geraldine began careers there. Jack Rubin and David Radler, pals of media mogul Conrad Black, became late-era owners until September 27, 1972 when 30 diners and a a few baritones were forced to abandon meals and arias as the building went up in a blaze that claimed many irreplaceable paintings by the Group of Seven.

Krausmann's *1195 Philips Square (1901—)* John Krausmann served weiner schnitzel and German beer on St. James, a few doors down from the courthouse, while women sat

upstairs in a separate space. He died in 1929 and the place moved to busy Phillips Square, where brother William served up pickled pork hock and other tasty fare in a two-level joint with low ceilings, 225 tables and dark paintings. Meals cost a buck with no extra cover charge to spy the modest chorus girl revue, as Krausmann's served imported German draught beer right through World War II. Jacques Fauteux revived it in 1964 after it closed for a few years. It shifted to 1093 Beaver Hall Hill from 1989 to 2007 when Brisket's took over the space, honouring Krausmann's with a space on its sign.

Edinburgh Café *786, 1628 St. Catherine W. (1907-1940)* Katherine Louttit and sisters Agnes, Julina and Annie, described as spinsters from the Orkney Islands, opened at the southeast corner of McGill College and St. Catherine, near the vaudeville house strip where business survived after ice

slipped from the roof and killed a passing four-year-old. The sisters offered discounts to groups holding meetings at the café and so unmarried men over 25 met there to organize opposition to the $10-a-year bachelor tax they were forced to pay between 1918 and 1925. Suffragettes made it their hangout, as the vote-hungry women postered its walls with slogans like, "Women suffrage equals lower infant mortality." Canadian Communist Party leader Tim Buck offered a fiery speech there in 1938, a decade after it moved 10 blocks west.

Ben's *990 De Maisonneuve W. (1908-2006)* Fluorescent bulbs pounded diners, while bow tie-clad waiters scribbled smoked meat orders on notepads at this timeless downtown deli where

diners were beckoned by beautiful loser ghosts from the past, as dozens of showbiz almost-stars stared down from framed 8 x 10 photo glossies. Ben Kravitz and wife Fanny "Mrs. Ben" Schwartz sold candy from 4078 St. Lawrence and then ice cream from 3993 St. Lawrence in 1915, then making it a deli. Kravitz is credited with bringing smoked meat to town but historian Eiran Harris claims it was around from 1893. Ben's moved to 1001 Burnside (NW corner Mansfield and De Maisonneuve) in 1929, where it lasted two decades before settling into its landmark corner location one block west. Ben's featured a lengthy melamine counter for diners who didn't mind

nestling with backs to the action on swiveling stools without backrest, while bathrooms were down a flight of stairs and a cashier sat in a glass-encased booth behind a metal cordon. Three generations of Kravitzes kept the joint hopping as diners renounced time and slumber,

strolling in past the early-edition newspaper hawker to kill post-closing time hungers. Leonard Cohen described Ben's in 1964 as a "funnel that draws everyone who happens to be up at night, committing the first rebellious act that a man can perform, refusing to sleep. So they come to Ben's." Author Hugh McLennan led a pre-emptive campaign to save it in 1982, as developers transformed downtown De Maisonneuve into skyscraper alley. But it survived until employees, including Ben's grandson Brian Kravitz, went on a four-month strike in 2006, leading to its closure. It was demolished two years later.

Northeastern Lunch *(1912 – 1962)* Irish Protestant

Andrew C. Cordner knew nothing about restaurants when he arrived in 1912 and opened a place offering baked beans for a nickel at the northwest corner of Clark and St. Catherine. The chain soon expanded to 429 St James W., the top floor of the Sun

Life building, and filled 51, 292, 470 and 903 St. Catherine W. as well as 1005 St. Catherine E., and a dedicated dining room for women. Porcelain, marble and steel were favoured, as Cordner believed they could be kept cleaner than wood. Business only grew during the Great Depression, as thrifty diners ate at solitary tablet arm desks lining the walls, devouring full meals that cost 55 cents in the 1940s. The chain teamed up with competing restaurants to fight a Sunday take-out ban in the early 1930s. It declared bankruptcy in 1943 but continued unabated under the name Cordner's, with outlets managed by former magician Howard McLeod and future senator Maurice Riel. Many still called

Cordner's by its original name, including a young Leonard Cohen who, at age 13, would lounge around with old timers at the original restaurant at Clark and St. Catherine. "I never understood why I was down there except I felt at home, at home with those people," he said. Cohen described those budget-seeking diners in an early poem as having "rotting noses and tweed caps, huddling in thick coats and mumbling confidential songs to ancient friends." The original location, as well as 468 St. Catherine and 6665 St. James W. were all that remained in 1960 and the chain disappeared two years later. Its memory was stirred in 2015 when a sign was removed from 1001 St. Catherine E., revealing the restaurant's name handsomely-chiseled into the stone facade of a former premises.

Murray's *(1923-2007)* Inhale the aroma of sweet steamed fruit pudding served by well-scrubbed waitresses in dress uniforms with hairnets, aprons and regularly-inspected

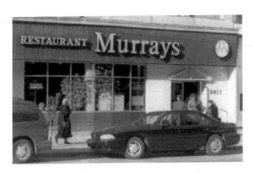

fingernails. You have arrived at Murray's, which stormed into Montreal in 1923 when American immigrants Fred McCracken and Murray Crawley opened a restaurant with cash earned from feeding logging camps. Diners would ingest rice pudding, mashed potatoes, English sausage and grab endless free coffee refills at any one of five locations on downtown St. Catherine alone, including at the corner of Bishop and also at University. Visiting comedian Red Skelton was at a Murray's on St. Catherine in the mid-1930s when he spotted a fellow diner dunking a doughnut in his coffee, which inspired him to come up with his legendary routine demonstrating the myriad approaches to eating doughnuts. The skit made Skelton a major comedy star. Diners could get that flaky Murray's apple pie experience in the Ford

Hotel, in the Sun Life Building, the Laurentien Hotel, Lucerne Shopping Centre, 4861 Park, on Queen Mary and on Phillips Square. Murray's was where aging waitresses in nursing shoes dutifully served elderly ladies in white gloves and was where writer Patrick

Staff at first Murray's

Waddington dined daily, as did anglo-rights activist Alan Singer, who favoured the Murray's near Claremont, which became a McDonald's after it closed in 1999. Murray's served its final meal at the Lucerne mall in the Town of Mount Royal in 2007.

FDR's *(1923-1965)* Frank De Rice quipped that his FDR chain stood for Feed Dem Rite but it would be more apt to call it Fire Department Required, as flames regularly claimed his outlets. De

Rice was an aspiring wit, once claiming to have a degree in MRO, Mustard, Relish and Onions. His minor restaurant empire began with a humble concession stand at Belmont Park in 1923. De Rice opened his pioneering place in 1931 and boasted that he brought Montreal car service, toasted hot

Former FDR's at 990 Gouin W.

dog buns and soft ice-cream and he was known to transplant palm trees around his restaurants. De Rice sponsored a football trophy, promoted boxing matches and managed prizefighters, who sometimes trained at his facilities. He was forced to pay up in 1938 after an employee complained to a judge that she was only paid in tips. His "FDR Wants You!" lured hungry bellies but his eight-year-old roadside eatery at 560 St. Joseph in Lachine burned down in 1941 and his St. Laurent outlet suffered the same fate two years later with $900 missing from the till and the night guard nowhere to be found. His outlet at the doorstep of Blue Bonnets at 7450 Decarie (later the Bonfire Restaurant), was hit three times by fire in four months in 1951, leading him to distastefully conflate his fire-of-the-week with a fatal blaze at the nearby race track: "Blue Bonnets lost 17 horses, I lost 1,700 hot dogs to fire." De Rice shifted downtown to 1237 Metcalfe and 1122 St. Catherine W. near Peel where window shoppers could watch cooks boil

FDR's in Lachine

industrial quantities of spaghetti. By 1959 De Rice had locations at 5322 Queen Mary, 5742 Sherbrooke W. and 4474 St. Denis but branches started disappearing in 1963 and the last FDR closed two years later as De Rice retired to a fishing life in Delray Beach, Florida where he died in 1971 at age 80.

American Spaghetti House 64 *St. Catherine E.*

(1941-1959) What Montrealers later knew as the barren expanse across from the Foufounes Electriques nightclub once housed a

American Spaghetti House fire 1959

wildly-popular pasta emporium that was felled by tragedy. High-profile pimping couple Angelo Bisante and Lucie Delicato snapped up most of the property around Berger Street and in 1941 took over the 17-year-old Venice Café, a jazz joint where hep cats once danced the jitterbug. Bisante borrowed a name from the recently-closed American Grill and soon his spaghetti house, along with Laurier BBQ and Dunn's, was one of three Montreal restaurants to remain open all night. The restaurant had no locks and welcomed many post-nightclub revelers, closing only one night in May 1945 for war victory celebrations. Authorities were irked by Bisante's brothel operations and yanked his license but Bisante, who also had interests in the Casino de Paris and Casa Loma nightclubs, blamed his wife, saying he had separated from the wicked woman and would only return to after she renounced her sinful ways. It was a minor blip at a place that popularized spaghetti in Montreal and snagged free publicity by dressing its staff in Union Jacks to wave to Princess Elizabeth on her St. Catherine Street parade route in 1951. Bisante's hard-working

Bisante

brother Dandy managed 160 employees in the mid-1950s, a time when the place served three tons of spaghetti in meals that cost less than a buck. On its final deadly night, 25 staffers, 11 diners and many residents from the upstairs rooming house fled a hellish conflagration that spread from a photography studio. Firefighters Edward Normoyle, 53, and Hubert Daudelin, 26, died of hypothermia following a roof collapse on February, 23, 1959. Three other firefighters died in separate Montreal blazes that same night. An attempt to reopen a block east failed.

Astor's *696 St. Catherine (1924-1985)* Revenge might be best served cold but Greek immigrant George Gavaris offered hot meals while nursing a lifelong grudge inspired by a snub he suffered as a young man. Gavaris developed an intense will to

succeeded in 1910, after staffers at the Astor Hotel in New York City slammed a door in his face when he asked for a job. Gavaris eventually got his own little fish-and-chips joint and then opened Astor's opposite Goodwin's department store, which became Eaton's the next year, naming his place after the hotel that had mistreated him. Gavaris offered no Greek fare at his 450-seat, 85-employee establishment, which was best known for its strawberry shortcake and soulful house pianist. Tables were jammed with soldiers during WWII, as seas of servicemen pushed staff to their limit. Gavaris's daughter Pauline, 20, a hat check girl, and pianist Billy Munro were among the 50 who escaped a 1944 blaze by fleeing down a fire escape out back. Most of the crowd had to walk home in the cold, as the streetcars were on strike. Gavaris also tried his hand at a few less-successful restaurants, including

one whimsically catering to a swimming pool in Cartierville, while his son operated the Howard Johnson's restaurant that sat adjacent to Astor's for many years. Gavaris still came downtown to greet customers until the age of age 92 and died at the age of 106, long outlasting the New York Astor Hotel. Part of the building was later used for the Super Sexe strip club, which closed in 2016.

Café Martin *1521 & 2175 Mountain St. (1927 – 1982)* Leo Dandurand, who purchased the Montreal Canadiens for $11,000 in 1921, became owner of this French restaurant that sat in a

mansion south of what's now De Maisonneuve, where a notable farewell party for Chicago-bound Hab great Howie Morenz was held in 1934 and the football Alouettes had an office in the basement. It expanded to three floors at a building closer to Sherbrooke, after its original home was demolished in 1958. Dandurand's son Gerard managed a place that included the upstairs The Flamingo Room, shunned by regulars who preferred the basement space. The family sold out in 1971 and other owners kept it going for another decade.

Schwartz's Hebrew Delicatessen *3895 St. Lawrence (1928–)* Many disliked Reuben Schwartz but everybody loved his sandwiches, which came out spicier than other smoked

meat competition after being cured for 10-days in an on-site smokehouse. "He was a miserable bastard and bad businessman," longtime waiter Morris Sherman told restaurant biographer Bill Brownstein. Schwartz's friend Maurice Zbriger rescued the eatery from bankruptcy a couple of times before buying the operation outright. Zbriger, with backing from well-heeled wife Mary, spent more time organizing gypsy violin music concerts than tending to his 61-seater but it ran smoothly nonetheless. Zbriger bequeathed the operation to his caretaker Armande Toupin when he died in 1981. The humble sandwich personified the spirit of The Main and of Montreal itself, as time added to its allure and lineups. Hy Diamond purchased the restaurant in 1999 and mused about opening a second branch on Crescent before selling to a group that included Céline Dion's husband René Angélil for $10 million in 2012.

Honey Dew *(1928–1975)* A sugary orange drink so enchanted investors that they launched dozens of Honey Dew restaurants almost simultaneously across Canada, the first of  which hit Montreal in July 1928 at St. Catherine near University. Full blitz mode ensued and by 1930 nine more Honey Dews were open in Montreal, many on downtown St. Catherine Street. Spacious booths, orange painted walls, cheap breakfasts—the chain's Chief Dietitian recommended Corn Flakes in print ads—and the sweet orange drink were all features of this chain which mega-investor E.P. Taylor eventually purchased. Honey Dew was everywhere on the main downtown strip, filling 481, 728, 966 and 1340 St. Catherine W., a spot in the Guy metro and Simpson's department store among others. Students protested its English-only menus in 1965. A half-dozen locations still lingered into the mid-1970s before it closed for good.

Ogilvy's basement *1307 St. Catherine W. (1929-1983)* Montrealers could time-travel in the 1980s by spending a night swaying on a dance floor in a sea of dyed-black Goth hair and then lining up the next day to be served by matronly, beehive-hairstyled Ogilvy's waitresses with names like Dot and Gertrude, all decked out in practical shoes and well-ironed aprons. Ogilvy's basement welcomed all comers as a heavenly throwback oasis with reassuringly comfortable booths and dim lights, offering not just solid and affordable square meals but also a taste of old-style kitsch that united the generations. But Montreal was determined to make a tragic break with its past and Ogilvy's basement cafeteria became a victim of the spirit of misguided modernization. The city lost the joy of this department store basement paradise where sausages and pancakes were offered for an obscenely affordable $1.50. An upscale Westmount-wallet-chasing food counter replaced the beloved cafeteria but nothing could replace the magic of the old reliable.

Orange Julep *3100 Sherbrooke E., 8000, 7700 Decarie (1932—)* The giant, hypnotic goofy prop landmark on Decarie didn't earn its domination in a single step. The bright orange 1965 dome is larger modular fiberglass knockoff of the cement

Sherbrooke E. & Moreau

original, built in 1945 one block north at 8000 Decarie, expropriated for the expressway dig of 1964. The concrete orb lacked the swag of its larger progeny but it came with a place upstairs where the Gibeaus planned to live but was used instead by roller-skating waitresses to snooze breaks between hauling trays of curb-service burgers. The Geodesic Dome-like precursor structures was funded by Hermas Gibeau's juice stand at Belmont Park, which grew into a mini-orb at Sherbrooke and Moreau and lasted until 2009. It served a juice made possible by railways that brought oranges to a huge warehouse at the old Bonaventure train station and by watering it down with egg whites and milk. Gibeau's life was not only orange-inspired joy, as his six-year-old son drowned after falling through ice on East End St. Just Street near the St. Lawrence River and his penny-pinching wife Irene was once fined $10 in 1939 by the Office of Reasonable Salaries for

Old Orange Julep at 8000 Decarie

destroying records. The bright orange orb, which eclipses the Guaranteed Pure Milk bottle as primo oversized oddball prop, offered rollerskating waitresses until 2005 when authorities ordered them into helmets. Gearheads still assemble vintage hot rods out front and pilots get their bearings from the ball. Gibeau himself lived mostly in Florida and was 92 when he died there in 1999.

Chez son Père *12 St. Antoine E., 907 St Lawrence, 5316 Park*

(1929-1977) Campy celebs like Liberace, Xavier Cugat and mail-order muscleman Ben Weider beamed over meals for newspaper

testimonials to promote French chef François Bouyeux, who didn't mind taking a circuitous route to being taken seriously. The first Chez son Père was expropriated for the courthouse, leading owner F.-X. Moissan to retire and sell to Louis Vaudable in 1959. It hauled its trademark bead curtains to the Main near Viger, where Pierre Trudeau's gang met in the 1960s with arch-rivals such as Pierre Vallières to debate federalism. That location was claimed by the Ville Marie Expressway and so it moved to a former adult vocational centre on Park Avenue where Outremont residents like Premier Robert Bourassa often dined. That costlier, larger location specialized in lobster for a half dozen years before being cooked by bad reviews.

Dilallo's *(1929—)* Luigi Diallo's crumbly burgers lured

appetites to 6801 Monk until it was expropriated for a metro in 1976, moving on over to its familiar spot at 2851 Allard. Sons Louis, Carlo and Tony took the reigns when papa died in 1959 and the Buckburger, served upside-down with capicole, hot pepper, onion and cheese, became a signature Montreal staple.

The chain rose to seven outlets by 2000, including at Notre Dame and Charlevoix, co-owned by NHL goaltender Gilles Meloche, one of many kids the family encouraged into the hockey team they sponsored. Mario Lemieux—whose parents kept living in their tiny home nearby throughout his hockey career—also played for the Dilallo-funded Ville Emard Hurricanes. Lemieux, alas, could not eat at Dilallo's, as he'd be swamped by admirers on each visit.

Eaton's Tea Room *677 St. Catherine W. (1930-1999)*

Losing this art deco, ship-inspired department store gem was as painful to the white-gloved tea-sipping set as losing the Montreal

Expos was to wearers of tri-coloured ball caps. The main room offered a knock-your-socks-off, jaw-dropping, majestic experience, as diners sat amid columns, a sky-high ceiling and impeccable artistic symmetry. To a city that cruelly never knew much art deco, Jacques Carlu's knockoff of the *Ile de France* ocean liner was like an orange to a sailor with scurvy, as one became instantly

uplifted before even before propping elbows on white linen tablecloth. The tea room, which opened about five years after Eaton's launched in 1925, had its rare troubling moments, such as when a 20-year-old woman from New Brunswick leaped to her death out one of its windows in 1943 and again when management was fined in 1983 for under-cleanliness, as a manager was known to recycle bread rolls from the trash. Then there was that awkward rebranding attempt in the early-1970s which saw the

restaurant renamed *Le Vieux Bonsecours*, painted in coral and its waitresses and busboys clad in red and white. The ninth floor tea room was a great place to finally reveal to you mother that you are gay, as one Eaton's clerk noted. The city lost a magical refuge when Eaton's closed in 1999. Quebec named the tea room a heritage site that year but it has remained mothballed ever since.

Miss Montreal *7600 Decarie (1935-1981)* A retired railway car became a transferable temple of tastiness in 1910 after being souped up with 20 stools to feed plane-spotters visiting the Cartierville Flying Field. Mike's Spot, as the diner was known, offered humble fare like hot buttered toast until it was slowly rolled down Decarie 25 years later, where it became Miss Montreal. Norm Silver and Jack Blatt came on board and injected more menu options and a souped-up decor on the west side of

Decarie near Paré. Ownership hyped the chicken-in-a-basket, fried chicken with fries served in a wicker (in later years plastic) basket. Waitresses would plant a bowl of coleslaw in front of all diners, then offer griddle cakes, PuPu platters served with a small sterno flame, corned beef Lantman's Special platters and strawberry shortcake, often while fawning over the jockeys who dropped in from nearby Blue Bonnets. At its 1950s peak Miss Montreal had 145

staffers and seating for 500 in comfy seats surrounded by driftwood. It claimed to be the first in town offering curb service, which allowed car showoffs to eat inside their vehicles, as waitresses fastened specially-designed skinny trays onto car windows. Owners included

Maurice Novek, who launched the Miss Snowdon and Miss Dorval knockoffs in the early 1960s and successor Johnny Whiteman, who moved it near to De la Savanne, as the Decarie underwent its big highway dig in 1964. The new location would never shine as bright as the original and police raided in 1973 for serving booze without a license, part of what they insinuated was a Jewish Mafia affair. It closed in 1981 and was demolished in 1997 to be replaced by a funeral home.

Piazza   Tomasso *8205   Decarie   (1935-1987)* Decarie

Boulevard was dotted with barns and cabbage patches back when Eminio "Tommy" Di Tomasso ditched his gigs as Montreal's top

trumpeter in 1948 to run his mom's restaurant. Tommy squeezed his Rolodex for quality musicians and snagged Magic Tom Auburn to host a Thursday afternoon Kiddies Cabaret from 1951 to 1975, which eventually had 25,000 members and 120 kids attending. Tomasso bought roller skates for waitresses who offered summertime curb service from 1953 until the early 1970s. Di Tomasso, a frequent Restaurateur of the Year and onetime head of the Canadian Restaurant Association, propped a billboard testimonial featuring Jackie Gleason on the roof, while also publicizing visits from Tony Bennett and

Dihanna Carroll and tag-lining ads with "where the stars dine." The restaurant closed for renovations after Tommy died at the age of 66 in 1973 and never recovered its shine. An ill-fated franchise in the downtown Les Terraces mall also drained resources. The Di Tomassos were embittered after being fined

for their English signs in the mid-1980s and served their final club sandwich on May 10, 1987. Its name survived on frozen grocery store pizzas but the land where all the fun once happened now still sits vacant as abandoned scrubland.

Curly Joe's *(1937-1990)* and **Joe's Steak House** *1453 and 1459 Metcalfe (1956-1998)* A pair of steak joints co-existed peacefully until the senior switched its name to mirror its upstart

neighbour, sparking an all-out charbroiled T-bone war. The Pollack brothers opened the Mount Royal Steak House in 1937, while Joe's Steak House launched two decades later 15 metres north. Mobster Willie Obront and pals purchased the Mount Royal in 1967 and renamed it Curly Joe's. Obront and co-owners Sam Rubin and Gerald Pencer ran ads describing Curly Joe's as "the original," a brazen piece of nominal mimcry. Management at Joe's had other problems, as they owed $360,000 in taxes, forcing the restaurant to close for two years from 1976. When it reopened, manager Joe Hanna switched from one place to the other a total of four times and was eventually accused of misdirecting Joe's-seeking diners from the sidewalk into the wrong place. Joe's owner Lillian Pollack sued Curly Joe's for $75,000 in 1985, alleging that Hanna, 50, slandered her place. A 1990 fire settled the rivalry. Joe's reopened a year later. Curly Joe's did not.

Dinty Moore's *1236 St Catherine W. (1938-1967)* George McManus immortalized restaurateur James Moore in his *Bringing Up Father* comic strip, so Moore took advantage of

his fame to open a chain that included an outlet beneath the Chez Maurice nightclub. Cartoon Jiggs loved corned beef and cabbage and so naturally that dish was front row centre at this place known for its window portholes and well-exploited liquor license. Charles Manella, who started the Metropolitan News at Peel and St. Catherine, owned it and other joints when he died in 1967.

Moishe's *3961 St. Lawrence (1938–)* Morris "Moishe" Lighter started busing tables at the Yankowitz and Julis restaurant in 1927 and 11 years later won ownership in a card game with his compulsive gambling boss Saffrin, whose descendants still rue the recklessness. Lighter renamed it The Romanian Paradise, and went head-to-head against the better-known Bucharest Steak House across the

road. But his old-country name itched for a switch after Romania found itself allied with Hitler. Lighter, who married late in life, rose at 5 a.m. to scrutinize beef at meat packing houses. He never ate lunch or sat with

customers and always returned home at 4 p.m. to dine with wife Beatrice and three kids. Lighter died in 1986 and son Lenny now oversees a unionized staff that includes some with over 50 years seniority, while a few dedicated diners come for lunch and dinner, making 10 visits a week. Branded grocery items now generate most of Moishe's profits.

La Binerie *387 Mont Royal E. (1938–)* Brothers Leo and Joachim Lussier's humble bean restaurant remains not just a time-honoured jewel of the common-folk gustatory Plateau

restaurantscape, its ownership was also the prize famously sought by Yves Beauchemin's protagonist in *Matou* (1981), the massive-selling Quebec novel. The 10-stool diner is "a grail of the ordinary, a mythical spot" that serves up 32 tons of homemade lard-cooked beans a year, cooked in the original cast-iron basement oven. Tortière, pork roast, fried eggs and salmon pie stayed popular after Leo's son-in-law took it over and remained so after Fernand Groulx took the baton in 1978. Jocelyne Brunet worked the kitchen for two years before purchasing it with hubby Philippe Brunet in 2005.

Chic-n-Coop / Indian Room *1198 St. Catherine W.*

(1939-1961) Montreal was a backwater for chicken when the Hill brothers opened the Chic-n-Coop on the day the Allies declared

war on Nazi Germany. Chef Dillard Smith—a striking black man in a bowler hat—perfected a sauce that got diners lining up for half-a-block, for a half-a-chicken, for half-a-buck. Diners could enjoy the soothing sounds of Henrietta Carrick on the Hammond organ or see stars like Montreal Royals pitcher Tommy Lasorda dining with Habs goaltender Jacques Plante, who designed the first goalie mask on a napkin at the restaurant. "I want a mask just like your baseball catchers wear," said Plante, who became hockey's first full-time masked man. The Hill brothers, who opened the Frolics nightclub on the Main in 1929 and launched Montreal's first Mexican restaurant, El Chico Club four years later at Metcalfe and St. Catherine, added the Indian Room next door to the Chic-n-Coop in

1949 where German artist Winold Reiss's murals offered tribute to the Blackfoot, while war hero flying ace Buzz Beurling greeted diners before his ill-fated trip to Israel. It served such treats as lamb-on-flaming-sword and marinated herring. The building at

Drummond was the former house of Father of Canadian Confederation Thomas D'Arcy McGee and was hit by fire in 1961. Two carved Irish lintel stones that adorned the building from McGee's time were donated to Loyola College. The Ville Marie Wax Museum later inhabited the premises and its wax figures of Sleeping Beauty and Prince Charming inspired a politically-inclined young man to smash the window with a hammer in March 1967.

Ruby Foo's *7815 Decarie (1945-1984)* Illegal gambling hustlers Leo Bercovitch and Max Shapiro—who reputedly won his ownership share at the gambling table—took over Gallagher's Restaurant, which lasted four years offering such fare as "frankfort grilled in pure creamy butter." They borrowed a Boston Chinese female restaurateur's name and filled the

700-seat, 300-parking space eatery—12 minutes from downtown!—favoured by taxi drivers eager for a higher cab fare. Waiters served Chinese food, prune juice, deviled eggs, $1.60 prime rib steaks, "exclusive French cuisine," while a silk-kimonoed Chinese cigarette girl sold smokes, a trio serenaded the lounge and photographers sold souvenir snaps.

Trampoline acts, stand-ups and torch singers supplied moderately ambitious show fare, featuring blonde bombshell Inga Andersen, "pert Parisian" Simone Dolphen and actor Buddy "Jed Clampett" Ebsen. Tyrone Power, George Raft and Rudy Vallee drifted in, as did Mafia chief Vic Cotroni. Ads boasted "an atmosphere that's just right for summer

bachelors" and bartender Benny Lajoie introduced defence minister Pierre Sévigny to honey pot Gerda Munsinger in 1960, leading to a faux espionage crisis. Habs great Maurice "Rocket" Richard often low-profiled it through the back but he marched in to wild cheers after helping beat Detroit for the Stanley Cup in 1956, while PM Pierre Trudeau routinely pestered chefs for the recipe for their *Duck a L'Orange* on his Sunday visits. While publicly traded, it declared $2.3 million in 1961 sales, making it "Canada's most successful restaurant." Owner Irwin Leopold added 118-hotel rooms in 1962 and managed a staff that later forgot that sprinklers would rain down when they smoked salmon, leading to a lengthy 1981 closure. Union strife preceded its demise.

Monsieur Neptune *1488 Mansfield (1945-1970)* "Enjoy

the thrill of catching your own live lobster or fish in our giant aquarium," implored ads for Monsieur Neptune, which sought to

entice diners by inciting piscicide, even lending a rod and a net to commit the grisly aquatic deed inside the old Mansfield Hotel at the southwest corner of De Maisonneuve. The restaurant's bland ads remained unchanged for years, as management boasted it was "specially requested by the City of Montreal to supply a fabulous banquet in Paris for Canadian and French delegates." The Neptune angled for guests from the adjacent hotel, but not of the lowbrow variety, once snootily telling tourists "this is not

a snack bar" when they ordered only hash browns in 1970. It was razed for what became a longstanding parking lot.

Corso Pizzeria *204 St. Catherine E. (1947–1958)* Pizza is a

"pie covered with tomatoes, cheese, anchovies and Italian sausage" that "needs tasting to really be appreciated," explained a

Mastracchio

columnist in 1947. This original downtown pizza building also housed a flying barbotte joint, one of many $1-per-toss dice gambling outlets that Diodato Mastracchio's gang operated. Mastracchio—whose wife Vittoria divorced him for adultery in 1949—stashed cash in a locker at the Montreal Pharmacy, which he would employ to spring found-in dice-rollers for $50 each. Mastracchio and three partners divided the building into a half dozen sub-parlours, so if police padlocked one gambling den, they would open another down the hall. Mastracchio was arrested and punished for his gambling sins and was busted again in 1952 after undercover RCMP officer Hugh Walker infiltrated his inner heroin-importing circle, leading to 23-months in prison and costing his heroin king crown. The Corso later burned down and insurers only paid $85,000 for a property that owners claimed was worth $1.5 million. Mastracchio died in 1969, aged 51.

Butch   Bouchard's *881   De   Maisonneuve   E.*

(1948-1983) Canadiens rearguard Émile "Butch" Bouchard broke into the NHL during World War II and after seven solid seasons he also scored as a restaurateur, one of several Habs to pad their

puck-pushing incomes with a Montreal eatery. (Others included Toe Blake, Henri Richard, Bernie Geoffrion, Shayne Corson and Sergio Momesso). Bouchard retired from his $15,000-per-season hockey career in 1956 and kept busy by running the softly-lit, green-and-pink restaurant that featured gleaming linen and glittering glasses. Bouchard ran his establishment while also serving on Longueuil city council and presiding over the baseball Royals. The occasional Habs-related event took place at this spot behind the Dupuis Frères department store, including the time Maurice Richard picked out a lotto winner for a giant $25,000 prize in 1960. Hockey prestige did not grant Bouchard immunity from police, however, as his place was fined in 1961 for serving beer without food on a Sunday. Pierre Bouchard followed his father's skatesteps as a large-framed, slow-footed Habs' defenceman who also toiled at the restaurant. Indeed, so attached was Pierre to his father's place that when the Washington Capitals acquired his contract, Pierre initially refused to join his new team, as he preferred to tend to the family biz. Butch sold his part-interest in the place in 1977 after a doctor told him to slow down or die of heart disease. He closed it six years later and died in 2012.

Rieno Milk Bar *3950 Sherbrooke E. (1949-1990)* Stratton Stevens got rich dealing Greek ships after World War II but he subscribed to the old adage that a Greek is nobody until he has his own restaurant, so he launched a place just west of Pie IX,

using an employee's suggestion to keep bits of its previous name, Crémi**èrie** *No*tre Dame. Stevens brought curb service to the car-friendly spot, selling burgers and non-alcoholic wholesomeness implicit in the bovine name. Stevens later opened strip malls, motels and the Tramway restaurant on St. Catherine near Peel. He managed over 1,000 employees, who he trusted to be honest, leading to an occasional disappointment. Jet-setting Stevens dated Ivanka Trump and was friends with Hilary Clinton but later said managing his business empire was too stressful and he would have worked at a regular job if he did it over. Moe's Deli now occupies the spot.

Dusty's *4510 Park (1949-2012)* A perfect Montreal day might entail a stroll on the mountain, a stop at the hippie Tam Tam bongo jam and a dorsal slide into a booth at Dusty's to slay that

growling hunger with a mishmash omelette, bagel burger, cheese blitnz or a massive Big D. Dusty's dodged bankruptcy in 1991 and closed for a time five years later. But the feisty, unpretentious joint returned and outlasted the feral McDonald's next door, axed after a union drive. What was first known as Park Avenue Restaurant broke fasts of many people who tired of waiting at the Beauty's line up a few blocks east. Late-era owner Peter Lymbariou called it quits in about 2010 and staffers took over until it burned down two years later. It has been a deserted eyesore since.

St. Hubert Bar-B-Q *(1951–)* Free restaurant delivery first came to Canada thanks to a car accident that forced René Léger to hang up his fireman helmet after eight years fighting blazes. He and wife Hélène pursued their dream of owning a business by scoping out restaurants to see which had the longest line-ups. The biggest lines were for barbecued chicken, so their first operation at 6359 St. Hubert saw René cooking up the birds and Hélène serving tables and driving the delivery car. They obtained a secret sauce recipe and a stylized mascot drawn up by Disney veteran and legendary drunk Jack Dunham. Their big break came in 1954 when a TV telethon host spontaneously expressed a craving for St. Hubert chicken and he and his gang then lustily feasted on a dozen chickens on camera. Sales skyrocketed and countless new outlets opened, allowing René to take frequent tropical golf vacations, while Hélène spent her loot on lavish trips to other far-off destinations. The chain had 13 restaurants in 1973 and 51 eight years later, over half around Montreal. Ontario-based Cara purchased the chain for $537 million in April 2016.

Émile Bertrand *1308 Notre Dame W. (1951-2006)* This hot dog joint was a haven for those pining for the bubbly pine needle spruce beer beverage until late-era owner Barbara Strudensky, who took it over in 1960, was felled by her smoking habit. It continued around the corner for a time and its spruce beer legacy now lives on at Paul Patates on Charlevoix. Founder Bertrand was at 1401 Notre Dame for a few years prior to coming to the familiar spot in the early 1950s.

Colibri *1485 Mansfield, 1202 Bishop (1952-1984)* Hungarian Johnny Vago bemoaned the dearth of homey establishments where he could conduct leisurely chit-chats, so he persuaded a countryman to open Montreal's first espresso bar in a tiny, 10-foot wide, eight-table space at the then-buzzing corner of Mansfield and De Maisonneuve. French chef Jean Bonnin took it over around 1966 and earned constant rave reviews before André Krysiewski and wife Ida bought it in 1974. The Colibri migrated west to a larger space on Bishop where a former restaurant supply shop was redecorated with red tablecloths, stained glass windows and a fireplace. Reviewers were unimpressed and bankruptcy ensued. St. Leonard-residing

Krysiewski & Hanriat

Frenchwoman Marie-Francoise Hanriat purchased the restaurant items at auction and arrived with a legal writ of seizure on January 4, 1984. Krysiewski—who lived upstairs with his wife Ida and 19-year-old daughter Isabelle—did not welcome her arrival and stabbed her to death in the adjacent alleyway. Krysiewski was previously *maitre d'* at Mayor Jean Drapeau's Vaissseau d'Or restaurant three blocks east, which waged a far more successful battle against seizure agents 13 years earlier.

L'Échouerie *54 Pine W. (1953-55)* Hungarian George and

George of l'Échouerie

his wife arrived in Canada with $100 in pocket and within three years were attracting a jammed house of fellow painters as well as poets and musicians at their fisherman-themed place, which featured twice-monthly basement exhibits of mostly abstract *automatiste* art, whose leaders included the notable iconoclast Paul-Émile Borduas. Chess boards, beards, espresso, cigarette smoke, musical jams and loads of artsy and political chit chat thrived amid a sometimes-threadbare clientele who ate on credit when they couldn't afford a meal.

Da Giovanni *572 St. Catherine E. (1954–)* Giovanni Poggi started busing tables at the age of six in a village near Milan and then failed in a pair of Montreal-area restaurants before hitting

pay-dirt with his pasta place. From day one custom was so brisk that Poggi and his wife barely slept on weekends for several years, as they closed for only 90 minutes a day on Saturdays and Sundays. Four expansions failed to shorten the frequent line-ups—present even in bone-chilling cold—as the place served 1.1 million diners a year by 1980, dishing out 50,000 pizzas and 100 tonnes of homemade pasta, covered in 28 varieties of sauce. Poggi humbly explained that he lucked out, as the area was underserved by restaurants at the time. He didn't

bother getting a liquor license and as a result diners rarely lingered, often freeing their coveted seats within 30 minutes, as he watched over the operation from a seat near the cash for 12 hours a day. Customers were mostly budget-conscious east-side folk but they

also included political deviants like Raymond Villeneuve who conducted covert auditions for the first wave of FLQ separatist terrorists over spaghetti. An infuriatingly catchy uptempo TV commercial jingle proved a memorable earworm and many recall the constant clatter, echoes and non-stop motion inside the 250-seat place, as a fast-moving swirl, created by mostly-longtime staffers deftly conveying fragrant plates of giant meatballs onto tabletops. Poggi, who also owned a mink farm, sold out in 1981 when he was 53. Veteran restaurateur Paul Nakis has owned it since and has changed little, although long lineups have abated.

Kon Tiki *1455 Peel (1958-1984)* Pity the fool who never took a kitschy trip to Polynesia in the heart of the downtown Mount Royal Hotel, complete with grass skirts, flaming rum and pineapple drinks served with tiny paper parasols. The windowless space with fake lagoons and colourful lights was launched by actor Stephen Crane, ex-husband of Lana Turner, who aimed to copy his Hollywood bar

The Luau. Opening night kicked off with a celebrity visit from a young

Tina Louise (later of Gilligan's Island TV fame) and chunky overactress Priscilla Alden. And yes, movie star Lana Turner would occasionally drop in to the Kon Tiki with daughter Cheryl. Waterfalls flowed from ceiling to pond, as a small bridge spanned a stream of coloured water. Popular dishes included Bo Bo and Bali Miki and of course the Pu Pu Platter but most guests came for drinks with names such as The Volcano, The Scorpion and the Blue Lagoon, which could be sipped in the Lover's Nest equipped with real palm trees. Roving photographers would sell souvenir photos for a couple of bucks, which inspired Leonard Cohen's *Death of a Ladies Man* album cover, shot by "Anonymous Roving Photographer At A Forgotten Polynesian Restaurant." The Kon Tiki was a hot ticket on grad night and the first pit stop for Wayne "The Vampire Killer" Boden, who dropped in while fleeing prison. Management relocated elsewhere in the building after it was remodeled but the new version failed. Early-era employee Douglas Chang launched his own **Golden Tiki**, which lasted from 1974 to 1990 on Sherbrooke E. and **Jardin Tiki** *5300 Sherbrooke E. (1986-2014)* where the drinks and decor were tiki-tastic but many grumbled that the buffet was not the best in town.

Carol's Snack Bar *1463 Crescent (1958-1986)*A brightly-lit greasy-spoon on the Crescent Street bar strip offered consolation burgers and a jolt of caffeine sobriety to dejected late-night pickup artists discussing Stones tunes and Camaros. Crescent Street had few bars when Nick Iadeluca and wife Fernande opened their basement place, which rapidly became an

essential icon of the strip, where posters of Elvis and James Dean sat next to a sign urging diners to "yell like hell when placing an order." Their son Ron, a former Satan's Choice biker, slung tiny burgers to customers seduced by the overhanging Coca Cola sign, too distracted to notice how minuscule the beef patties were. Carol's did not serve fries, which irritated many among the drunk-dining crowd. Tragedy struck in June 1986 when Ron Iadeluca, 30, died taking a turn in Hudson on his customized chopper, leaving a widow, two kids and heartbroken parents. It was soon after incorporated into an adjacent bar.

Moe's Corner Snack Bar *1455 Lambert Closse (1958-2015)* Moe Sweigman cast a wide net. "The Westmounter, to the down-and-outer, the show people, the kids from the discos, waiters, barmaids, cops, taxi drivers, insomniacs and ladies of the night," all sought nourishment at Moe's, the place to grab a plate of bacon and eggs before or after a visit to the Forum,

Seville Theatre, or El Morocco (later the Mustache). Moe put up 8 x 10 framed glossies of visiting stars such as Sophie Tucker and Jackie Mason but longtime waitress Cecile tired of cleaning the glass. For years black-clad Rosie perched all day on a stool slurping soup and Canadiens' goaltender Lorne "Gump" Worsley fielded unsolicited netminding tips from diners, who might have claimed partial credit for the Habs bagging 10 Stanley Cups in the 18 years Sweigman ran the joint. Many starving musicians playing bargain gigs at the nearby Mustache scored free meals from soft-hearted Moe, while others would just drop in to buy from the 129 variety of cigarettes on offer. Sweigman was humble about his legacy. "People will still come here after I'm gone. As long as you serve good food at good prices, you can put a baboon behind the counter with a cigar in his mouth and they'll still eat." Peter and Bess Thomas took over n 1978, serving 200 breakfasts daily until Peter's son Eddie closed it.

La Crêpe Bretonne *2080 Mountain (1961–1976)* The French crêpe rivaled smoked meat as Montreal's quintessential dish and the place to get your paper-thin pancakes was the

bizarre haven of barrel chairs and rope-covered benches, where sailor-clad waiters served up superskinny stuffed pancakes inside an imitation prow of a French Louis IV galleon. In another room waiters with handlebar mustaches served crêpes named after girls. Frenchman Louis Tavan was a 30-year-old under-employed truck driver living in Ste. Adèle when he started selling his wife Josette's Brittany-style crêpes to skiers. They sold so well that the couple moved their operation to Mountain Street into a building that Tavan later bought from Sam Silver for $100,000. Tavan, who was as small as his moustache was large, opened crêperies at 5182 Côte des Neiges, 808 St. Catherine W., and 360 St. François-Xavier, indeed he opened a new restaurant every year between 1957 and 1973, when he had 240 employees on his payroll. All were charmed by the Crêpe Bretonne's upstairs room with its miniature cannons, fish nets, polished oak tables, Breton hats, green lagoon and ship wheel, but waiters grew weary of their cute costumes and cooks started skimping on the peaches, asparagus, chicken, sausages, lobster, ham and honey that were meant to jam the crêpes.

Competition crept up among Montreal's 6,000 restaurants in the 1970s and the fad eventually walked the plank. Tavan, who had an apartment in Côte des Neiges and a turkey farm on the Eastern Townships, faded into obscurity, other than a kerfuffle in 1982 when he complained to police about a goon shakedown before he moved back to Europe. The Mountain Street strip, once  known for such lively establishments as Le Bistro bar and later the Jaggerz alternative nightclub, is now occupied by retail outlets.

Stage Coach / La Diligence *7385 Decarie (1961-1993)*

The square-footage didn't get more impressive than the place launched by serial restaurateurs Eli, Cecil, Victor and Louis Hill in 1961. The brothers had opened the Indian Room downtown

 years earlier so they went for a cowboy theme at the Stage Coach. Sam Rubin bought it in 1969 and rechristened it La Diligence in 1971. Rubin, who had also owned Curly Joe's downtown steakhouse, loaded the giant space with country antiques suspended from the ceiling, including spinning wheels, farm implements, milk cans and rocking chairs, which left some feeling claustrophobic and wary of death by falling ceiling display. One summer morning in 1984 four armed robbers walked in with ski masks tied up 10 employees, including Rubin and 62-year-old kitchen helper Pappy who told a reporter, "I figured they were trigger happy." The salad bar was a hit, as was dinner theatre with such stars as Patsy Gallant. Former boxer Manny Gitnick bought it in 1991 but never made a cent and closed two years later. A trio of restaurants now inhabit the premises.

Tokyo Sukiyaki *73 Mountain Sights Ave.*

(1961-2002) Montreal's first Japanese restaurant plopped chopsticks down at 5612 Decarie just as the massive depressed expressway was being dug. So management carted the wasabi to a spot a sushi-toss away from Jean Talon and Decarie, placing its delicate and serene presence next to warehouses and tire shops.

Diners were required to remove shoes at the door and wear colourful slippers as they crossed tiny bridges spanning goldfish-filled streams to tami rooms, private cubicles with shoji screens, red lanterns and straw tatami mats. Management cheated tradition by modifying cross-legged floor seating with dug-in leg-wells, allowing diners to sit on the floor while still dangling toes. Although dog-eared in later years, Tokyo Sukiyaki attracted high-rollers like Prime Minister Pierre Trudeau and actor Jean-Paul Belmondo, were served by soft-spoken kimono-clad waitresses who followed Japanese custom by serving men first, delivering delicious plates of chicken *yakitori*, shrimp tempura and *shabu shabu*. The operation quietly disappeared around 2003 and a much-less-graceful *Centre de Collision* now inhabits the site.

Bill Wong's *7965 Decarie (1962-2007)* Montreal's first-ever

Chinese buffet sprouted up amid the noise and dust of highway construction in an oversized space that had faltered in

its previous incarnation. Owner Bill Wong was known as a bad cook and an introvert who secretly felt burdened by having to deal with customers. None of that mattered, as the restaurant proved a smash. Wong rose to restaurant hero status after paying his way through McGill engineering school with a newspaper route. He then toiled briefly for Bell Canada before quitting to manage a Chinese restaurant and then opened his own House of Wong on Queen Mary, said to be Montreal's first Chinese restaurant outside of Chinatown. Wong caught the eye of a landlord who gave him a sweet offer to take over the fully-equipped Candlelight restaurant on Decarie, once dubbed Canada's biggest. Wong hired 15 cooks and the buffet restaurant was a hit, thriving in spite of hokey newspaper ads with such catch-phases as "What's Wong, Bill?" and  "Everything's Wong Here." When food inspectors found a dead mouse in 1990, Wong apologized in large newspaper ads. Crowds only grew. Wong's son Earl took over when his dad retired at age 81 in 2001 but he shut it down six years later citing long hours that took him away from his kids. Bill Wong

Bill Wong

died in 2014, aged 93. His survivors, including his daughter, the noted journalist Jan Wong, have since been in litigation over the building.

Le Gobelet *8405 St. Lawrence (1963-1994)* Bernard Janelle despised even the smell of beer but needed to fill a vacant space in his building, so he replicated a pub he saw in Covent Gardens,

London. Janelle spent a fortune in artwork and bucolic items salvaged from a 19th century barn in Rosemere so clients could sip 20-cent beer near a massive fieldstone fireplace that roared even in summer, singing budgies and a

once-banned Robert Roussil nude sculpture displayed in a police jail in 1949. Menu items ranged from Brome Lake duckling *a l'orange* with Bordelaise sauce to pork and beans, served amid the sound of chirping songbirds, a red tile floor from Wales and a confessional, which served as a phone booth so drinkers could plausibly inform wives that they were at confessional. Intellectuals *Les gens du livre* penned the influential *Carnets du*

Gobelet based on their meetings at the place. One hundred feminists, with more men than women, marched on the tavern in January 1969 to protest female exclusion. "Men can go to the tavern if they want to get away from the outside world; we have no place to go," declared Brenda Zannis. Police fined Janelle for serving the women, which Janelle fought in court. A blaze forced a one-year closure in 1971 and Janelle, who doubled as an art lecturer, reopened as the province's first brasserie, essentially a tavern that allowed women (Bill 44 also lowered the drinking age from 20 to 18). Few taverns made the switch

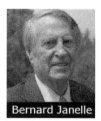
Bernard Janelle

initially, as it required adding a bathroom and owners also claimed women were fussier and drink less. The newly-redone brasserie came with a two-tiered beer garden, bidet-style urinals and a heated roost to welcome pigeons. Georges Durst purchased the establishment in 1987 made it a branch of his thriving *La Cage aux Sports* empire but it struggled and shut down for good in 2002 after a brief return as Le Gobelet. Janelle died in 2011 and the building now houses an antique store.

Sambo's *5666 Sherbrooke E. (1963-1983)* The Montreal franchise of a fast-growing coffee, pancakes and burger chain wasn't launched with any intention of having a racist name, as

Sambo was taken from its Califor nia founders **Sam** Battistone and Newell **Boh**nett, although that claim was belied by table mats emblazoned with comical caricatures of Africans. One thousand parking spots offered curb service, which meant a long trek for waitresses carrying trays to parked cars. The 1,000-plus branches in the United States almost all changed their names over the years but this one kept calling itself Sambo's to the bitter end. Tiny Sambo Pizzeria at St. Catherine and Joliette now bears the name.

Café Prag *1433 Bishop (1964-1988)* A family of eight German-speaking Bohemian Czechs fled the Soviet Bloc in 1952 and all found employment except for oldest brother Kurt. So the Sperlich clan remedied his work woes by purchasing a downtown building and opening a restaurant that soon became a magnet for girls with bob cuts, velvet miniskirts and shaggy-haired boys clad in Nehru suits and hush puppies. Leonard Cohen penned *Suzanne* while drinking espresso in the corner. Novelist Robertson Davies debated an FLQ supporter at one of the long wooden tables near stucco walls. Playwright David Fennario did some productive people-watching at the Prag while rocker Robert Charlebois and film star Geneviève Bujold also dropped in regularly. English and French-speakers both frequented the Prag, which a 1967 *Reader's Digest* guide book described as a "hangout for separatists." Bikers moved in and killed the early buzz, prompting Sperlich to keep a loaded gun in his drawer, while a group of rough kids tried to torch the place after being ejected in 1969. The Prag persevered, hosting live jazz, Dixlieland Thursdays and cheap meals of soup, bread, pastry and coffee for $1, all served until well after midnight, a godsend for hungry students. The Sperlichs also opened The Annex bar next door, notable for its film screenings. The Prag closed in 1988 and Sperlich died a dozen years later. Early-era regular Bob Abitbol memorialized the place in his award-winning 2003 novel *Les Amants du Café Prag.*

Chez Bardet *591 Henri Bourassa E. (1965-1981)* Montreal was home to a French restaurant so outstanding that *The New York Times* frequently urged readers to strap on tuques and travel

André Bardet

north for a meal. Owner André Bardet, a tall, solidly-built Frenchman took over a steak house with a mission to teach Montrealers *haute cuisine*, which he whipped up with his tiny dog at his side. The interior featured cane black chairs, low ceilings, tapestries, wall sconces and decent reproductions of French impressionists, with 25,000 bottles of wine in the basement. A typical meal included chicken liver with pistachios and fresh strawberries *a l'angevine au Cointreau*. The restaurant was busiest at lunch and three-quarters of diners were English-speakers, over half of them American tourists. Bardet was affable to clients and stern with staff who later took over cooking all that that cream, butter, shallots and endives. He still spent 15 hours a day at his restaurant before retiring to France in 1979. Chef Michel Dunas took over but went broke within a couple of years. Bardet died in 1995 at the age of 77. The replacement building now offers pizza by the slice.

The Image *3435 Park (1968)* Flower-power bloomed in 1968 and the stoner scene centered around this coffee shop that replaced The Op, just south of Prince Arthur. The Image served no booze or entertainment but that failed to slow the flow of hippies, bikers, draft dodgers and dealers that flocked down its

3435 Park 1966

three steps. Owners Cliff Gazee and drug dealer Sam Fried were in their early twenties and many customers even younger, with all sharing an appreciation of mind-altering medicines easily obtained from a drug store of dealers, including members of the fledgling Satan's Choice biker gang. Gazee named his place The Image for his artsy plan to snap photos of everybody who entered but he found himself too busy to get his camera out, as police targeted the spot and often arrested hippies for little reason. Customers included cape-wearing chess whiz King John, who dealt a higher-quality of Mexican marijuana, Mike French, a brutish biker prone to sexual assault and Reet Jurvetson, later mysteriously killed in Los Angeles. The Image lasted less than a year and the building was later demolished for the La Cité apartment towers. Fried overdosed on laughing gas in 1974 and Gazee became a social worker.

La Banquise *994 Rachel E. (1968–)* Pierre Barsalou tired of endlessly staring at the fire station ceiling on Rachel, so he slid down and rented a fire-damaged store across the street where he started spending his non-blaze-dousing time mixing milkshakes. He named it *banquise*, the French word for ice floe but soon

realized that nobody buys ice cream in the winter so he made it a greasy spoon and passed it on to his 19-year-old daughter Annie in 1994. She spruced it up on a tight budget, ditched the cigarette-burnt rugs and video lottery machines. One day a diner asked for a bunch of unusual ingredients on his poutine and the new dish was placed on the menu in his honour. Other diners became creatively competitive and soon the menu was full of poutine variations, eventually making the place Montreal's world-acclaimed go-to spot for that Quebec fries-gravy-and-cheddar curds poutine treat. The place doubled in size and is now jumping 24 hours a day, proving that sometimes one has to wait 35 years to realize one's true mission.

Decarie Hot Dog *953 Decarie, St. Laurent (1969–)* Tom Vriniotis's earliest memories include the moment his father Nick examined what would become a St. Laurent tube steak

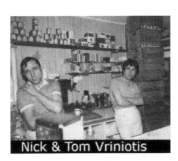

Nick & Tom Vriniotis

institution. It was love at first site as Nick signed a lease to replace the Carnival Snack Bar and went on to purchase the building a decade later. Nick, now in his eighties, still comes six days a week to serve up steamies and poutine to the hundreds who occupy the eight stools, some past 1 a.m. Tom and his sister have taken charge and changed almost nothing, including the original flawed sign offering TOATS. Tom, who works the evening shift, attributes the loyal following to his tangy coleslaw and homey friendliness. "Whether a customer comes in wearing a suit or pants hanging down, we treat them the same," he said. Prior to launching his St. Laurent hot dog emporium, Nick owned a similar place at Ontario and Alexandre de Sève where a worker stabbed boxer Tony Percy to death in 1962 while fending off a broken bottle attack.

Vaisseau d'Or *1100 Cypress (1969-1971)* Mayor Jean Drapeau gambled that Montreal diners wanted seven-course meals for $10 served over the sounds of a 20-piece orchestra. So he opened such a place inside the Windsor Hotel, where his 300-seat Golden Vessel was decked out in chandeliers and paintings of poets like Émile Nelligan. Opening night proved a disaster, as diners walked out after waiting forever for food and those more patient gave thumbs-down to the no-talking-during-music rule. Protesters of every stripe relentlessly targeted the

mayor and bombed the restaurant in the fall of 1969 after doing the same to Drapeau's Rosemont home a few weeks earlier. Business wasn't helped by tanks rolling through streets during the October Crisis of 1970 and the restaurant closed in January 1971. The Webster family, which owned the

Windsor Hotel, noted that Drapeau had gone over a year without paying rent and attempted to to seize $30,000 of restaurant items. Drapeau's henchmen moved in and cut the bailiff's locks and moved the items out while Drapeau sat barricaded in the basement. Police decided that Drapeau had acted legally. "Would you do something against your own boss?" one cop was sheepishly heard asking. Drapeau's arch enemy, scrappy longtime Point St. Charles city councillor Frank Hanley, had been working as a public relations consultant at the hotel, leading some to suspect he was behind the mayor's humiliating battle to defend his forks and knives. Another theory suggested the hotel brass was irked at Drapeau for neglecting his promise to try to open a casino in the hotel.

Reggio Bar *5880-5884 Jean Talon E. (c. 1970-78)* Mafia boss Paolo Violi's place in St. Leonard served up tasty gelato with a side dish of mob drama, complete with betrayal, brutality and

murder. Violi, a chubby, mid-fortyish, white-Cadillac-driving, separatist-hating, father-of-five, had wealth and power after rising to the top of the local mob. But he was also a hotheaded bully who once held a gun to the head of his window-washer and had henchmen beat a competing merchant with a wooden paddle as punishment for also selling gelato. Violi was also shareholder of Reggio Foods, which illegally sold dog food meat to humans. Bartender Jimmy "Rent-a-Gun" De Santis proved a loyal employee, accepting a year in jail for refusing to testify at a crime commission hearing in 1975. He was released after one month. Violi's secrets seemed safe until electrician Bob Wilson rented the upstairs apartment in December 1970. Wilson was really Bob Ménard, an undercover cop assigned to record Violi's restaurant conversations. The recordings spelled doom for Violi, who sold Reggio's to Guiseppe and Vincenzo Randisi. Violi was briefly jailed for contempt and police warned him that his Mafia brethren had a $50,000 contract on his head. Yet Violi did not flinch when invited to play cards at Reggio's where two masked men leaped out of a Camaro and shot him in the head with a 12-gauge Italian-made Zardini shotgun. "The pig is dead," said one. Ménard later expressed admiration for Violi for bravely facing his execution. Three men pleaded guilty to murder charges. Violi's two brothers were also killed, leading to ascendancy of the Sicilian Mafia Rizzuto clan. Impeccable and entirely respectable La Bella Italiana Restaurant now occupies the space. Gelato remains a popular menu item.

Skala *4869 Park (1970-2005)* Grungy heroin chic collided with a mellow Greek fisherman vibe in this existentialist-friendly spot where patrons sucked on smokes and swigged directly from quart bottles. The meeting of slacker and Mediterranean cultures began when musicians started appreciating Skala for its cheap food and beer, attracting groups like Three O'Clock Train, whose entourage included hard-drinking Howie, who would routinely pass out on the floor, forcing co-owner George Karygiannys to do his closing-time vacuum session around his prostate limbs. The sound system consisted of old-style jukeboxes, much appreciated for not drowning out artists mumbling about film funding and how best to finger guitar frets. Nicoletta Marcolefas' establishment started next door at 4871 Park in 1970 before new owner Karygiannys and his brother Christos brought to its familiar premises in 1978, taking over a beauty parlour. The trendy transformation of Park Avenue in the early 1980s saw business rise about sixfold, according to management, and new clients were not coming for the decor or sound system. Former regulars insist that the bar's reputation as a place to buy heroin and cocaine was largely unwarranted, while others recall it as a tense United Nations of dealers where clients wouldn't hesitate to fire up a crack pipe. The owners eventually opted for retirement.

George Karygiannys

Dunkin' Donuts *(1970–)* It was time to make the doughnuts—as the TV catchphrase repeated—after the Boston chain expanded into Quebec in the mid-1970s, occupying 250 oulets across the province within two decades, making it the clear king of the Quebec doughnut market. Canadian competitor Tim Horton's, emblematic of Toronto Maple Leaf hockey, might not have seemed a serious threat to the doughnut throne during a time when Canadiana was a non-seller in Quebec. But the big crowds at an early Tim Horton's at Ontario and Bercy proved ominous and Dunkin' Donuts saw its market share and outlets halved by 2002. Some franchisees pleaded with U.S.-based corporate headquarters to permit menu modifications for regional tastes. Their request was refused and almost all of the remaining Dunkin' Donuts outlets closed shop. Thirty of the franchises sued HQ and won an $11 million judgment. Years of

mockery on *Bonjour la Police* comedy skits on the popular *Rock et Belles Oreilles* TV program and undercooked dough possibly harmed the bottom line. The pink and orange signs have almost all now disappeared from Montreal.

Stash's Café *461 St. Sulpice, 200 St. Paul W. (1972–)* The scent of pierogies and stuffed cabbage floating into the narrow streets of Old Montreal form part of the legacy of

ink-stained freelance journalist Stanislas Pruszynski, who ditched the newspaper world after witnessing the assassination of Robert Kennedy in Los Angeles in 1968, his audio tape recording remaining one of the more chilling artifacts of the event. Old Montreal was a quasi-barren wasteland when the aristocratic Stash welcomed artisans to sell their wares at his fledgling flea market in Old Montreal at 338 Notre Dame E (just east of City Hall) in 1969, as he leveraged his media connections to shame city hall for allowing the old city to go to rot. Stash opened a modest Polish place next to Place D'Armes in 1972 and closed his flea market the next year, bitterly denouncing greedy landlords and tax collectors. Stash's restaurant proved a hit with diners and he sold it to waitress Eva Bujnicka in 1978 and moved back to Europe three years later. Fire ravaged the building in February 1992, forcing the operation to relocate to St. Paul Street. Bujnicka retired to Ontario and sold the restaurant to waitress Anita Karski in 2010.

Café Santropol *3990 St. Urbain (1973—)* Doorknobs that fall off when turned, creaky, crooked floors and windows that need to be jammed with hardcover books to stay open: Montreal was full of such homes in the early 1970s and a frequent remedy was to tag 'em and bag 'em. Noble buildings were routinely demolished, bricks carted off and new parking lots christened.

Garth Gilker rented an apartment in a such a building at the southwest corner of St. Urbain and Duluth. Demolition clouds loomed, so Gilker appealed to heritage groups to save the building but they just shrugged. When a plumbing company moved out from the first floor premises, Gilker stepped up with the $50 monthly rent. He started selling sandwiches to fund his renovations, which included landscaping the front and back. His sandwich business bloomed, so he set up a terrace out front, which led to much bickering with the municipal authorities, who were clearly not fans of outdoor snacking. Gilker learned that he had a solid ally in his corner, as his landlords were nuns who eventually agreed to sell the property (and several others nearby) for a co-op, thus ensuring

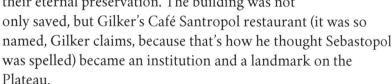

Garth Gilker

their eternal preservation. The building was not only saved, but Gilker's Café Santropol restaurant (it was so named, Gilker claims, because that's how he thought Sebastopol was spelled) became an institution and a landmark on the Plateau.

Giustini Steak House *6657 Paul Emile Lamarche (1974-1978)* Montreal's *sexy serveuse* naked waitress trend arrived when Melvin Deutsch and wife Esther defied nudity laws by hiring 30 waitress-strippers to serve meals topless from May 1974. Their establishment, set in deepest St. Leonard, stayed open around the clock, with nude dancing starting at 8 a.m.

Police raided the restaurant 68 times over eight months from October 1974, keeping the female talent in jail cells for a couple of hours before freeing them. Mel was not discouraged and opened four other steak houses, including one at 2 Le Royer in 1976, which met with similar police hostility. Deutsch attempted to sue police for $260,000 after they aggressively raided the new

Mel Deutsch at work

bar. But the 1977 Monique McCutcheon court ruling declared nude shows legal, inciting Mel to announce plans to launch a chain of topless waitress restaurants across North America. Deutsch, who called himself The King of Topless, moved to Ontario in 1978, citing police harassment after he was charged with hiring a 13-year-old girl to dance at his establishment. He met similar resistance in Ontario and made judicial footnote status by requesting that his trial be held in French, even he did not speak it fluently. Deutsch was later charged with many other offences and once offered a job to a woman on the condition that she sign a contract reading "I _____ agree to have sexual relations with Mr. Melvin P. Deutsch." *Sexy serveuse* restaurants enjoyed a revival during the early-1990s recession, with several modest Montreal restaurants trying out the gimmick before authorities made it difficult for them to operate.

Maison Egg Roll *3966 Notre Dame W., 3471 Wellington (1976–)* Retired Prime Minister Pierre Trudeau did more than General Tao to put this Chinese restaurant on the map, as he offered fiery political lectures in its meeting hall as part of his duties at a revived *Cité Libre* magazine, an influential 1960s publication resurrected in 1991. Trudeau's constitutional speech—described as a "wok on the wild side" by one headline—attracted 350 people who plopped down $20 to hear him talk about "the trouble with nationalism." The same venue also hosted The Replacements soon after, as the punk band rocked out for a considerably younger demographic. Forty-four-year old father-of-six John Mark got the The Egg Roll rolling during the Montreal Olympics and was known for traveling all the way to his home in Canton, China to buy garlic and soy sauce. He later branched out with another restaurant in Brossard. The building was demolished and replaced by a large grocery store around 2004 and reluctantly made news again in its new home on Wellington in 2006 when inebriated boxer Alex Hilton served up a plate of Sum Ting Wong by fighting with his ex-wife at the restaurant, landing him in jail.

Lentzos *1515 St Catherine W. (1978 -1986)* Where now towers the Concordia University behemoth at corner of Guy sat a homey 24-hour place midway between the Stork and the York (nightclub and theatre, respectively). Nightclubbers from nearby gay, punk and disco establishments would convene in its dim and comfy booths for submarine sandwiches and nocturnal pizza experiences. In the early 1980s veteran waitress Cecile was so beloved that diners would wait extra to get tables in her section. Lentzos sat kitty corner from a blindingly-lit doughnut shop where scruffy strongman The Great Antonio would sell his self-aggrandizing postcards. Lentzos was owned by a Greek, as were many—perhaps most—Montreal restaurants for a time. Vasilios Lentzos later moved to Plattsburgh, where he opened another place, while another Lentozos restaurant sat on Beaubien.

Consenza Social Club *4891 Jarry E.*

(c.1980-2007) Anybody could sip espresso alongside genuine Montreal Sicilian made men just by strolling into this generic spot in this strip mall near Viau.

Customers might be asked why they strolled in to that particular place but would get served in a friendly manner and sometimes offered free cake. The café had stools and a monster espresso machine but the real Mafioso sat in a separate sparsely-furnished room in the back. Passionate discussions could be seen taking place on a white couch beneath posters of racehorses and boxers and at least one car bomb exploded out front, unsuccessfully targeting mob boss Vito Rizzuto. Police planted surveillance devices in the place in a daring anti-Mafia operation that saw 80 cops and many technicians amass 28,000 hours of videotaped conversations between 2002 and 2006, resulting in scenes of an aging Nicolo Rizzuto stuffing huge wads of cash money into his socks. Police recorded the license plate numbers of all visitors, so anybody who innocently enjoyed coffee at the Consenza might now be listed deep in police files. The location is now occupied by a clothing store.

Euro Deli *3619 St Lawrence (1982-2013)* Attention-seekers who tired of sitting on their Plateau-district spiral staircases would raise the stakes and relocate to "The Beach," a ledge under the canopy of Vincent Scanzano's landmark eatery, which opened on a Main reborn by a slacker generation of hip culture vultures. A slice of pizza, ham and cheese calzone, eggplant lasagna, pasta or soup and espresso could be picked up at the cash and carried over to tables where artsies were known to linger. Regulars included musicians from Men Without Hats, The Nils,

Doughboys, Voivoid, Idées Noires, photographer David Sanders and filmmaker Stevie Way-Gone. The joint became a coffee-scented homeland for a generation that lingered over alternative weeklies while sipping Black Label beer in dive bars across the street. The Eurodeli Twins, Marco and Mauro La Villa, ran affairs before departing to make films in New York City. The Euro Deli stayed open until 4 a.m. before the late night post-bar bedlam became too much to handle. Property taxes rose and the rent doubled, leading to its surprise summertime closure.

Mad Dog Burger *(1988-1989)* Mad Dog Vachon served up headlocks and piledrivers on Saturday morning pro wrestling TV matches but conquering the world of fast food was also on

his bucket list. Sadly, his franchise dreams were pinned to the mat almost from the start, thanks to a crooked accountant. The chain began when electrician Martin Gilbert plopped down $50,000 to launch the maiden franchise at St. Catherine and St. Elizabeth, where Mad Dog and other pro wrestling friends found a home away from the mat. It took a year to get a second franchise open on Masson but Mad Dog missed the launch party after losing a leg in a hit-and-run. A third outlet opened briefly in Place D'Armes but the business failed fast. Former Union National president Jean-Marc Béliveau was in charge of the accounting and that was not a good thing, as he scattered the

Mad Dog Vachon

funds around in complex deals in China and Africa. "It was a very bad experience," the late Mad Dog said. "It was a good idea but he wanted to take all the money."

Other notables

Bagels Bagels Etc. *4320 St. Lawrence (1939—)*Main Lunch fired up the skillet on the eve of World War II and became Cookie's Main Lunch in 1957. Bagels appeared on its shingle in 1983, as the general fare joint helped feed the Plateau-area Renaissance amid old-style touches including the tin-stamped ceilings. It's most often mentioned as a Leonard Cohen hangout. **Fairmount Bagel** *74 Fairmount W. (1919—)*Jacob Drapkin and Isadore Shlafman started the Montreal Bagel Bakery at 3835 St. Lawrence in 1919 (although records peg it at 1932). Drapkin kept it going until 1956 but Shlafman launched his own in 1949 with his son Jack and family lodged in the upstairs duplex on Fairmont. Sesame bagels gained their dominance in the 1950s after a customer brought his own supply, claiming that the standard poppy seeds hurt his dentures. Third-generation Irwin Shlafman runs the place with military precision. **St. Viateur Bagel** *263 St. Viateur W. (1957–)* Myer Lewkowicz and wife Emma teamed up with Hyman Seligman (of the Fairmount bagel clan) to open his place after surviving Nazi death camps. Employee Joe Morena bought an interest in 1974 and took over two decades later along with Marco Sbaino. Writer Don Bell's whimsical *Saturday Night at the Bagel Factory* helped bring it fame in 1973.

Chicken Montreal became a mecca for barbecued bird around 1940 and friendly debate has raged ever since concerning the city's finest. **Laurier BBQ** *381 Laurier W. (1936-2011)*A giant rooster weather vane crowned a mansard roof on posh Laurier in a building where the Laporte family brought one of the best-loved chicken dishes before selling to a group that rebranded it for British celebrity chef Gordon Ramsay in 2010, an ill-fated venture that preceded a swift closure and legal action. **Chalet Bar-B-Q** *5456 Sherbrooke St W (1944–)*Hitler was on the run in 1944 but the real great news for Montrealers was that Marcel Mauron helped open the this timeless treasure, offering .35 cent thighs and .15 cent fries. Diners have since sat in orange booths, crayons on place mats for kids, all savoring poultry cooked in four charcoal ovens, as mature waitresses smoke out front. Daughter Louise McConnell took over after the founder died. Franchises were short-lived, including one where a cashier was killed by thieves in 1978 at 6825 Decarie. **Chalet Lucerne** *1631 St Catherine W. (1949-1989)* Swiss Bar BQ, as it was first known, offered a spicier sauce under a sign reading "a person never lingers, he lays aside his knife and fork, and eats with his fingers." Marcel Mauron's place across from Toe Blake's Tavern was fined for uncleanliness after being sold to a numbered company. The many successors at the space included the O Noir restaurant which offered meals in total darkness. **Marina Sweets** *196 6th*

Ave. (1950-56) William Calogeridis hired newly-arrived Greek Jimmy Essaris to wash dishes and he suggested they copy Chalet Bar-B-Q. Custom grew and by 1956 Essaris opened his own Quick Lunch and used those profits to buy a parking lot downtown, which he grew into a parking empire, that he later built skyscrapers upon. **Côte St. Luc BBQ** *5403 Côte St-Luc (1953–)* Maple char grilled poultry is still cooked in original ovens at a place that made news when a loan shark was shot dead while dining in a booth during a surely-delicious meal in 2000. **Poulet Frit Kentucky** *(1963–)* Tommy Tomasso's maiden Montreal KFC franchise at 5249 de la Savanne opened after Colonel Sanders moved to Toronto after selling his U.S. interests. It offered home delivery. The chain briefly became Scott's Villa du Poulet and is now known as PFK. A dozen outlets closed in Quebec in 2012 and as many still inhabit the island. **Coco Rico** *3907 St. Lawrence (1970–)* The Castanheira family, who founded the sit-down Janos restaurant, offers the fast-food version of deliciously greasy roasted Portuguese chicken to be eaten at a counter, which some note is cheaper and healthier than Schwartz's next door. It's recognizable by its rotating chicken window display, a throwback to when edible beasts were featured in many storefronts on the strip.

Chinese Dumplings and fried rice have long lured Montealers into the culinary ghetto of Chinatown, as the eastern eateries remain a treasured mainstay in the local gustatory heritage. **Nanking** *50 La Gauchetiere W.(1933-2000)* This eyewitness to old-time gambling dens and Tong wars kept its finger on the Chinese pulse until the 1990s, hosting public events under owner Woon Lam "Bill" Wong, who became president of the Montreal Chinese Chamber of Commerce. It was fined for uncleanliness in 1986, 1996 and 1998 and ditched its popular dim sung for a generic buffet. Wong, who was close to Mayor Pierre Bourque, was later nailed for an immigration scam. **Jasmine Café** *62 La Gauchetière W. (1945-1991)* Sweet and sour ribs and chicken chow mein starred on Chung Fun Tou's menu before he sold to the Yees, whose sons David and Howard were popular students at Montreal High School. **Silver Dragon Café** *1800 de l'Eglise (1958 – 2016)* Neon-lit dragons—sadly fallen into dark disrepair in later years—caught eyes at the gateway to Côte St. Paul. In early years staffers often worked 365 days a year and all remained under-the-table cash for decades. Locals targeted it with nasty jokes about stray cats ending up in the soup.**Yangtze** *4645 Van Horne, 6066 Sherbrooke W. (1961—)* Snowdon residents found a place to hang out on Christmas Day and still sing its praises decades later. Owner Marco Yao shifted it to another former Chinese restaurant on Sherbrooke, where the menu remains unchanged. **Van Roy** *1095 Clark (1958-2010)* This mainstay on the shady and narrow strip was first called the Kwong Chao Café but its fortune cookie read bad things in 1997 when inspectors found enough dirt for a fine. It was doomed by a complex legal dispute between rival Chinese Nationalist League groups claiming to own the building. **L'Orchidée de Chine** *2017 Peel (1987—)* Geoge Lau's Sechuan flavours were an instant hit and its fans included visiting movie stars. Lau's seven chefs from Hong Kong all eventually opened their own places. He said that the rise of sushi cost him customers, as did an aging clientele. "People who once came in with glamorous women are now coming in with walkers or wheelchairs," he told reporter Lesley Chesterman. **Le Piment Rouge** *1237 Metcalfe, 1170 Peel (1982—)*Hazel and Chuck Mah borrowed $20,000 to open their first place on Metcalfe, where their spicier cuisine drew crowds that allowed them to pay off their loan in just three months. A 1988 fire forced them into the much-posher former Windsor Hotel. The duo expanded to five restaurants in Montreal and Toronto, with a scary $1.5 million loan that they eventually paid off. They moved out of Peel in 2013 and now run the Piment 2 at 201 St. Jacques. **Kam-Fung** *1008 Clark, 1111 St. Urbain (1979—)* Dim sum dumpling brunches served on carts thrilled Montrealers when this place started the trend. The lively spot, known for also holding charity fundraisers and celebrity cook-offs, moved over to a tower one block west in recent years, changing its name to Kim Fung, as the Ruby Rouge took over the original place. **Beijing** *92 La Gauchetiere W. (1982 –)* Spicy northern food has lured the Chinese culinary cognoscenti to this place opened by Desmond Wong and sold to Dannic Lam and William Ma in 1989.

Deli Deathbed regrets rarely involve eating smoked meat sandwiches, even though they probably should. **Dunn's** *892 St. Catherine (1927–)* Myer Dunn sliced cold cuts on Papineau just north of Mont Royal before shifting to the downtown movie theatre strip in 1955. Staffers red-eyed it all night, serving 75 strawberry cheesecakes daily and many meaty meals. Grandson Elliot Kligman took over after Meyer died in 1993 and handed control to a pair of employees, while he concentrated on selling franchises and grocery store products. The new owners closed at night and business faltered and closed. It reopened not long later at 1249 Metcalfe. **Wilensky's Light Lunch** *34 Fairmount W. (1932–)* Moe Wilensky opened a humble cigar and soda shop at 115 Fairmount before its 11 stools were transported a block east in 1952 to the spot which remains Montreal's primo ramshackle throwback eatery. Paradox-of-choice misery was relieved after the restaurant stopped serving smoked meat and other items to concentrate on The Special, a fried salami and balogna sandwich on a kaiser bun. Staff will not serve it without mustard. Author Mordecai Richler claimed that his happiest moment took place when he won $2 at Wilensky's informal weekly pinball competition and he later returned the favour by featuring the restaurant (in its newer location) prominently in the film version of Duddy Kravitz, shot on site in October 1973. Widowed Ruth Wilensky worked until the age of 93, finally retiring in 2013. Her descendants now operate the place. **Chenoys** *3616 St John's (1936–)* Brothers Morty, Sam and Joe Chenoy had their first deli at 4447 St Lawrence, which lasted until 1949 when it moved to 5274 Queen Mary, renaming it Chenoy's Boys. They stayed until 1960. Morty then worked at Dunn's before teaming up with colleague Nick Sigounis to start the 24-hour place on St. John's. Morty sold out a decade later to Sigounis and his brother and died with Alzheimers in 1999. Franchises have come and gone. **Beauty's** *93 Mount Royal E. (1942—)* What has become best known as a breakfast place was launched by Hyman Skolnik and wife Freda, who transformed a candy store to launch what would become a landmark. Until he died in 2016 at age 96, Hyman still greeted customers amid throwback photos in a place that hasn't changed in decades. **Ben Ash** *1 St. Catherine E. (1944-1998)* Ben Ash served up smoked meat after taking over the Tucker Deli at 1335 Van Horne where he lasted until 1950, then moving to St Catherine and the Main in 1954, serving regulars like nearby novelty store owner Richard Whiteford who dined there daily for 40 years. An ill-fated franchise in the Côte des Neiges Plaza was where a young rowing champ shot five dead on June 25, 1972. **Snowdon Deli** *5265 Decarie (1946—)* Brothers Joe, Abe and Phil Morantz worked part time at Ben Ash then invested $3,000 each (including $1,000 war compensation for Abe's shrapnel wounds) to open their own place. Staffers included waitress Elizabeth Armstrong who logged over four decades and Sarto Orsino, who worked the kitchen for over 30 years. The brothers had all died by 2016 but it remains largely unchanged under descendants and in-laws. **Lester's** *1057 Bernard W. (1951—)* Bill Berenholc has fed Ordinary Joes as well as bigwigs at a place his father purchased in 1956 and later bequeathed him. The deli locked horns with a larger namesake for the right to sell plastic-wrapped smoked meat under the Lester's name. Lester's Foods (originally a deli at 4105 St. Lawrence as of 1931) prevailed in that dispute. **Le Roi Du Smoked Meat** *6705 St Hubert (1954—)* Many of Abe Kligman's dress shop customers lied when they promised to return after grabbing lunch next door. So he opened his own restaurant. Son Melvin took over in 1994. His son, in turn, later owned Dunn's. This place with throwback booths remains little changed, including its red peppers in window jars. **Brown Derby** *4827 Van Horne (1955-2000)* Quipsters dubbed this 250-seat non-kosher restaurant at the Van Horne shopping centre, "a Jewish Fellini movie" and a "meeting place for a local branch of the Israeli Parliament where all of the world's problems were solved over sandwiches and coleslaw." Characters included owner Sam Kolatacz and 30-year waitress Molly Gosselin, a British immigrant who dispensed blintzes, latkes and knishes and wry quips before retiring at age 75. Late-stage owner Harry Fleischer declared bankruptcy with $400,000 in debt after his 90 workers set up a union in the early 1990s and the strip mall eatery reopened under new ownership a month later with mostly the same staff but minus the union. It lasted a few more years before closing in 2000. **Gerry's Delicatessan** *3982 Ontario E. (1963–)* Gerry's opened at 4641 St. Catherine E, at the dog-eared corner of Aird where cops shot a robber dead outside after nabbing $300 from the till in 1993. It has morphed into a general fare restaurant since moving 10 blocks northeast in 2002. **Manny's Deli** *5274 Queen Mary (1959-1969)* Snowdon teens loitered out front with transistor radios while speculating whether it was a wooden leg causing former boxing champ Manny Gitnick to limp as he served up hot fare to locals at the former Chenoy's Boys Deli. Gitnick later tossed a big bash, featuring professional dancers, to christen his short-lived early-day discotheque Manny's Place at 5018 Decarie in 1964. **The Main** *3864 St. Lawrence (1974–)* Peter Varvaro was a student of smoked meat before founding The Main with his wife Diane on St Lawrence, where late night meals with latkes were munched under hand-drawn caricatures looking down from the walls. The clan has since shifted to Smoked Meat Pete's on the West Island. The Main's new owner Orlando Cardemil oversees the place where Céline Dion and hubby dined often before buying Schwartz's across the street.

French **Le 400** *1490 Drummond (1941-1958)* Jolly owner Edouard Lelarge was as large as his name implied, as the 240-pound veteran Parisian chef presided over the 400 Club, a place recognizable for its *"Je mange chez moi"* sign. Lelarge's mother owned the Cordon Bleu restaurant on Berri, where "hearts beat as one and life was happiness," according to one description. **Le Caveau** *2063 Victoria (1949-2010)* Well-heeled diners ate power breakfasts or dinners of steak tartare, oyster mushroom, marinated salmon and lamb in the cave-like Parisian-styled eatery a stone's toss from McGill's Roddick Gates. Some early-day meals cost just .88 cents after Albin McLaughlin opened it during the war. His son Gaetan later assumed ownership with a staff managed by long-timer Alcide Bernard. **Le Fournil** *361 St. Paul E. (1964-1968)* Thieves grabbed cash and 90 bottles of booze from Maurice Riopelle's embattled place near the Bonsecours Market. They did the same a week later. Countless promotional photos still falsely imply that the restaurant was a success. **Les Halles** *1450 Crescent (1971-2005)* Jacques Landurie and Jean-Pierre Beauquier started casually in a former Chinese restaurant but soon went upscale, making it the pricey place to go, serving up to 400 customers a day. Forty chefs, many from France, whipped up exotic dishes like lobster-and-grapefruit. Landure eventually bought out his partner and bemoaned the day he could not longer refuse men not wearing suits and ties. **Mas des Oliviers** *1216 Bishop (1976-2016)* Architect Ray Affleck, PM Brian Mulroney, Habs GM Serge Savard and author Morty Richler and other notables all flocked to Jacques Muller's discreet downtown circus of misfits and aging scenesters. The onion soup and garlic snails brought joy to this place across from the longtime eyesore parking lots of Bishop. Muller retired and closed at the age of 72 after a rent disagreement **L'Express** *3927 St. Denis (1980—)* Sophisticated dining, mixed with a charming ambiance and superstar service made Mario and Collette Broissoit's place on St. Denis the favourite of many food critic and fan of French cuisine. Joël Chapoulie ran a kitchen that rarely disappointed with flavours ranging from chalottes, butter and pistachios. The much-loved Broissoit helped organize a food stand in the Théâtre du Nouveau Monde (which brass had threatened to rent out to McDonald's) before she died in 2014. **Le Passe-Partout** *5563 Monkland (1981-2004)* Ingenious pastry chef James MacGuire propelled his power of obsession to create a den of smoked salmon, ice cream and bread considered best in town, all done with just a dozen staffers. High rents forced him to shift east to 3857 Decarie near Côte St. Antoine in 2001.

General Fare John's *4350 Notre Dame W. (1919-2012)* Two generations held this St. Henri fort for over 90 years, as John Volkakis toiled for over five decades at the place his father opened after World War I and shifted one block over to St. Marguerite in 1938. Diners ranged from artists to politicians. Social justice warrior types revived it with predictable results, as employees eventually protested non-payment following its closure in 2016. **Nick's** *1377 Greene (1920—)* Greek newcomer Nick Alevisatos opened Maryland Ice Cream Parlour with his cousin after World War I, leaving it to his son five decades later, as the clan bought up much of the block. Rob Callard bought the deli 1995, keeping the name but offering healthier salads and burgers cooked in canola oil. Actor Harvey Keitel (who married a Montrealer) sometimes pops in, as does Ben Mulroney who got down on a knee to propose at Nick's in 2007 (two kilometres east of the Mount Royal Tennis Club where his parents Brian and Mila met 35 years prior). Nick's claims to be Montreal's oldest restaurant still in its original location. **Au Select** *365 St. Catherine E. (1924 1986)* Irascible late night diners enchanted playwright Michel Tremblay, whose memories were so solid that decades later he penned a novel starring one of the waitresses who carried trays at the northwest corner of St. Denis. It became part of mega-restaurateur Paul Nakis' portfolio in 1955 and was demolished for a CEGEP building. **Green Spot** *3041 Notre Dame W. (1947—)* The place under a green-shingled, barn-like mansard roof has duked it out from a couple of locations near Greene against culinary competition, including a late-era McDonald's and The New System, with its orange delivery car fleet, since early in the postwar boom. It began in a location across the street and booths with jukeboxes salute its vintage allure. It's not old enough to earn a mention in St. Henri misery novel *The Tin Flute*, whose beleaguered heroine works at Two Records, likely Two Minute Lunch at 1842 Notre Dame W. **Blanche Neige** *5737 Côte des Neiges (1959—)* Dishwasher Nick Triandosa bought this crowd-pleaser from his uncle in 1978 and has been laying out the budget meals to thrifty diners, many from the nearby Jewish General Hospital, ever since. A diner forced another to dance with bullets blasting underfoot outside in 1973. **Johnny's Hideway** *481 Sherbrooke W. (1960 – 1985)* Johnny Goldstein blew jazz saxophone and sewed suits before devoting his life to serving homemade soup, low-cost breakfasts and the "best coffee in town" to diners on stools at two counters. It attracted McGill Ghetto youth hostel drifters and regulars who earned a photo on the wall near a caricature of blue-eyed, silver-haired Johnny reading "Yas theess es de place." **Cosmos** *5843 Sherbrooke W. (1978—)* Tony Koulakis was the face of this 11-stool greasy spoon known for its massive breakfasts and wide variety of toast, at a place folksy enough to merit a documentary film. Koulakis was disappointed when language inspectors forced him to remove a sign reading "delicious breakfasts" before leaving the place to his kids Nikos and Niki in 2002. Another son, suffering from mental illness, killed him in 2013. **Fontaine de Johannie** *3666 St. Denis (1962-1981)* "A filthy restaurant frequented by small time hoods," was how Dany Laferrière described this dark place in his semi-autobiographical breakout novel. A pair of bikers were shot dead inside on July 21, 1974. It briefly relocated to 4736 St. Catherine E. **Picasso's** *6810 St. James W. (1979-2009)* Peter Sergakis owned nine restaurants when he demolished a Texaco and moved one of them to his big-windowed place on the St. James strip above his Amazones strip club. It rocked the 24-hour clock. Friends were made, conversations had and 4 a.m. appetites were soothed. Sergakis rented it out in 1995 but his nearby P.J.'s lured diners away, leading to its closure. **Le Rapido** *4494 St. Denis (1988-2014)* Celebrated waitress Carmen Iacianio hauled tasty fries and burgers to after-hours diners in cozy booths at this corner spot with great window views. It closed after a dispute with a landlord over unrepaired pipes.(The Fameux restaurant across the street still offers a similar dining experience, as it has since 1958). **Galaxie/Pizzaiolle** *4801 St Denis (1993-)* This vintage diner has been serving since 1952 but only had its fist

Montreal customer 41 years later. Collector Daniel Noiseux snapped up Uncle Will's Diner, which served up griddle cakes and other treats in Shrewsbury, Massachusetts between 1952 and 1983. Noiseux towed it north and popped it onto an empty lot at Gilford. He hired Richard Gutman to re-do the interior in hopes of making it a sort of French equivalent of Beauty's. He renamed it Pizzaiolle in 2000.

Greek **Arahova** *256 St Viateur W. (1971–)*Nick Koutroumanis enabled a hunger for little-known souvlaki pitas by giving away free samples when he opened his tiny 400-square foot, two-table joint. Neighbours protested in 1979 when it expanded to take over an adjacent barber shop and Levine's 30-year-old grocery store. Arahova's marched forward with capitalistic zeal with a new generation launching franchises and vacuum-sealed packs of seasoned meat. **Jardin de Panos** *521 Duluth E. (1978–)* Neighbours of tiny, adjoining Chateaubriand laneway have long complained that the 350-seater with a gorgeous outdoor terrace disturbs their peace but squid and other tasty dishes have kept it immune from serious blowback. **Marven's** *880 Ball (1976–)*For decades the Kostopoulos clan has served up sumptuous calamari under wall-mounted moose head in a cramped hunting-lodge ambiance. **Kojax** *1389 St. Catherine W. (1977–)*Drunken post-Crescent street nightmares have long been planted by chatty employees at this brightly-lit Greek fast-food place launched by four Italian-Canadians. **Tripolis** *679 St. Roch (1985–)* Old-school doners rule at this lower-duplex festooned with pictures of Greece, a summer terrace and a loyal following. Joseph Eliopoulos kept it open all night in the 1990s but Philadelphia-born Sokratis Kokkinos, who purchased it in 2009, lets it sleep.

Hamburgers **Dic** **Ann's** *10910 Pie IX (1954–)* Anne Collecchia saw little future as a jazz accordionist so she zoomed up from Rochester with hubby Dick Potenza to serve up razor-thin burgers at Papineau and Cremazie, leading to several others around the island 25 years later. The skinny burgers were quick to cook and allowed them to set a world record for numbers of burgers served in an hour. **Harvey's** *(1967—)* Richard Mauran, whose dad launched the Chalet Bar-B-Q, moved to Toronto and opened up a burger joint as a summertime place in 1959. Its first charcoal broiled burger was cooked in Montreal at the still-operational 7100 Sherbrooke E. in 1967. Its best-known outlets were at Drummond and St. Catherine (SE corner) and one still standing across from the Côte des Neiges Plaza, where two employees were killed in a 1996 robbery. An employee stabbed a thief to death at another branch eight years earlier. **McDonald's** *(1972—)* Ray Kroc's chain was founded in 1955, came to Canada 13 years later and made its Montreal debut on Nov. 23 1972 at 6415 Sherbrooke E., with 2895 Concorde E. in Laval and 1565 Côte Vertu being among the 18 Quebec outlets that sprouted up in and around Montreal within 18 months. The McDonald's at La Ronde set a world record $5,360 in sales in an hour in 1985.

Hot Dogs PM Pierre Trudeau once shamed Quebec premier Robert Bourassa for being a "hot dog eater." Bourassa responded by posing for a magazine cover munching a Montreal tube steak. **Montreal Pool Room** *1200, 1217 St. Lawrence (1922—)* So many boots trod Bulgarian Darko Filipov's floor over time that the impact left craters underfoot. The Bulgarian Hadjiev clan long held out against pressure to demolish for various lower Main street-sanitizing Disneyfication proposals before they were finally forced to move after authorities condemned the premises for electrical issues. It relocated across the street in 2010. Its pool tables—where Al Capone supposedly once played—moved as well but still remain covered, as they have for decades.Though it claims its origins at 1912, this hot dog place shows up in listings a decade later. **Lafleur** *(1951—)* Farmboy Denis Vinet set up a hot dog van on Lafleur in LaSalle, which did brisk sales to hurried factory workers. He got a roof at 475 Lafleur a decade later, his first employee being an eight-year-old potato peeler who stayed over four decades. Vinet owned 19 Montreal-area Lafleur outlets at one point and about a dozen remain. **Vieux Montreal Pool Room** *3496 Frontenac*

(*2003–*) Bulgarian Sote Petkov sold the Montreal Pool Room on the Main in 2000, a decade after he inherited it. He then opened a namesake further east, co-run by his son Todd. The joint was featured in the 2012 box office flop *The Factory* starring John Cusak.

Hungarian A postwar influx of Soviet-fleeing Hungarians pioneered a paprika-powered surge of Magyar flavours. **Carmen's** *2063 Stanley (1954-1995)* Spanish artist Jesus Carlos de Vilallonga received $500 and all the sandwiches he could eat in return for painting the murals at this place. Crescent Street king Johnny Vago designed the premises where daytime diners chose between 17 flavours of coffee. Office workers crammed in after work and rubbed shoulders with an artsy who's-who. Carmen's expanded upstairs with George's, named for its owner. The building later sat abandoned for many years. **Pam Pam** *1425 Stanley (1952-1984)* Owners Eugene and Elizabeth Gotlieb served standard $3.25 specials (until 1991 only meals above that price were taxed in Quebec) including soup, goulash, roast beef, while 40 types of coffee were purportedly available. **Coffee Mill** *2046 Mountain (1961-1987)* Management of the former Kiss Mocha restaurant invested big money in an espresso machine but at first people hated it and spat it out, according to Olga Penzes who became sole owner after widowed in 1966. Roast duckling with braised cabbage and bean soup were on the menu but many diners knew the Hungarian joints for their spicy salami sandwiches, poppy seed rolls and cakes. Other long-gone Hungarian restaurants include the Continental, Rose Marie, Tokay (2022 Stanley) and Opera.

Ice Cream Montrealers ate penny ice cream out of semi-washed bowls in Victoria Square from the 1880s and have continued their quest for icy heaven in more sanitary forms since. **Seatltest Dairy** *7470 St James (1927-1978)* A trio of cow's heads oversaw long lines waiting for shakes and 15 flavours in cones at the dairy founded by Thomas Trenholme, also known as independent NDG's last mayor. The cow heads disappeared in 1999 and Parmalat finally returned them to display in 2017. **Dairy Queen** *(1956—)* DQ brought its soft ice cream to Western Canada in 1953 and within three years christened still-standing outlets at Beaubien and 9th and the exquisite old-school 4545 St. Catherine E. Other vintage locations include 4604 Park and 955 Jarry E. **Swenson's** *930 St Catherine W. (1983-1996)* This downtown people-watching heaven was so equated with ice cream when it went up that passersby still imagine seeing Au Coton-clad early-eighties girls giggling and wriggling their noses over sundaes. **MacDougherty's** *6707 Sherbrooke St. W (1975-2002)* Bill Doherty lured West Enders into family strolls to his place at the corner of Montclair until an overall dip in ice cream popularity in the 1980s scuttled his plans to grow an empire. Successor Sam Berlin's ambitions were similarly doomed. **Crème de la Crème** *152 Ste. Anne (1988—)* Monique Vézina dined on the picturesque Ste. Anne's boardwalk and later spotted a defunct fish and chips shack. She rang the number, signed a lease and raked in the cash by selling cones to ice-cream-starved waterside tourists. Son Patrick Bird now runs a modest takeout place which has easily outdone countless challengers.

Italian **Roncarelli's** *1429 Crescent 1912-1947)* Roma

Restaurant first served pasta on Osborne before moving to Crescent in 1935, where it was called Roncarelli's, (not to be confused with Roncari's at the Main and Dorchester). Owner Frank Roncarelli took to springing fellow Jehovah Witness co-religionists from jail for selling religious literature on the street. Premier Maurice Duplessis sought revenge by rescinding Roncarelli's liquor license, forcing him out of business. Roncarelli later won a personal lawsuit against the premier. **Fontana di Trevi** *6717 St. Hubert (1957-1968)* Before getting massive awnings, majestic vertical neon hugged every joint on St. Hubert. This Italian eatery also boasted a smaller replica of the famous Trevi Fountain in Rome. Diners would feed it coins that would later be given to charity. **Frank's** *65 St. Zotique E. (1960-2006)* Pizza profits were too tiny, so Francesco Scalise pushed fancier dishes like gnocchi in a dark and mysterious place that returned to its pizza vocation in 2006. **Paesano** *5192 Côte des Neiges (1962-1986)* Students appreciated the $1.25 spaghetti meals but ownership kept souping this place up, adding a fancy Michaelangelo Room and statues and fake stone. It became a Gothic shrine of stained glass but slowly lost its favour. Family infighting led to its sale in 1982 and closure for years later. **Tre Marie** *6934 Clark (1966—)* Sisters Rosina and Maria Fabrizio saluted their Abruzzo home province by bringing in budget diners with their veal stew, chicken cacciatore and salt cod. **Place Tevere** *(1968—)* Frank Reda came from Calabria in 1958 and set up his first restaurant in Ste. Geneviève on the West Island a decade later. With cash from partner Oreste Pulice, the chain grew to a half dozen other Montreal-area outlets, including in downtown food courts and the Olympic Stadium. Its best known was likely at 285 Dorval (1970-2014). Reda, who married a member of the billionaire Saputo cheese clan, was gunned down by an assassin early one morning in May 1994 outside of his cold cuts company at 10035 Plaza in Montreal North. A handful of outlets still serve up tasty pizza and other Italian dishes. **Le Piemontais** *1145 De Bullion (1977-2012)* Owner Romeo Pompeo graduated to Montreal after running a restaurant for a decade in Baie Comeau. His chic Italian-and-French place attracted politicians on expense accounts and hosted a tense sit-down of political rivals René Lévesque, Pierre Trudeau and labour leader Michel Chartrand. Rent hikes forced its closure. **Casa Napoli** *6728 St Lawrence (1979-2013)* Roving musicians played Italian melodies amid busts of Roman emperors at Joseph Napolitano's fancy place, as diners got up to dance in the grotto room. Director Sergio Leone shot a scene for his epic marathon *Once Upon a Time in America* at the restaurant. **Da Vinci** *1858 St. Catherine W. (1987—)* King of Pizza opened in 1958 and became Da Vinci in 1972 and was where hockey-playing Habs came for carbs. It moved to a posh space at 1180 Bishop in 1993. **La Cantina** *9090 St. Lawrence (1985-2014)* Tasty and affordable Italian dishes made this spot a hangout for Italians of all stripes, including mob bosses. It hit a snag in 2009 was mob-connected co-owner Federico del Peschio was shot dead outside. **Le Latini** *1130 Jeanne Mance (1979-2014)* Wine merchant Moreno di Marchi, an obsessive collector of olive oils and enthusiast of white truffles, gladhanded businessmen at this pricey joint, which he sold prior to its closure. **Café Presto** *1244 Stanley (1995—)* This homey place buzzes at lunch in a space where mob boss Harry Davis was shot dead in July 1946. It forms an Italian bookend with the nearby Santa Lucia (formerly La Delizia), which has sat a few doors up since 1989.

Pizza Montreal has long boasted a higher concentration of university students than almost any other place in North America, helping make pizza an essential food group. **Napoletana** *189 Dante (1948—)* Old country gentlemen convened at Montreal's most Italian street to play cards and shoot pool at this place, but its culinary supremacy became known and pizza-hungry crowds eventually required a 2009 expansion, creating a bring-your-own-bottle madhouse where waiters aren't out to get to know their customers on a deep level and cash is king. **Pines Pizza** *4520 Park (1959-2004)* Peter Kefallinos moved on from his brother's Gazette Restaurant (near the old Gazette building) to open his own place at the southwest corner of Pine and Park. He had no lease so he moved up from Mount Royal in 1981, at a place one fifth the size but where 90 percent of business was takeout. People would ring up from around the world just to hear his trademark phone reply "PI-I-I-IINES!" Cleanliness fines preceded its sale and closure. Kefallinos died in 2007 at age 76. **Amelio's** *201 Milton (1985—)* Christopher Phillip Scodas's popular basement place in the McGill Ghetto coped with fussy student idealists quick to complain about delivery snags. It closed briefly under bankruptcy protection before returning as Amelia's. **Angela's** *1662 De Maisonneuve W. (1970—)* Angela Bella sat in a tiny ground floor space at the southeast corner of Pierce, equipped with side-by-side black rotary phones, sparking giggles when employees routinely answered the wrong phone. It moved to a larger space across the street in 1983 and two years later former employee Nick Tsotzis purchased the establishment that still closes just four hours a day.

Sexy Serveuse Fully-nude waitresses served meals in the flesh in Montreal until outlawed in recent years after considerable legal exertion. **Les Courtisanes** *2533 St. Catherine E. (1995-2008)* Windows were covered as a waitresses clad in only runners, a belt and tattoos hauled dishes to booths. Coffee refill offers from a stark naked middle aged women were unforgettable, not necessarily in a good way, for many who dropped in. **Restaurant Mini Bouffe** *6043 Notre Dame E. (1997-2001)* This now-replaced building across from the port made news when a waitress was busted for indecency going outside clad only in a translucent veil. **Princesses d'Hochelaga** *4970 Hochelaga (1998–)* Raynald Morissette fought to keep his waitresses naked, a feature that attracted one customer to drive 35 km almost every day for 10 years. Police investigated for seven years from 2000, as undercover officers were given the tough assignment of sipping coffee in front of naked waitresses. Lawmen forced the waitresses into bikinis in 2011. **Sexy Bernie**'s *4000 Thimens (2005-2010)* Aficionados of semi-or unclad-table service gave this place solemn approving nods. It closed and was replaced by bikini-clad waitresses as St. James Pub. **Chez Lidia** *2205 Rosemont E. (2007-2014)* Jacinthe Vigneau sometimes went solo as nude waitress, cook and cashier from 5 a.m. with the standard mix of porn on TV and a claw crane game which gave a chance at picking up vibrators and porn DVDs. Other short-lived naked waitress restaurants could be found at 4040 Jean Talon E., 8520 Parkway in Anjou, 8527 Notre Dame E, 167 Mountain and 8803 Hochelaga.

Submarines Lord Sandwich and Cornelis Drebbel's famous inventions combined to make a Montreal specialty, according to Director Ivan "Ghostbusters" Reitman who noticed that the long sandwiches were popular in Montreal, while unknown in Toronto. He pitched a relative for cash to open such a place there but opted to make movies instead. **Mikes**

(1967–) This restaurant empire expanded as stealthily as a submarine attack, starting with a single restaurant in 1967 (at 2560 Centre), rising to five by 1971 including at 6543 Somerled and 1813 St. Catherine W., a total that doubled in five years, with the popular All Star sub helping it morph into a pizza chain. It is now a corporate-run giant with over 75 outlets. **Mr. Submarine** *2192 St. Catherine W. (1978-1988)* Assorted cold cuts were loaded into long bread and slammed onto counters at such places as Closse and Ste. Catherine, after it took over from West End Hamburgers in a barebones, low-overhead, microwave-only, stylistic forerunner to a typical Subway outlet. Its decade of survival was a success on a strip where doomed eateries included a Harvey's, Swiss Chalet, Fat Joe's and The Texan. The chain remained Montreal-based until 2011 when it had 2,000 outlets, but few in Montreal. **Momesso's** *5562 Upper Lachine (1978–)*Alessandro Momesso learned fast that his adoptive country didn't have much need for amateur soccer stars after he came in 1951, so he opened NDG Snack Bar Pool Room. He renamed it in the late 1980s after his son Sergio scored a bunch of goals for his hometown hockey Habs. It shed its pool tables and son Paolo took over, serving up Italian sausage subs.

Others: **La Bodega** *3456 Park (1969-1999)* Studly waiters in white shirts and black pants toted sangria and paella to tables in a stubby building later demolished for condos, while a student-friendly terrace beckoned a younger set. **Café Toman** *1421 Mackay (1976-1993)* George Potuzil, wife Bela and son Robert served 50 types of pastry, apple strudel, sandwiches upstairs in a candy-castle type building that survived a park-expansion demolition threat in 1988. **Bar-B Barn** *1201 Guy (1969–)*Manny Barnoff's wood-paneled place attracted endless athletes, office workers and even rock stars like Iggy Pop. It was known for ads featuring radio star Ralph Lockwood and its still-thriving West Island branch. **Mazurka** *64 Prince Arthur (1963-2012)* The first restaurant to thrive on Prince Arthur served up pierogis with love, leading other restaurants to move in. Soon the street was transformed into a sprawling pedestrian mall before diners soured on the once-popular strip. **Iskcon** *1626 Pie IX (1977—)* A couple of dozen vegan and vegetarian places now thrive on the island, with this religious recruitment place being one of earliest, as it offered a slice of eastern faith along with cheap meals. It was hit with uncleanliness fines in 1991. **Le Maharaja** *1175 Crescent, 1481 Dorchester W. (1994-2016)* Ali Khan moved his Crescent Street buffet to a 300-seater just west after a fire. It bagged many consumers choice awards until it started getting hit with regular fines for uncleanliness. Like most of Montreal's Indian restaurants, it was owned and run by Bangladeshis. **The Vientiane** *6330 Victoria Ave (1985—)* Now largely forgotten, this place was the first to bring yellow curry and coconut milk, lemon grass, chicken tamarind and other flavours of Thailand. **Saigon** *3525 Lacombe (1970-1980)* The first Vietnamese restaurant in Montreal, possibly the first in Canada offered a businessmen's lunch for $1.24 in 1972. **Katsura** *2170 Mountain (1973-2007)* This was the first Japanese joint to culinary colonize once-trendy Mountain Street with raw fish nigiri sushi and maki roll sushi. The more casual Sakura then opened two doors down and grill-tastic Toyo moved in nearby. Noriko Ishii's Sakura took over the old Katsura premises in 2007. **Le Commensal** *2115 St. Denis (1977-2013)* A vegetarian restaurant where customers paid based on the weight of their food, such was the concept that made this chain popular enough to expand from St. Denis to six other places, including one at McGill College and St. Catherine before diners started staying away due to its high prices. Some were not happy when the chain added chicken to its fare in its dying days. Owner Pierre-Marc Tremblay, who bought the chain in 2006, reoriented it to provide packaged products for grocery stores.

3

Hotels

Beds of straw, horse stables, a roaring fireplace and protection from hatchet-wielding attackers was considered luxury service at Montreal's earliest inns. Hospitality has rocketed forward since. Here's the key to your room from the past.

Auberge St. Gabriel *426 St. Gabriel (c. 1688—)* Patrons now

snap food selfies where grunting hunters swapped beaver pelts for French coins. The stones for The Old St. Gabe were first laid where the courthouse now stands but were relocated a half block south in 1963, as the versatile building served as a private home, restaurant and a place for weary travelers. Two resident piano-

playing ghosts, still irritated by a fiery-and-fatal fur exchange gone wrong, keep the secrets of what some say is the oldest inn in North America. That version has a French soldier acquiring the property in 1658 and launching the hotel 30 years later, while another account

dates the inn to 1757, its first liquor license issued by the new British overlords a dozen years later. Many black slaves later served wealthy widow Dolly Hart, who called it home for 24 years, while Dr. Michael McCulloch,

Monique Proulx film launch at the St. Gabe

the doctor who detected the typhus outbreak 1847, lived there for three decades before it returned as a hotel under Edouard Domptail Gauthier in 1875. It was The Hotel St. Louis, The Metropolitan Saloon, The Riendeau, The Franco-Canadien, Cecile Hotel, The Grand Hotel and Hotel Florence before Ludger Truteau finally purchased it in 1914 and renamed it the Auberge St. Gabriel. Police detectives partied there with mobster Joe Di Maulo after he was acquitted of murder in 1973 and three years later Ziggy Wiseman met with an officer at the St. Gabriel to offer him $5,000-a-week to turn a blind eye to his porn and prostitution empire. The Truteaus sold to the Bolays in 1987 and today singer Garou and billionaire circus impresario Guy Laliberté also own shares in what's now strictly a restaurant.

Donegana's Hotel *NW corner Notre Dame E. and Bonsecours (1846-1880)* An impressive mansion was inhabited from 1813 by a succession of "Handsome" Toussaint Pothier, American globetrotter William Bingham, Lord John Durham and briefly by 167 Montreal High School students before former Rasco Hotel manager Jean-Marie Donegana was hired to oversee it as Montreal's fanciest guest house. The 150-room Donegana's

was on "the Broadway of the city," as an ad ambitiously described the stretch east of city hall. It featured Doric columns, drawing-rooms, card-rooms, a reading-room, a concert hall, 200 square-foot dining room, a great view from the roof and a magnificent ballroom. But it burned after a concert on April 26, 1849, one day after rebels torched Parliament a few blocks west. On that fateful night a group of spectators led by Sabin Têtu persuaded performer Mr. Laborde to sing the French *La Marseillaise.* The tune irritated some English-speaking spectators and flames suddenly erupted. A falling wall killed William Douglas, who became the first Montreal firefighter killed on duty. Donegana, by now sickly, returned to Italy

Donegana's c. 1880

and the hotel moved a few doors down and became home-away-from-home to Confederates who settled in Montreal during the American Civil War. The sweet-talking Southerners stayed at Donegana's, while American federal agents were denied rooms and forced to stay at the Ottawa Hotel. The villainous Dr. Blackburn met allies at the hotel to gain support for his insane and unworkable Confederate plot to kill enemy Yankees by sending clothing infected with yellow-fever.

St. Lawrence Hall *139 St. James (1851-1910)* At a time when

food was dirt cheap, Montreal's top hotel insisted all guests sample fish, steak, chops, ham, chicken, turkey, rissoles, and 10 other dishes, along with jugs of milk and coffee, and that was just

breakfast. Owner Henry Hogan—whose Battle of Waterloo war veteran dad drowned after tumbling off a steamboat into the St. Lawrence River—sported big whiskers, curly mustache, *pince nez* glasses and would hoist three fingers in the air while talking, meanwhile vigorously shaking people's hands with his other paw. Hogan felt protective of his guests and once stood guard outside the room of Pope-critic Alessandro Gavazzi, whose 1853 visit sparked a nine-death riot near Victoria Square. The bustling street outside the 200-room hotel was jammed with carts, cabs and carriages, while inside sat a barber shop and a reading room with an all-night telegraphic bureau for newspaper reporters. Hogan hosted annual Christmas dinners for ink-stained wretches and the kindness was returned, as one critic described the hotel as a "fine handsome house after the style of the new hotels in London and Paris." The hotel attracted Confederate military men and Montrealers warmed to the Southerners during a time when many were not keen on Abraham Lincoln. While playing billiards, guest John Wilkes Booth boasted—likely under the effects of cocaine—about his plan to assassinate Abraham Lincoln, a promise that he unfortunately kept. Hogan earned praise for charging 10 cents for a glass of Scotch, long after

Henry Hogan

competitors charged five cents more. Hogan died just after the turn of the century, before hard-drinking federal Train Minister Henry Emmerson resigned after being caught with two women in his room in 1909. The hotel was demolished and replaced by offices in 1910. A Craig Street annex stayed open until 1933.

Hotel Iroquois *454 Jacques Cartier Square (1852-1984)* A period of mid-1970s barbarism forms only a tiny sliver of this hotel's 130-years but the shocking tale offers an eye-opening

lesson in the depths of human depravity. The St. Nicholas Hotel opened in 1852 and became a home for Grenadier Guard officers a decade later before returning as the Richelieu Hotel in 1879. Ten years later "Black Joe" Riendeau rechristened it with his last name, which it kept until 1922 when it became The Iroquois Hotel, with an added fifth floor. It was renamed The Taft Hotel midway through World War II, charging just $11 a week for a room in the early 1950s. Owner Gaston Gariépy died at 56 in 1962 and The Taft united with the adjacent Plaza Hotel to become Leo Rueland's Hotel Iroquois in 1966. Many came out to its plastic-themed Plexi discotheque, which attracted a steady stream of groovy youth clad in mini-skirts and bell-bottoms. Being in a hotel allowed the pulsating lighted stalactites over the dance floor to flash until 3 a.m. while most other places closed one hour earlier. DJs spun mellow tunes while mercury slithered and danced beneath the glass bar. The much-feared Dubois brothers gang of St. Henri became regulars with blessings

Dubois brothers

of doorman Pierre Ménard in 1975. The gang forced the manager to promote the brutish Ménard, leading many of the unionized staffers to quit. In a bizarre firing ritual, Dubois thugs spat on employees, threatened and beat them with sticks in a beat-down session that cost an employee an eye. They then replaced the workers with loyal gangster associates and launched a drug distribution operation from the hotel that netted up to $9,000 a week. The province of Quebec rented it after 1984.

Hotel Nelson *417   Place   Jacques   Cartier   (1856-1983)*

Patriotes sucked on corncob pipes while plotting the Rebellion of 1837 at a sailors' drinking hall on Jacques Cartier Square later

rebuilt as The Nelson. The Grand Trunk Railway moved in for five years but it returned as The Nelson in 1875 and was where a veteran police officer supplied Paris Green rat poison to distraught store clerk Mamie Lalonde, 18, who died at the hotel in 1904. The cop was demoted for inciting teen suicide, a grisly resolution to her indiscreet romance. It was rechristened Hotel Roy, then went vacant during World War I before becoming the Jacques Cartier Hotel. Three generations of Benoîts tried to squeeze coin from the place after

buying it in 1927 and restoring its Hotel Nelson name in 1941. Owner Pierre Benoît boasted of raising revenues tenfold to $1.3 million after taking charge in the late 1970s. Manager Gaétan Proulx hired 19-year-old punk rocker Johnny Spike to book

musical acts, which included Lou Reed and Heaven 17. The bar was soon jammed to its 144-soul limit but the hotel's New Wave Music Festival proved too much for the owner, who frowned on bands like Blew Genes and Electric Vomit and cleared house in 1979. The hotel briefly became the Friendly Inn before becoming office space.

Turkish Bath Hotel *140 St. Monique (1869-1913)* Wallets

opened as fast as pores at this oft-expanding steam bath inn at what's now the southwest corner of Place Ville Marie. D.B. Macbean's steamy cures promised to heal coughs, bronchial affections, consumption and catarrh (sinusitis) when it opened two years after Confederation. Dr. J.R. Alexander took over in the mid-1890s and invested in five expansions, which saw the hotel grow to 175 rooms. The hotel promised health aplenty but not for employees, as bellhop George Laurent had his head crushed by an elevator while attempting to save a child from danger in 1902. A boiler explosion killed another worker in 1909

and in July 1912 a guest from Chicago went bezerk, shooting bartender Frank McKenna dead and then taking aim at the owner's son, Dr. Roland Devlin. Killer John Sheppard dropped his gun and surrendered. Canadian Northern Railway purchased the adjacent properties for a through-the-mountain train tunnel line to the Town of Mount Royal. The railway was ready to pay any price to purchase and demolish the hotel but hotel brass caught wind of the desperation after the CNR's purchase agent mislaid documents in the lobby in 1911. Ownership got its price. It was demolished and the land remained part of the massive downtown pit that stayed five decades.

Windsor Hotel *1160 Peel (1878-1981)* The gem overlooking Dominion Square was launched after James Worthington inked a $40,000 annual lease to operate the

magnificent monolith on Peel, Canada's first grand hotel and Montreal's first fancy hotel outside of the old city. Early-day celebrity guest Mark Twain famously nailed the spirit of the city by telling a hotel audience that "you couldn't throw a brick without breaking a church window," in Montreal. Power brokers cut big deals within its walls, giving birth to the NHL at the hotel in 1917 and the Montreal Expos in 1968 while royalty, heads of state and entertainers hanged hats and crowns on Windsor racks, including Sarah Bernhardt, Rudyard Kipling, John F. Kennedy, Hailie Selasse and the Queen Mother, who was cheered while standing on the balcony flanked by Mayor Camilien Houde, who quipped to her, "some of that cheering is for you." Fire struck in 1957 but the hotel was soon back to form with its famous Peacock Alley—complete with glittering bird atop the entrance—as a classy option for tea-sipping ladies. The gleaming gold-and-white Versailles Room featured Canada's largest chandelier with its 1,700 pounds of glittering crystal, while *La Reserve* served up French cuisine in front of bucolic murals. The Lantern, with its mounted hunting trophies, was the place for a quick lunch, cooked in a kitchen known to whip up 1,000 meals per evening. Fires and partial-demolitions shrunk the Windsor, which needed massive repairs that the Webster family proved hesitant to invest. Staffers who toiled on its final day on Halloween 1981 included 88-year-old waiter Alfred Mercier and manager Arthur O'Dette who started 52 years earlier. Part of the building still stands as offices.

Oxford Hotel *1250-1254 University (1879 –1948)* Irishman Joseph Kearney overcame vigorous opposition led by abstentionist Dr. Bazin to obtain a liquor license in 1892 and made sure everybody knew about it by advertising as "Montreal's

first fully licensed uptown café under the liquor laws of the province of Quebec." Former Ottawa police officer William S. Hamilton bought it in 1902 and was charged two years later with murdering Irish soldier John Fitzgerald by ejecting him into a snowbank. New owner John J. Whyte paid a princely sum for it in 1907 and kept up its boastful hype, declaring it in ads as a "landmark," "most unique in Canada." "You never tire of our meals, they are so wholesome and so daintily served."Author Stephen Leacock was a late-era regular at the grill, which also offered a "ladies dining room at moderate prices." It was replaced by a much-larger post office after World War II.

Queen's Hotel *736 Windsor (Peel) (1883-1970)* An indestructible structure just a stone's toss from Bonaventure train station, such was the superhero formula meant to give The Queen's eternal life at its inception. Marble and iron were

favoured and wood was shunned in an effort to prevent blazes from spreading in this lavish red stone structure jammed with artsy *bas relief* images of Prince Albert and Queen Victoria. The hotel had 100 rooms at birth and doubled in size in 1909, while another 150 rooms were added in 1923. Guests would hop off trains and lounge to the soothing sounds of the Markowski Orchestra, as they sucked cigars, sipped wine and enjoyed solid meals under seven-metre high ceilings. Management offered the less-sedentary a

heart-stopping boat ride down the Lachine Rapids. Hotel czar Donat Raymond started in the kitchen, rose to management and eventually became owner before snapping up many other local

businesses and becoming president of the Montreal Canadiens. His brother, the famous aviator Adélard Raymond, bought an interest after World War II but business plummeted after the Bonaventure Station was demolished in 1952. When a suicidal hotel guest blew himself up in his room in 1955, management demonstrated it as proof that the hotel was fireproof. The Raymonds sold in 1962 and a long line of schemes all failed, including one which would have turned it into student dorms in 1970. The province shot down plans to protect the building, which was demolished in 1980.

Arbour Hotel *1057 St Lawrence (1897-1960)* This "pest hole of immorality," was known for exuberant, unaccompanied women who favoured knee-length skirts and danced until 4 a.m., showing off their alluring legs with high kicks, a dance that Manager Johnny Bertrand defended in 1913 as being in the Scottish tradition. Cops raided and seized its liquor license in 1937, arresting "a large number of persons found in the premises, particularly in the rooms on the upper floors." Its bar later had an equestrian theme, as racing fans met amid race-track souvenirs. At the time it closed for good, the Lower Main was so overrun by thugs, drug dealers and pimps that some urged young people be banned from the area.

Viger Hotel *510 St. Antoine E. (1898-1935)* All admire Quebec City's landmark Château Frontenac Hotel but Montrealers never warmed up to its local east-side imitation.

The Canadian Pacific Railway-owned hotel proved a poorly-located flop, in spite of being designed by Bruce Price as a knockoff of his Quebec City boardwalk gem. The Viger aimed to be a city-within-a-city, not unlike the Hays House, which burned down one block south in 1852. It had an electricity plant, elevators, 40-foot bar, billiard room, barber shop, gentlemen's writing room, ladies reception room and gold leaf ceilings and walls. Mayor Raymond Préfontaine applauded the CPR for building in the overlooked French-speaking part of town but it lacked identity, billing itself as "handsome, well-furnished, comfortable," sitting near "Montreal's

Bruce Price

"Ocean and River Steamship Landings and business centre," and CP's Viger Station. It closed in 1935 and later housed City of Montreal offices before going vacant awaiting a succession of redevelopment schemes that have yet to bear fruit.

Carslake Hotel *571 St. James (1898-1912)* A horse racing sweepstakes hustle brought George Carslake wealth after he sailed from England as a 28-year-old in 1873. Carslake invested

in the Queen's Hotel in 1883 and sold his shares soon after it opened. He launched a competitor 15 years later, with the Zetland Lodge Freemasons chowing down at its first dinner three doors east of Peel. Visiting Brits wore snazzy Knickerbocker pants and toted Gladstone bags at a time when tourism fluctuated wildly, as hotels were jammed in 1906 but empty two years later. Carlsake, who endowed various sports with trophies named after himself, sold to a consortium of miners and returned to England in 1910. His hotel soon went the way of The international Journeymen Horseshoers of United States and Canada, one of many groups that met under its roof. The *Montreal Herald* accused feds of overpaying when they purchased it for a post office, leading to a libel suit and debate in Parliament. It was demolished in 1944.

Corona Hotel *1431-1449 Guy (1906-1938)* Diners could feast on mutton chops while baritone Thomas Cowan sang over the sounds of Professor Shea's Orchestra, as part of William

Strachan's downtown real estate empire, which included the adjacent His Majesty's Theatre. Rooms with bathrooms cost double the standard $1.25 back when Charles Thomas shot Frank Angus in the thigh during an argument in the hotel bar in 1916. Uniformed police officers, in another minor scandal, were reprimanded after drinking and joining women in an upstairs room. Neil R. "Foghorn" MacDonald, a "rolicsome, frolicsome and fervent" soldier of fortune died of pneumonia at the hotel in 1923. A decisive fire forced 75 "scantily clad" customers out into the cold in March 1938 and left barkeep William Peek, 32, badly burned.

Ritz Carlton Hotel *1228 Sherbrooke W. (1912—)* Service

so attentive that a waiter would rush to a room to pour from a bottle sitting at a guest's elbow, the Ritz-Carlton sought to be that kind of place after it was launched at a posh New Year's Eve

opening bash scheduled to narrowly avoid the unlucky 1913. The five original investors included a few Sirs, as in Holt, Allan and Gordon but the hotel was run by Charles Meredith, as the first franchise of Euro-luxury hotel mastermind César Ritz. The "most wonderful demonstration ever witnessed by any gathering in this city," took place at the Ritz on Valentine's Day 1916 when the first transcontinental phone call was placed from Montreal to Vancouver. Attracting high-rollers wasn't always a cinch through the wars and The Depression and management reluctantly permitted male guests to dress in regular suit-and-tie rather than black-tie tuxedos in 1940, and after World War II many mansion owners downsized and moved in permanently. The hotel enjoyed its greatest moment when Richard Burton and Elizabeth Taylor tied the knot there in 1964, while other big name guests included Winston Churchill, Charles de Gaulle, Marlene Dietrich, Liberace, Tyrone Power, Maurice Chevalier, Paul Newman, Robert Redford and John Wayne. Eccentric tycoon Howard Hughes spent a month at the hotel in 1957, running up a $20,000 phone bill while Marlene Dietrich and former McGill music student Burt Bacharach later dined at the Ritz nightly while performing together at Her Majesty's Theatre. Prime Minister Brian Mulroney and wife Mila were among the regulars who enjoyed the whimsical charm of the duck-laden pool. The hotel lost its five star rating to the Four Seasons in 1992 after being taken over by a less-fancy German chain. It has since sought to recapture its luxury reputation through major renovations.

Mount Royal Hotel *1455 Peel (1922-1984)* Hustlers, loiterers and weary-footed downtown wanderers lounged on couches in this often-unhinged 1,000-room city-within-a-city created after Canadian Pacific Railway chief Edward Wentworth Beatty sought to create the fanciest hotel in the British Empire.

He aimed to purchase, gut and renovate the Queen's Hotel but instead built a 10-storey giant on a two-acre field where a school previously sat. A half-million bricks, 2,000 telephones and 25 kilometres of electrical wiring was laid and the hotel opened doors in December 1922, with a golden key turning a lock that management vowed never again to use. Jack Denny's 30-musicians played the hotel bars upstaged by the drum-intensive Xavier Cugat Orchestra. Boss Vernon Cardy and lifelong-bachelor assistant George "Never Forget a Face" Morrisette watched over oddballs like the elderly Newspaper Lady, who'd snag papers from the lobby, creating a massive pile of old dailies in her room. The Hat Lady bought a new lid every day and had piled up 600 in her room when she died. Mayor Camilien Houde lived in the hotel for nine years and stockpiled dozens of canes in his room. Bars included the Polynesian Kon Tiki, Brit-themed Picadilly and the Normandie Roof, where management persuaded flamboyant Liberace to ditch his first name and rejig his last name with a hard pronunciation. The hotel had a press club, long rows of wooden telephone stalls lining the mezzanine, Turkish baths and legendary moocher Jockey Fleming, who was banished in the early 1960s. Guest Sarah Smith Scollard died of pneumonia in July 1932, her $15 million fortune never to be found. Thieves exploded a Trans Canada Airlines safe in the building in a daring 1957 heist and an elderly woman perished in a 1972 third-floor fire. The slowly-fading hotel fell into disfavour, as guests preferred newer hotels that offered shorter walks from elevators.

Berkeley Hotel *1188 Sherbrooke W. (1928-1978)* Tryhard

megalomaniac John Scofield reinvented this sleepy 81-roomer in 1967 after longtime Austrian co-owner Hubert Stein died and

went to the big hotel in the sky. Scofield oversaw Montreal's first street terrace café, while at basement Johnny's Bar waitress Doris hauled trays full of three-ounce martinis past jukebox and nude paintings to red vinyl booths containing preppy Westmount teens and Air Canada stewardesses-in-training. The Ambassador Hotel was launched in 1928 as a residence for wealthy bachelors from good families and was transformed into The Berkeley three years later, the year police arrested a receptionist for tipping a felon off to their impending arrival. Mayor Camillien Houde fired an employee for plotting against him at the hotel in 1939 and after his wartime internment Houde visited the hotel

and charmed wary anglos from the Fossils Club amateur theatre troupe by belting out a jolly version of *Alouette* on the hotel piano. American Nazi party leader George Lincoln Rockwell checked in on a 1962 visit that aimed to rouse

Berkeley Hotel street terrace 1950

fascist support. Instead management kicked him out and Rockwell left town and was shot dead five years later in Texas. Constantly-scheming owner Scofield loved Canadian football and handed out an annual trophy to the best Montreal Alouette. He formulated an ambitious $10 million expansion in 1974 but it all went sour. The hotel was incorporated into the Alcan building in 1980. Billionaire Guy Laliberté later mused about returning it as a hotel.

The Alpine Hotel *2015 McGill College (1932-1962)*

Smith & Zoda

Traveling snake charmer Edward E. Smith, aka Abdul Saud, was dejected after his snake-vs.-cobra battle fizzled out. The slithering duo dozed off, prompting audience derision. Smith, staying at this modest inn at the northeast corner of McGill College and De Maisonneuve in 1936, underfed the snakes to put them in a combative spirit. But one hungry serpent bit him. Smith fled and a dozen killer snakes slithered away. Doctors amputated Smith's arm to the elbow and police searched 12 hours before finding his assistant Florence Zoda, who only fed the panic. "They are wild and ferocious," she declared. Authorities killed the snakes by pumping lethal gas into the inn. The Alpine was originally an apartment building, and was home to Vere E. Johns, a Jamaican-born former New York City celebrity journalist, whose wife petitioned the American government in 1935 to block his return to the United States on grounds of moral turpitude.

Ford Hotel *1425 Dorchester W. (1929-1948)* Prices were

reasonable at the Rochester-based budget chain's 750-room hotel spanning Mackay to Bishop. Floor shows at the downstairs Bishop Grill (later replaced by a generic Murray's restaurant) all

failed, so action went to a hotel bar popular with wrestlers, entertainers and newspaper staffers. The soda counter at the 24-hour Ligett's pharmacy was manned by soda jerks famous for their deadpan quips. Al Palmer—whose novel *Sugar Puss on Dorchester Street* saluted the then-lively strip—recalled guests square dancing in snowshoes and burlesque star Beverly King improvising a peekaboo costume from Ford curtains. The structure, built of 4,000 tons of steel and 2.5 million bricks, was a carbon copy of Ford's Toronto hotel, demolished in 1973. The CBC moved in for two decades after 1948.

The   Laurentien   Hotel *1130   Windsor   (Peel)*

(1949-1976) Postwar Montrealers stared into the pit across from Dominion Square to catch an eyeful of hardhats toiling away at Charles Davis Goodman's Streamline Moderne building (a style seen at Ben's, the Jewish General Hospital and Snowdon Theatre), as the rubberneckers hauled chairs to watch the building go up in the spring of 1946, with one hustler selling drinks and membership cards. The Ford chain embraced Mayor

Camilien Houde's suggestion that its new hotel bear a French name. They called it the Laurentien and offered a radio in every room with four stations to choose from. But there would be no loud rocking out, as volumes were controlled by a master unit. The Laurentien couldn't compete with the classier Windsor and Mount Royal but Muzak serenaded halls and elevators and the Kiltie Scottish-themed lounge and Au Ballon Cocktail Lounge was where The Montreal Men's Press Club met at booze-ups overseen by lovable barman Joe Servant. Canadian Pacific Railway purchased the building in 1969 and sought to demolish it in order to replace it with a massive Bank of Montreal head office that would have dwarfed Place Ville Marie in size, although planners complained that adjacent Place du Canada wrecked the continuity of the row of downtown towers. The Laurentien was slated to close in November 1974 but stayed open through the 1976 Olympics. Employees, including 73-year-old Charlie Baldwin, were unenthusiastic about the reprieve, which delayed their severance settlements. The 1,110 room, 22-floor hotel closed soon after the Olympics. Its senseless demolition ensued and CP abandoned the replacement project to focus on its Toronto properties. The structure disappeared less than three decades after its foundation was poured. It was the third-largest demolition in Canada at the time. An unremarkable office tower now occupies the site.

Queen Elizabeth Hotel *900 Dorchester W. (1958—)*

Pyjama-clad John Lennon and Yoko Ono pleaded to "Give Peace a Chance" in Room 1742 in May 1969 but the 1,000 room hotel built above CN Station was rife with strife even before General

Manager Donald Mumford became its first resident 11 years earlier, as the booming 1950s saw downtown grow over the hideous 45-year-old train crater. Bickering began when Quebec nationalists attacked Canadian National Railway president Donald Gordon's choice of name, as 200,000 signed a petition urging *Le Reine Elizabeth* be rechristened *Chateau Maisonneuve*. Gordon then claimed that he could find no qualified French Canadians for top brass positions, a remark that attracted 700 to a raucous 1962 protest. Nurse

Gloria Baylis sued the hotel in 1964 for anti-black discrimination after they declined to hire her and a judge compensated her $25 but brass appealed the ruling. Boss Mumford—who once jokingly claimed that he would fire any wine steward

John Lennon in Queen E bed

who shaved his beard—retired in 1972 and was succeeded by Reg Groome, who was with the hotel from the start. Charles de Gaulle, Fidel Castro and George W. Bush stayed there, as did Queen Elizabeth herself, who visited four times. What else? Employees were spoiled for a few years with deep discounts at other CN hotels, the provincial government commandeered rooms during the 1970 October Crisis, the NHL held its entry draft at the hotel 10 times from 1963, a Chilean tourist was stabbed to death in Room 1849 in 1979 and police arrested 108 poverty protesters for raiding the buffet in a 1997 bread riot.

Peg's Motel *1980 Westmore (c. 1962—)* The Piggery was so nicknamed for its floor "constantly wet with spilled beer, vomit and blood," and was where drivers from the nearby Sealtest Dairy would race trucks to arrive first at the end of the day.

"Chico, Peg's bartender tried to keep everybody in line by the strength of his presence. He looked like a grizzly with a migraine and the weight of his nightstick, a length of two-by-four that he swung like a Montreal Expos baseball player in the warm-up circle," read a memoir. Country tunes lightened the pain for regulars who included hulking pro wrestler Sailor White. "Fistfights broke out over a single ill-spoken phrase or even an innocent glance," continued Frank O'Dea, who became a Toronto panhandler before co-founding the Second Cup coffee chain. Owner Peg O'Neil said she had no connection to crime but

streetwalkers were rounded up inside in 1964, thieves stole a whiskey truck outside in 1967, police found weapons in unrented Room 14 in 1976 and a gunman shot at cops parked outside that

O'Dea, White, Slawvey

same year, his bullet sailing through the police cruiser. Police killed the suspected shooter John Slawvey soon after, gunning him down in his indoor parking lot after a night of drinking at Peg's, in what many consider a cold-blooded assassination in May 1976. The bar, later named Spurs, was featured in a fight sequence in the hit film *Bon Cop/Bad Cop* and scenes from *The Favourite Game*, based on the Leonard Cohen novel, were shot at the motel. Mafia bigwig Frank Cotroni wrote Peg's a $500 cheque that remains uncashed 50 years later. The bar was demolished in 2010 but the Motel St. Jacques, as it is now known, remains open.

Belvedere Motel *7250 Ste Anne de Bellevue Blvd.*

(1962-2004) The   Belvedere's original Longchamps restaurant was ably run by Adalbert Galecz, hired away from the French Embassy in Ottawa but disaster struck in 1975 when 20 guests, most about to fly to Europe, fell ill after eating rancid tuna and coleslaw. Leo Constant spent 21 days in hospital and was awarded $54,000 after a decade-long court battle. Cocktail lounge waitresses would overcharge tab-running businessmen over the soothing sounds of live organ music but in later days crack hookers found the rundown spot handy for meet-ups. Marcellus François picked up a woman at the Belvedere before getting shot dead by police in an outrageous case of mistaken identity in 1991. A Canadian Tire outlet now occupies the land.

Motel Raphael *7455 Ste. Anne de Bellevue Blvd.*

(1965-2009) Developer Raphael Ruffo's multi-tiered 100-roomer at the gateway to all roads west started off as Ruffo's Motel,

featuring a dining room, swimming pool and cocktail lounge, where guests might groove to seductive piano stylings of Cliff Carter. It failed to fill during the tourist rush of Expo 67, perhaps because it was a favourite for criminals on the lam, with cops occasionally launching tear gas into rooms where fugitives holed up. The Nittolo family launched the Casa Mezza Luna restaurant in the motel in the late 1980s, serving up decent fare amid atrocious décor. A man was found stabbed dead in a bath in 1993, a woman held captive for five days by a spurned ex the next year and a man died in a fire in 2006. It long sat crumbled and empty before finally being carted off in 2016.

Hotel Colonnade *1366   Dorchester   W.   (1965-2002)*

Cadillacs and skyscrapers were Morris Stahl's favourite things but he was able to acquire only half the land required for his planned downtown apartment tower. So he hired a team of fledgling architects, all under the age of 25, to design a slender 10-storey apartment building to jam onto the postage stamp-

sized land. Cost overruns ensued, so Stahl scrapped the precast facade in favour of cheaper glazed bricks, a gaudy but briefly-popular style. The mortar didn't match the shiny bricks and architects Morris Melamed, David Croft, Jim Grainger and Mike Fish were unfairly blamed for the unimpressive result. The apartment building became the 65-room Majestic Hotel in 1965, renamed Hotel Colonnade the next year with

rooms costing $7.50 a night during Expo 67. The big-eyed landmark structure perched atop the hill like a thin sail in the wind, with the broken EL on the its HOTEL sign often unlit, leaving passersby wondering what exactly a Hot Colonnade might be. A group of 100 investors paid $4.5 million for the building in 1986 and pumped $3 million into renovations. It was removed in 2002 and replaced by an office tower.

Hotel de la Montagne *1430 Mountain (1982-2011)* Sun-

baked afternoons admiring a luscious skyline alongside insolent poolside party babes, such was the urban paradise on tap atop

this 16-floor concrete behemoth created after a bank handed a juicy construction loan to Thursday's bar owners Sonny Lindy and partner Bernard Ragueneau. The last bucket of cement was poured in 1982 at the site of a wartime whorehouse run by Madame Blanche, a small building that had conveniently burned down three years prior. A tunnel linked the hotel to Thursday's on Crescent, forming an

under-celebrated booze-seeking subterranean pathway, while

the piano bar was peopled with semi-discreet hookers and heartbroken divorcées. The rooftop bar remained a beloved primo hotspot for Grand Prix weekend excesses, enjoyed by guests that included Robert DeNiro, George Segal, Pierre Berton, Woody Harrelson, Pierce Brosnan and Lee Majors. Co-owner Lindy eventually exited and opened the Crocodile restaurant on the Main, which thrived for a few years. Ragueneau, as sole owner, overloaded the restaurant with trinkets collected on his world travels. The building was still sturdy when demolished by the Weston family for a condo project, which would have been

even more massive had Wanda's strip club and other structures on De Maisonneuve agreed to sell. Ragueneau pocketed a reported $160 million, of which he kept about one-third after debts and taxes. About 300 hotel workers lost their jobs when it closed.

Other hotels Albion Hotel *143 McGill St. (between St. Paul and Le Moyne) (1854-1909)* L. W. Decker's $1.50 rooms on St. Paul proved so popular with business travelers that the hotel

grew like a fungus, expanding every three years until it reached McGill Street. The hotel hosted serial killer Dr. Neill Cream in 1880 and boasted beds with new spring mattresses. It was where "attractive looking" Mrs.

Sicker from Albany New York fled with her child and her husband's life savings, to be with another man. The hotel disappeared after the Anti-Alcoholic League persuaded a Liquor Commission judge to order it sold. The building was replaced a large structure at 407 McGill. **American House** *St. Henry Street,*

between Notre Dame and St. Maurice (c. 1840-1894) Between Griffintown Haymarket and McGill Street sat a hotel that housed the 21 Confederates who attempted to burn down St. Alban's Vermont in the fall of 1864. Courts refused to send the Confederates back to face trial, as the attack was deemed an act of war. Montrealers cooled on Southern rebels following the violence. The once-buzzing block has sat barren for decades. **Freeman's Hotel** *182 St. James (east of St. Pierre) (c. 1912-1932)* The

Freeman's

Freeman name was associated with scandal after Mrs. Freeman of the Freeman House on Notre Dame W. poisoned herself with Paris Green in 1880. But young Irish-Montreal bookkeeper Frank Gallagher and his investors used the name for their restaurant regardless until it was closed by fire. So they launched the 150-room Freeman Hotel, offering rooms without bath for a nifty $1.50. It prospered and gobbled up the nearby St. Regis Hotel but World War I put the brakes on profits and Gallagher, who acted in amateur dramas with Montreal's Young Irishmen's Literary and Benefit Association, died in 1917 in his early forties, leaving a widow and small children. The hotel was demolished and the land sold for a stunning $3.5 million in 1923. The Insurance Exchange Building was later built on the site. **Nittolo's Garden Motel** *6590 St. James (1957-1997)* The Nittolos bought a farm near the cliff in 1923, built a restaurant on it in 1957 and added a motel soon after, run by Blanche Nittolo and her eight kids until they sold out in 1988. A worker died out back in a construction accident in 1961, management was fined a decade later after nitroglycerin was found hidden in the basement and West End Gang leader Dunie Ryan was shot dead in Room 40 on Nov. 13, 1984. **Hotel Dorchester** *1484 Dorchester W. (1958-c.1985)* People-watching geriatrics plopped bottoms onto frayed vinyl seating strips of rusty metal lawn chairs outside of downtown's most brazen welfare hotel. The six-storey hotel aimed high after being built on land emptied by the widening of Dorchester, as it filled the void with its rooftop "fabulous Starlight terrace," Catalonge Lounge and *La Regence* restaurant, an eatery that lasted no time at all. The hotel was afflicted with accelerated aging syndrome, quickly falling into disrepair, as competitors at 1005 Guy (now Hotel Espresso) and at 1155 Guy (Maritime Plaza, closed in 2013) fared better. Owner Raphael Fleming sold in 1969, with new management renaming it *Hotel de Province*. The Montreal Folk Workshop were regulars, offering performances by bands like The Dregs of Tradition until the bar was padlocked in 1973. The hotel lasted almost a decade longer and was demolished soon after its closure. The subsequent empty lot served as a rogue parking lot for decades.**The Cavalier Hotel** *6951 St. James(c. 1962—)* Businessmen were pampered in the bar upstairs, while younger folk danced under a mirror ball, as Greek manager Daddy Vince showed a brave face to tough guys in the late 1960s.

Nittolo's

German barmaid Maria Hillebrand met assassin Jackie McLaughlin at the bar but the couple was later murdered in New Brunswick. The hotel later became The Chablis and is now The Chabrol. **The Inn** *St. Sauveur (c. 1970s)* An Irish-Canadian proprietor hosted Mafia hit men at this homey hotel one hour north of Montreal. The assassins, flown in from Italy, were usually discreet but one such killer pulled his gun on another motorist after a minor fender bender. **Youth Hostels** *(c. 1970-72)* A bed cost just 50 cents when the provincial education ministry gave cash to schools to fund youth hostels. Loyola Campus welcomed 6,000 guests in 1972 while another 100 beds awaited in the heart of Old Montreal at 461 St. Sulpice.

4

Venues

Academy of Music 9 *Victoria (1875-1910)* Crowd-surfing, a blind piano prodigy and an early anti-racism lawsuit coloured the history of this 2,000-seat venue, which made the mistake of being built on swampy terrain at downtown Victoria and St. Catherine, a site later filled by the western half of Eaton's department store. Blind Tom a "wholesome-looking negro" proved an early-day draw, as the sightless Georgia-born ex-slave pianist played to full houses before returning to live a quiet life near New York

City. A revolving door of managers and vaudeville acts ensued, including the hit "Bathing in the Nile" show in 1877. Kids would participate in "pit tossing," a forerunner of crowd-surfing, which allowed a small body to get passed overhead from the back row to the front, if the passenger dared to endure the manhandling. The business started sinking, literally, one evening in 1896 when the structure descended five inches into the muddy soil, leading officials to condemn the building. It reopened after extensive repairs but trouble returned two years later when owner John B. Sparrow refused to honour a black man's orchestra-section ticket. "The patronage which occupies that part of the house does not want them there. And so naturally I exclude them," said Sparrow. The snubbed ticket-holder, a Queen's Hotel employee named Frederick Johnson, sued for $500 and was awarded $50. The adjacent W.H. Scroggie department store building collapsed in 1899 and demolition of the entire swamp-challenged area seemed imminent but the venue gave it once last try as *La Théatre de la Comedie Française* in 1909. The building was demolished in May 1910 to allow the neighbouring Goodwin's department store—the former Scroggies and future Eaton's—to expand.

Gayety Theatre *84 St. Catherine W. (1912-1953)* The Bowery Burlesquers kicked off this 1,600-seater, which hosted films, boxing matches and political meetings but was best-known as "the only 100 percent vaudeville in the entire Dominion."

Authorities threatened to shut down Thomas Conway's venue in 1930 and briefly banned burlesque in 1945 but The Gayety snagged higher-priced "comedians, vocalists, musicians, acrobats and skaters" than the Esquire, El Morocco, Samovar and Normandie Roof. But its real draw was seductresses like Joan Mavis, "the blonde bombshell of exotic dancers" and Miss Noel Toy, "the first Chinese fan dancer," while better-clad Montrealer Fifi "I'm a Dreamer Aren't We All"

D'Orsay dropped in from Hollywood for a 1950 stand. The possibly-tragic conjoined-twin Hilton Sisters also performed that year as did French singer Jean Sablon, who walked out after a week, scorning his scantily-clad co-stars and the lowbrow crowd. Joan "The Original Radium Girl" Meller glowed in the dark in 1948, 13 years after

Hilton twins

radioactive powder landed her in a hospital bed awaiting certain death. Other acts included Ray Rogers, an argumentative xylophonist who quarreled with the Len Howard Orchestra house band for giggles. Lili St. Cyr became its biggest star when she did her Chinese Pavilion and Bird of Love acts, which were carefully evaluated by police but mostly permitted to proceed until she split town in 1951. Reporter Al Palmer proposed a statue of St. Cyr in the lobby, and informed readers that the sidewalk outside was the go-to-place to purchase cocaine, which was "not addictive." It continued as The Radio City from 1953 to 1956 and playwright Gratien Gélinas then turned it into Comédie Canadienne. It has housed the Théâtre du Nouveau Monde since 1972.

Her Majesty's Theatre *1421 Guy (1898-1963)* A former "weed encumbered spot," as "well-known elocutionist" May Reynolds described it on opening night, was transformed into a

playhouse that featured top stars like Edward G. Robinson, Charles Laughton and Lon Chaney, all performing for audiences clad in gowns and tuxedos. Architect Peter Lyall designed the ornate theatre for the West End Theatre Company at a spot where the Guy metro station would later sprout up. Early management rotated until J.B. Sparrow leased the theatre in 1903, producing shows by such stars as an elderly Sarah Bernhardt, who was hauled on stage on a Louis XVI chair, after having a leg amputated in France. When local opera singer Pauline Donalda performed in 1915, the bill enthusiastically announced that "Madame Donalda (Herself) will positively sing." The venue, renamed His Majesty's for all but 15 of its 65 years, was nearly transformed into an indoor garage—not unlike Mansion's across the street—in 1929 but Consolidated Theatres (later United Theatres) kept it going with veteran impresario Phil Maurice bringing in talent. The theatre was left to rot in its later years, as the the Place des Arts was expected to supplant it. The curtain fell at on May 27, 1963 and its demise was rued by thousands, including theatre critic regulars Herbert Whittaker and Sydney Johnson. "It seems incredible that the laughter and applause will forever be stilled when the asbestos is lowered on this esteemed theatre. This is not the end of an era; it is merely the pause before another era," said producer Rupert Caplan. Once-lively Guy Street was never the same after theatre closed and neighbours like The Stork Club (later Oz disco), The Royal, Gay Apollon and Lentzos all-night restaurant were all eventually demolished.

Bennett's Theatre 525 *St. Catherine W. (1906-1966)*

Eastern Townships-born bombshell Eva Tanguay rejected a lucrative offer in the United States to honour her one-week

contract at Bennett's, in July 1909 where she did four 20-minute shows for 2,000 admirers. "In an apotheosis of sartorial abbreviation that is calculated to throw any conscientious Rainy Daisy into an attack of the Green-

Eva Tanguay

Eyed-Monster, Eva Tanguay, she of the cyclonic temperament and correspondingly distended salary, has come and been seen. Having developed at least a 40 horse-power lung action, she simply tore her songs up by the roots," read a review. Young juggler W.C. Fields also took the stage at what became The Orpheum after World War I, a venue that started showing movies in 1926. The Théâtre du Nouveau Monde used it for plays until it was demolished and replaced by drab offices.

The Princess 478 *St. Catherine W. (1908-2007)* W.D.

Ogilvie's 2.000-seater was Canada's most-lavish when it launched across just east of Phillips Square across from rival Bennett's Theatre. Visitors watched burlesque amid ivory

sculptures, painted flowers and nymphs, all lost in a massive 1915 fire. Its replacement opened two years later with an early-day escalator and telephone switchboard. Live shows shifted to silent films and then to talkies but its signature moment came in October 1926 when magician Harry Houdini performed. The megastar was later

surprised at his hotel by a punch to the stomach tossed by McGill student Jocelyn Gordon Whitehead, who claimed to be testing Houdini's stomach-of-steel trick. Houdini died soon after. It became Le Parisien multiplex and closed in 2007.

Empress Theatre *5560 Sherbrooke West (1927-1992)*

Egyptian sculptures, Ramsesean heads and Tutankhamen's funeral masks made this West End movie house one of Montreal's most ornate. After serving for decades as a theatre

and live drama venue, J.C. McNicoll and Gaby Richard overcame considerable resistance to turn the 1,500-seater into a the Royal Follies, although they never built a promised a 15-storey hotel where cars would parked on the same floor as each room. When the club opened in 1963 it had an orchestra pit suspended a dozen feet above the stage as Parisian crooner Jean Philippe stole hearts and leggy showgirls impressed nightclub columnist Al Palmer who exclaimed "All those pretty girls! Hoo boy!" Teenage boys would stand outside in hopes of catching a glimpse of scantily-clad women until it closed in September 1967. Michael Costom then

ran it as an artsy movie venue until 1975 when Stephen Miller, 23, transformed it into the Cinema V, Montreal's third repertory cinema. The two-roomed Cinema V printed 60,000 schedules, which film fans affixed to fridges to consult and ponder whenever they had an

explicable urge to watch *Chinatown*, or *Catch 22* yet again. The Famous Players chain battled to make it a viable first-run movie theatre in the parking-challenged spot from 1988 to 1992, when it was struck by fire. Endless committees, chinwags and do-gooder community consultations have since failed to move the rehabilitation chains forward.

Seville Theatre *2155 St. Catherine W. (1929-1985)* Many recall the Seville's painful 25-years as the crumbling embodiment of Montreal decline but for decades the structure hosted

sermons, songs and gender-bending film screenings that saw celebrants toss toast at the silver screen. The building opened in 1876 as the Douglas Methodist Church, named after the blind, paralyzed Rev. George Douglas, whose disabilities could not deter him from inspiring a healthy fear of God. The McConnells and other moneyed worshipers filled pews, while its church women launched the Old Brewery Mission in 1899. The Methodists shifted over to The Boulevard in Westmount after joining the United Church, so designer Emmanuel Briffa transformed the structure into an atmospheric theatre with a blue sky ceiling and silver stars in 1929 and Frank Sinatra, Nat King Cole, Louis Armstrong, Sammy Davis Jr., Sarah Vaughn, Rosemary Clooney, Patti Page, retired boxer Sugar Ray Robinson and Johnny Ray all took to the Seville stage over the years. Television wiped out the audience for live acts, leaving projectionists to roll films like *The Sound of Music*, which played daily for almost two years straight. The Seville went repertory in 1978, which meant a mishmash of low-cost older films each night and *The Rocky Horror Picture Show* became a big weekly draw, as it attracted flamboyantly-dressed fans who transformed screenings into wild parties. David Stein purchased the building in 1985 and quadrupled the rent, forcing manager Andy Simon to shut the theatre down, leading at least two people to threaten to handcuff themselves to chairs to prevent its closure. Stein failed to come through on his promise to create a dinner theatre venue and the vacant building just kept falling apart, as authorities prevented its demolition by declaring it a heritage monument. The building became a public health hazard after a wall collapsed in 1994. After many false starts it was demolished in 2010 and replaced by condos.

Eden Wax Museum *1168 St. Lawrence (1892-1940)*

Scowling Chinese opium pushers, a devil child with hooves and tail, a murderous gorilla and a triple homicide from Rawdon

were on wax display at The Eden, nestled in the stately *Monument National*. The Eden's nadir came when it displayed the recently-deceased corpse of corpse of 8'2" giant Édouard Beaupré in 1907. The show packed them in, or went broke, or was cancelled by its horrified directors, depending on varying accounts. Beaupré's real embalmed corpse was later replaced by a wax likeness which stood near Mrs. Thomas, famous for sleeping 18 months straight. Jack the Ripper, bloody scenes from World War I and the Devil's Kitchen, which featured Satanic imps roasting a man over a fire, completed the fun. The *Société Saint-Jean-Baptiste* evicted the museum in 1940. The wax museum had already had been supplanted by its crosstown rival, which aimed at supplying more uplifting, religiously-correct Catholic fare.

Montreal Wax Museum *3715 Queen Mary (1935-1989)*

The Wax Museum was marketed as a stop for organized bus tours of the nearby St. Joseph's Oratory when it opened in a

building designed by Paul Lemieux of Atwater Market notoriety. Sculptors Robert Tancrède and Albert Chartier razzled up the place with suffering religious martyrs, scenes from the Roman catacombs and dramatic Canadian history displays, attracting an impressive 350,000 visits in 1960. Catholic clergy feared the museum might attract worshipers away from the Oratory but in later years attendance plummeted by 90 percent from its peak, leading Tancrède and Chartier to return to their native to France in 1989. The 200 figures were shipped to the *Musée de la Civilisation* in Quebec City. The building now houses a pharmacy.

Show Mart *1600 Berri (1954-2001)* The Show Mart—aka *Palais du Commerce*—was built on sprawling vacant fields and kicked off with a pianist sitting playing for 21 hours straight in a

display window. André Mathieu's piano marathon world record, alas, was topped one day later. The Sportsman's Show introduced visitors to Chief Poking Fire and his Iroquois Indians from Frontier Village and "Frog Men" who conducted "fancy riding and driving demonstrations." Car shows, absent from Montreal since 1939, returned at a space that hosted The France in Canada Show, The Exporama Industrial Display and conferences dealing with everything from construction to fashion. Chubby Checker, Pierre Lalonde, Jenny Rock and The Ink Spots were among the music acts that rocked the venue while CJMS radio called it home for many years. Sarto Fournier's Greater Montreal Rally was headquartered in the building in 1957 prior his only mayoral victory. That same year nationalists booed Prime Minister Louis St. Laurent and Taxi Fraternity boss Eddy Giller, 52, died of a heart attack after a

Sévigny & Munsinger

scuffle at a drivers' meeting and a hoped-for Elvis Presley show failed to materialize, as brass rejected him for unexplained reasons. Sadly, Elvis never shook hips in Montreal. Sexy faux-spy Gerda Munsinger snooped in on federal defence minister Pierre Sévigny at a 1965 event, while megapimp Ziggy Wiseman rented an office there before killing himself in prison. The Palladium roller skating revived the fading structure, as 1,500 skaters wheeled around the oval in the early 1980s, a time when the site was considered as a location for a new concert hall but rejected as too shabby. It was razed in 2001 and replaced by the BANQ provincial library.

Paul Sauvé Arena *4000 Beaubien E. (1960-1992)* When the province gifted the venerable old *Palestre Nationale* sports organization with its own rink, none could have guessed how many memories the 4,000-seat arena would create. Jimi Hendrix rocked out in a truncated 1968 concert, with legend suggesting that he denied Jim Morrison's request to join him on stage, while groups from Abba to Johnny Hallyday also played the venue. Police officers met at the arena before launching their illegal strike in 1969, while a bizarre pro-FLQ terrorist meeting was

held there in the midst of the October Crisis of 1970. The boxing Hilton brothers and stylish Eddie Melo were among the flashy pugilists triumphing in its ring while Tarzan Tyler and Mad Dog Vachon starred in the sometimes-televised Wrestling Aces bouts from 1965 to 1975. The Rosemont venue offered warm ambiance, terrible sound and hosted junior hockey, Olympic volleyball, roller skating, curling, bowling, bingo, the circus and some of the most crucial political moments in Quebec history, including a couple of No-side rallies in 1980 which saw Pierre Trudeau passionately defend Canada, while his rival Premier René Lévesque gave his historic *"à la prochaine fois"* referendum loss speech at the arena the same year. The cash-strapped *Palestre Nationale* returned the arena to the province in 1978. The city took it over and it was later demolished and turned into condos.

New Penelope *378 Sherbrooke W. (1964-1969)* Gary Eisenkraft was the irrepressible Duddy Kravitz of local folk music impresarios, as his innocence, youth and hustle propelled four short-lived folk music venues, the most famous being the 300-seat New Penelope that ran from 1967 to 1969. In its brief existence the club hosted a young Joni Mitchell (in front of seven spectators), Gordon Lightfoot, Frank Zappa and Paul Butterfield.

Eisenkraft—who boasted of being the man (or boy) with the longest hair in Montreal—left home in his young teens to play music in the United States, travels that convinced him that Montreal needed a dedicated venue for the new youth. "They are pushed around and mistreated when they go out but we will treat them with respect here," promised the 17-year-old after taking over the The Fifth Dimension Club at 1455 Bleury. He renamed it the Fifth Amendment and hosted acts like Muddy Waters and

Rev. Gary Davis. Unpaid bills piled up so the next year he opened Café Penelope next to Café Prag on Bishop. The owner disliked the hippie crowds, so after five months it moved to 1432 Stanley where the landlord was so impressed with the turnouts that he took the venue over for himself, leaving Eisenkraft without club yet again. Eisenkraft found a new home on Sherbrooke near Hutchison and unlike the previous spots, this one had a box office, movable bleachers and changing rooms. It had no liquor license, so some fans would dash next door for beer relief. "The Pen was founded as a non-profit thing and it certainly succeeded at that," wrote columnist Dave Bist when it went

Eisenkraft

broke in November 1968, in spite of a trio of benefits by "The Society for the Preservation of the New Penelope." The New Penelope was doomed, as the entire strip was demolished for high rises. Eisenkraft gave up show business and moved to northern California to farm. He died in 2004, aged 59.

Sohmer Park *Panet and Notre Dame (1889-1919)* Ernest Lavigne was an entrepreneurial extrovert who enlisted to fight for the Italian Papal Zouaves, toured the States in a brass band and played music at Place Viger before selling musical instruments with partner Joseph Lavoie. Lavigne's shows with

The Montreal City Band at Viger Square proved popular, so he pitched the Sohmer Piano Company on a musical park. The company funded the riverside park that was eventually equipped with a 5,400-seat bandstand, making it Montreal's largest venue. Often-perilous attractions helped attract audiences, including hot-air balloon rides and a 150-foot daredevil leap onto a mattress perched on a net. Acrobat George Fyfe was severely injured doing a double somersault in a 1897 show, with his newspaper prognosis described as "he cannot live." A net broke in a similar 1889 disaster but Jean-Baptiste Peynaud survived, only to be killed soon after doing the same stunt in Cuba. Sohmer

Park was officially known as The Zoological Gardens of Montreal and animal acts were plenty, including one which saw dogs conduct a funeral and elephants dine at a formal meal. The handsome, white-haired Lavigne struck a majestic figure in his top hat as he organized his 200 employees at a venue that had a license to sell beer on Sunday, in spite of objections from opponents of alcohol. Vaudeville acts—jugglers, contortionists, acrobats, barrel jumping—were many and boxing and wrestling matches were standard and included a battle between strongman Louis Cyr and giant Édouard Beaupré. Yussif Mamhout, The Terrible Turk, Farmer Burns, Strangler Lewis, George

Lavigne

Hackenschmidit, Raoul de Rouen and Zybzscko also thrilled with their wrestling feats. Lavigne died in 1909 and its once-impressive zoo was reduced to a mere parrot, bear and monkey when it fell victim to fire in 1919. Philanthropist Charles S. Campbell purchased the property and turned it into a children's playground (along with three others across town), later swapped for a park on Plessis Street.

Dominion Park *Haig and Notre Dame E. (1906-1937)* It

took a one-hour tramway trek from downtown to get to this
Coney Island-style thrill zone, which featured snake charmers, a
photo gallery, a shooting gallery, and an infant incubator where
premature babies were put on display. But the main thrills at
stock broker Harry Dorsey's amusement park came from rides

like Myth City, Bump
the Bump, The Crystal Maze,
The Laughing Gallery, Ye
Olde Mille, the Scenic
Railway, Shoot the Chutes
and The Tickler. Grisly
displays were also rife, such
as one display celebrating
The Titanic, which killed

1,500 in 1912 and another
imitating the Johnston,
Pennsylvania flood of 1889,
which killed 2,200. Boxing
matches, trapeze artists and a
diver who leaped into four feet
of water from 125 feet in the
air were also typical fare.

Movie cowboy Tom Mix was gored by a bull in 1912 but insisted
in participating in a bucking bronco event and was then tossed
and hospitalized, as heartless onlookers jeered his
departure. Firefighting boats shot water from the nearby St.
Lawrence River after the place caught fire in 1913. A lit cigarette
caused another fire six years later, this time killing seven roller
coaster riders: three men, three women and a boy. Sousa's Band
kept playing throughout the disaster, which left seven burned
bodies unrecognizable. Dominion Park faced competition from
Belmont Park starting in 1923 and business dipped further with
The Great Depression. The Dominion Park Amusement
Company leased the premises to new operators 1933 who kept it
going until 1938. Its remains were carted off in April 1940.

Belmont Park *Highway 117 at the Back River, Cartierville (1923-1983)* Generations of Montrealers had their neural

pathways reshaped by the terror and enchantment on rides such as The Whip, The Wild Mouse and The Matterhorn, while   the gruesome papier-mâché Laughing Lady greeted customers with her unnerving peals of laughter. The Cyclone, which hit speeds of 100 km/h, was the world's tallest wooden roller-coaster until 1946 and the Laff in the Dark Haunted House pitted visitors against terrifying Tiki gods and The Shiverin' Indian. Shows included Oscar Babcock's Death Trap, with loop-the-loop

cycling stunts in 1935 and the Demanati Brothers' aerial act, as well musical visits from Martha and The Vandellas and Bo Diddley. Charles-Emile Trudeau, father of Pierre Trudeau, was a minority owner when it opened in 1923 and Jacques Favreau took over a dozen years later. Paul Pappas and his group purchased Belmont Park in 1948 and added a dance hall, roller rink and illusion room. The amusement park—by now part-owned by Prime

Minister Trudeau—took a hit when two children were seriously injured after falling eight metres from the Parachute Paratrooper ride in August 1979. Police raided a week later and shut down its games of chance, targeting the weekly Florida holiday raffle. Owners won a $100,000 lawsuit against Montreal police but a subsequent $1 million renovation failed to stem its decline, as thrill-seekers preferred competitor La Ronde, leading to its closure on October 13, 1983.

Olympic Stadium Only grizzled Montrealers feel the complex mix of dismay, derision and sentimentality evoked by the East End Olympic Stadium that took 40 years to pay off. All-powerful Mayor Drapeau endorsed French architect's Roger

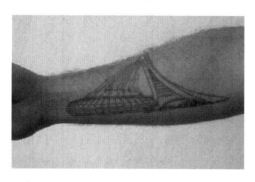

Taillebert's extravagant design for a stadium with super curtain cables hoisting a retractable roof, sparking a shameless orgy of corruption. Workers would clock in and return home to sleep, while construction materials were pilfered for private homes and replaced by substandard replacements. Extortionist union thug Dédé Desjardins led an illegal construction strike in 1974 aiming to discourage police from probing his drug and loansharking operations. A worker was killed and four others injured in August 1975 when a concrete support beam tumbled from the roof. Six months later four workers more fell 55 metres to their deaths. Athletes also suffered, as boxer Cleveland Denny was killed by punch from Getan Hart in July 1980. Promising Expos outfielder Terry Francona's career ended when in an on-field collision in 1983. Giants pitcher Dave Dravecky's cancer-afflicted arm snapped grotesquely while pitching in 1989, leading to amputation, Moises Alou broke his left fibula after his foot got caught in the artificial turf and André Dawson suffered years of knee pain caused by running on the unpadded outfield turf. Fans also suffered with a variety of falls from the stands, including part-time drummer Michel Bergeron who fell to his death into the bullpen on August 27, 1979 during a 2-0 shutout loss to Atlanta. For many years the stadium has remained closed in winter due to the poor condition of its roof. Demolition has been ruled out as an option, as the cost of protecting the metro line below would prove prohibitive.

Drive-ins Tail-finned sedans laid rubber to road to drive-in theatres across North America during the 1950s but Quebec kept the brakes on the outdoor cinema experience, banning all open-air cinemas until 1967. The powerful Catholic Church opposed what many saw as "passion pits," a name earned by couples who got frisky during films. But the ban irked families, as the drive-ins allowed parents to catch a flick while their children dozed in back seats. Quebecers on a quest for drive-in movie action were forced to motor to one of the thousands of

theatres beyond Quebec's borders until the Union Nationale finally reversed the ban. (The same legislation finally allowed kids under 16 into movie theatres, reversing a ban sparked by the 1927 Laurier Palace theatre fire, which saw Montreal 78 kids perish on St. Catherine E.) The drive-in theatre fad was in decline elsewhere by the time Quebec got its first such facilities, with a trio of Montreal-area drive-ins (including one on-island in Dollard Des Ormeaux) opening within weeks of each other in June 1970. The drive-ins proved massively popular for a while and helped feed provincial tax coffers, leading authorities to question why they had kept them outlawed.

5

Sports & Rec

Diligent, hard-working Montrealers sought to live fulfilling and meaningful lives but many others were happy chasing pucks, flying kites, riding roller skates and lighting firecrackers. These are their stories.

Alouette insanity The CFL Montreal Alouettes racked up prodigous losses in the 1960s but the floundering team also offered ample off-field entertainment thanks to coach Jim Trimble and owner Ted Workman, both inveterate maniacs. Workman supported the Moral Rearmament movement, a fringe cult that aimed to prepare for an upcoming cosmic military showdown. So he had his gridiron stars study and distribute group literature. Workman also caused the greatest blunder in franchise history when he met Hamilton brass at the Mount Royal Hotel and traded them star receiver Hal Patterson without consulting General Manager Perry Moss. Workman didn't realize that Patterson had a no-trade clause which made him a free agent if traded. The Alouettes lost their star player for nothing. Workman sold in 1969 and the Als won the Grey Cup the next season, ending a 21-year drought. Coach Jim Trimble, for his part, kidnapped and tortured sports reporter Ian MacDonald in Toronto while attending the 1965 Grey Cup. Trimble had tired of MacDonald's constant taunts and brought the scribe to his hotel room where he beat him and left him with two black eyes and a broken rib. Trimble was fired but then helped revolutionize football with Hudson's Joel Rottman and Alcan engineer Cedric Marsh. The duo sought Trimble's help in marketing their new invention, a one-legged football goalpost, which they hoped would replace the old-style extended soccer net design. The unipod uprights were showcased at Expo 67, unveiled at the Autostade and adopted by the NFL the same year. It was not the only standard goal structure invented in Montreal. In 1927 Art Ross redesigned the NHL hockey net two-inches wider with a modified crossbar and a double-curved back-side to reduce bounce-outs.

Patterson

Workman & Trimble

Starving the dolphins New Yorker Joseph Geraci was

hired to run The Montreal Aquarium, aka The Alcan Aquarium, on St. Helen's Island for Expo 67 but Mayor Drapeau wasn't keen

on keeping the tanks full after the world fair shindig, so he cut its budget in 1975. Five years later city blue collar workers went on strike and let the lovable fish go hungry. Management tried to get them fed but to no avail. Brigitte the Dolphin, aged 20, died of starvation in May 1980 while three months pregnant. Fannie, the star attraction, was the next to die, then down went Judith. The three surviving dolphins, Pierrot, Kim and Carole were relocated to The Flipper

Sea School in Miami. The federal government pledged $100 million to rejuvenate the aquarium by moving it to a new facility at the Old Port in 1988 alongside a new science museum and the relocated St. Constant train museum. But the massive project never came to life and the Alcan Aquarium was drained in September 1991. Most

of the remaining aquatic wildlife was transferred to the Biodome but four sharks were killed, one with a sledgehammer to the head. Entrepreneur Jim Pattison proposed building another aquarium in 2000, while The Granby Zoo promised to build one in Montreal the next year. But Montreal still has no dedicated aquarium. Some bemoan the loss of dolphins, particularly for autistic kids who some believe might benefit from swimming with dolphins, an idea that not all embraced. "Why not have programs where sick children walk with giraffes or sleep with gorillas?" one skeptical critic asked.

The war on pinball

The war on pinball Hip-thrusting, ball-smacking pinball seemed like an indecent activity when it exploded in Quebec after World War II, so authorities launched raids from the first

Jacques & Gerard Tremblay

day springy plunger bopped steel ball. The policy was deemed justified by its classification as a slot machine device, even though pinball became a game of skill when flippers were added in 1947. The Pax Plante-Jean Drapeau mayoral duo accused it of undermining juvenile thriftiness, calling it "a perpetual invitation to spend money recklessly." The Supreme Court outlawed pinball in April 1955, sparking more efforts to halt the rolling balls. "Nickel suckers have corrupted our young for too long," wrote a Montreal editorial. "Kids steal change from their mothers' purses to play them or coins from neighbours' milk bottles and spend lunch money on it and go hungry." Montreal cops seized and crushed half a million dollars worth of pinball machines between 1955 and 1971, thanks to the limitless enthusiasm of Morality Squad chief Steve Olynyk, whose selective busts included one on the Monte Carlo Gameland at 19 St. Catherine E., in which 14 were charged with keeping a common gaming house. Brothers Jacques and Gerard Tremblay of North Star Coin Machine were not deterred from building hundreds of legendary Sea Breeze pinball machines before their efforts were killed by cheaper American competition. A Montreal bylaw banning minors from playing was finally overturned in 1977 but kids had already migrated to other coin-sucking games. A Montrealer inspired the world's most famous fictional pinball champ, as Pamela Marchant shuffled around London with boyfriend Nik Cohn, who introduced her as a mute pinball champ. Cohn's friends in The Who caught on to the character and extended it to become the deaf-dumb-and-blind pinball champ of the Tommy rock opera.

Tragedy on ice Many a ferocious Montreal hockey warrior was felled not by rival pugilist but rather bad habit or fortune. John Kordic served up the knuckle sandwiches between 1986 and 1988 before being traded to Toronto.

John Kordic

After his premature retirement, Kordic moved to Montreal to live near his kickboxing centre and put his fighting skills into practice by taking on a group of Somali newcomers at 4460 Ontario E. Kordic said that the group had been bullying and taunting passersby. A full-blown neighbourhood riot ensued and the Somalis were resettled elsewhere in town. Kordic died of a cocaine-related heart ailment in 1992 at age 27.

The Canadiens signed ultra-muscular bodybuilding champion Normand Baron to a minor league contract in 1983, at a time when he was not even playing organized hockey. Baron's designated role was to be a backup brawler and he eventually rode the Habs pine for four games. After retirement, Baron attacked a West Island strip club doorman with a knife but avoided punishment. The Habs' most accomplished pugilist, Chris Nilan (aka

Tony Demers

Boston crime lord Whitey Bulger's former son-in-law), battled heroin addiction before getting clean. Other troubled Habs included Brian Fogarty, a Montreal-born junior defence phenom who played parts of two seasons with the Canadiens before dying in 2002 at the age of 32 following a drinking binge. Montreal Maroons defenceman Hobie Kitchen was benched for the playoffs in the Stanley Cup-winning season of 1926 and became a vagrant in Manhattan.

Hobie Kitchen

Habs' hard-shooting wartime right winger Tony Demers was nailed in a ringer scandal for impersonating a lesser player in an amateur game that attracted heavy betting. He was sentenced to seven years in prison for beating his girlfriend to death in the Eastern Townships in 1949.

Where kids ruled Kids didn't only fly kites and toss balls in parks, they also ran. Ran for election, that is. A longtime summer ritual saw kids elect park mayors from among their

peers in a playground democracy that began in a modest 10 parks in 1941. By the the early 1960s 55,000 kids cast votes in 244 Montreal park elections, totals that don't include municipalities like the Town of Mount Royal which alone elected 16 park little park bosses. Only 10 percent of races went uncontested and the winner was typically lofted onto shoulders and carried around in an impromptu victory lap, although the victory speech might be interrupted by young hecklers urging the winner to "shut up!" The winners met with Montreal's mayor who'd listen to wish-lists, which often included "add a swimming pool." Popular attachment to parks gradually declined for reasons too depressing to enumerate.

Fingers on frosty facades Vaudeville star Jack "The Human Fly" Lamonte vowed to climb the six-storey La Patrie

building at City Hall and St. Catherine in 1923 but he awoke to frosty -25 C weather, far too cold for such a perilous stunt. But 20,000 braved the chill to watch his climb, so who was Lamonte to disappoint his frosty fans? Lamonte, using his bare hands, braved the bitter winds to successfully scale the icy structure. The building was no stranger to entertainment, as 15-years earlier Léo-Ernest Ouimet had projected some of the earliest film screenings onto its front wall. The building went vacant in the early 1970s and was later purchased by the Church of Scientology. Frenchman Alain Robert pulled off Montreal's biggest building climb in 1999 when he scaled the 25-storey Crown Plaza hotel at Berri and Sherbrooke.

Curling rocks A group of investors believed that curling was in decline because the sport required participants to join clubs before laying down the slippery double takeouts. So they

The Haunted at BCC 1967

launched The Bonaventure Curling Club (6055 Côte de Liesse) with a pay-to-play policy, so anybody could pay by the hour to slide rocks from the hog line. Organizers went big with a 300-space parking lot and Chinese restaurant inside, all just south of what's now the Ikea on Cavendish Boulevard. Their marketing plan missed the target, as the curling was overshadowed by weekly rock-outs starring psychedelic rock bands like The Rabble, The Haunted, The Influence and Our Generation. The rockers would pack in 4,000 teens at a weekly Canadian Hopsville event, hosted Saturday evenings by radio host Dave Boxer in 1967. Owners eventually came to terms with the diminished appeal of curling, noting that young people preferred skiing on weekends in spite of irresistibly alluring ads insisting that "Curling is fun! Healthy, relaxing and inexpensive." The curling club became a hockey rink in September 1973. An industrial warehouse now occupies the site.

Fine day for kiting Flying a kite is a pastime that exemplifies joyous freedom but reeling out that gravity-defying twine was once a punishable offence in Montreal. The stringed aerial amusement ban brought strife to the life of 12-year-old Frédéric Pariseau, who learned that Montreal police were serious about enforcing the rule when he was fined 50 cents for flying a kite on Durham Street, later known as Plessis, according to *The Montreal Daily Witness* of June 7, 1879. Pariseau was offered the alternative punishment of spending 24 hours in jail. He's probably no longer around to report which option he chose. The reason for the ban remains unknown. The masses of phone and electrical wires that obscured the urban firmament only went up several years later, so the municipal interdiction was not likely inspired by overhead obstacle.

The fast and the furry horse Montreal daredevils once did their street racing with horses. Fearless competitors raced buggies down Upper Lachine Road (which included what would become St. James) until spoilsports started complaining. "The habit of racing on the streets is too prevalent and the police should be on the alert for offenders," opined a Montreal editorialist in a halfheartedly denunciatory opinion piece from 1879. On February 15, 1914 authorities aimed to eradicate the longstanding races. Chief Campeau and Captain Marwick of the NDG police station set out to snag speeders but watched helplessly as three racers blew by without stopping. The police adjusted their approach by blocking the roadway south of what's now Oxford Park to the next set of eastbound sprinters. One of the three racers escaped but the other two were captured and detained and forced to ride up to the NDG police station. The races had been a regular event since at least the 1860s.

Why try? Defenceman Robin Sadler's skill lay not as a heart-and-soul grinder willing to block pucks with his face, but rather as a man capable of recognizing his limits. Sadler was  drafted a lofty ninth overall by the Canadiens in 1975 but instead of going all-out to make the team, the offensive defenceman shocked the squad by quitting and returning home to British Columbia, handing back his $250,000 signing bonus. Sadler was honest in his self-assessment, as he later explained that he ditched the squad because he knew that he would never be good enough to play in the NHL. Few players from the 1975 draft went on to impressive hockey careers, although the Canadiens landed reliable Pierre Mondou, while 210th pick Dave Taylor had the most success of anybody in the entire draft. Sadler attempted once again to make the Canadiens the next season, scoring a goal in nine games in the minors. He went on to push puck for 14 years in various obscure European leagues before returning to become a realtor in British Columbia.

Juggler's fame fleeting Nine-pound cannonballs were no match for Edmond Gingras' powerful torso, as the Montreal entertainer would not only allow the fast-flying projectiles to blast his six-pack, he would then catch and juggle them after impact. Gingras wowed fans at New York's Madison Square Garden in 1915, sharing a stage with songbird Eva Tanguay on the Albee-Keith vaudeville tour. Gingras' juggling rivaled the legendary German Paul Conchas and he also impressed crowds with his feats of balancing, bodybuilding and wrestling. Gingras lived a charmed life until the Great Depression killed vaudeville and wiped out his livelihood. He attempted a comeback in 1934 at Montreal's *Théâtre Français* but learned that cannonball blocking is a young man's game. Gingras, then 50, was humiliated as spectators offered derisive jeers. Gingras spent the rest of his days as a recluse, moving from one cheap apartment to another until he was found dead in 1953. His body was brought to the Fullum Street morgue where he went unrecognized and unclaimed for some time.

No race to justice Montrealer Hilda Strike was the fastest female in the women's 100 metre dash at the Los Angeles Olympics of 1932 but she never received her gold medal. Strike  and competitor Stella Walsh, aka Stanislawa Walasiewicz, were both clocked at 11.9 seconds for the 100 metres on August 2, 1932 but judges awarded the photo finish victory to Walsh and the hulking Polish-American towered above the Montrealer on the medal stand. The injustice was exposed much later when Walsh was shot dead in the crossfire of a grocery store robbery in Cleveland in 1980 and a subsequent autopsy confirmed that Walsh had a non-functioning penis and lacked a uterus. The revelations were not enough to persuade the Olympic Committee to award Strike the gold medal. A polite Canadian-style outcry changed nothing. After the Olympics, Strike married, moved to Ville St. Laurent and died in 1989.

Walsh & Strike

Fire for the queen Victoria Day in Point St. Charles long involved firebombs, arson attacks and all the mischief one could accomplish with wood, matches and kerosene. Montreal's

Irish immigrants started lighting bonfires on Victoria Day in the early 1800s in Goose Village, some to display affection for the British monarch and others to express the opposite. "Montreal boys, both the young and old variety, got out the good old sticks of punk last night, muffled their ears with their hands and blew another 24th of May up in smoke, stars and thunder," read a 1934 report. The events grew as hordes gathered wood and mattresses, discarded couches and fences, then stored them in sheds for the big blaze and lit them up, pulling every fire alarm lever in the area to confuse firemen. Participants graduated to tossing Molotov cocktails and barricading streets. Some torched a vacant house at Shannon and Ottawa, just a block from the fire station in 1946. Rioters set over 40 fires in 1955 and lit up billboards and injured two police officers the next year. They torched a grain elevator and two sheds in 1959, while one industrious incendiary celebrated by shooting flaming arrows from his window. Vandals convened from all over, as police arrested between 20 and 40 every year in the 1980s. Rowdies once hit a cop with a brick and then did the same to an ambulance attendant, necessitating a second ambulance. Kids fed a fire with wood ripped out of a front balcony, leading a woman to walk out and break a leg. "There's nothing they don't do, except kill," laughed a cop in 1983. The ritual slowly went extinct in the 1990s, as authorities held outdoor rock shows with controlled bonfires. "It was like having St. Patrick's Day for 200 years and then suddenly you didn't have it," said one rueful rioter.

Equine airport If you hear the echoes of hooves from equine ghosts sprinting at Trudeau Airport, do not be shocked, for those are the stallions that raced on the grounds lifetimes ago.

Samuel Holman opened the half-mile thoroughbred Dorval Race Track in 1914 after a scheme to use the lands for a military barracks were nixed. The facility was built as a replica of the Terrazas Race Track in Juarez, Mexico and did solid business in its early days, raking in $90,000 daily in bets in its first year. The take matched its competitor Blue Bonnets but lagged far behind the Mount Royal half-mile track, which took in triple that total. The Dorval track proved too remote for horse fans and Habs owner Leo Dandurand purchased it in the 1930s and started a long process of trying to sell it off. Sir William Hildred finally got a deal done for $1 million in 1937 and four years later it was earmarked to become Montreal's main airport, putting an end to the notion of building it in South Shore St. Hubert.

Dutchman drowns The Canadiens once had a coach who never lost a game. Babe Siebert, who was known as the Flying Dutchman in spite of his German heritage, starred for the

Siebert

Montreal Maroons before ending his playing days with three seasons on the Habs. Siebert did much of the housework after his wife lost the use of her legs in a birthing mishap, although he also managed to find quality time to spend with his mistress Audrey McMorran on Monkland Ave. The Canadiens chose Siebert to coach the club soon after his retirement in 1939. Later that summer Siebert swam into Lake Huron to fetch a rubber dinghy for his daughter. He got caught in an undertow and his body was found three days later. He never got to coach a game in the NHL.

Wrestling heartbreak Pro wrestling exploded in Montreal after 1939 when all pretense of noble battle was replaced by hammy story lines acted out by such local products as Johnny Rougeau, Yvon Robert and Larry Moquin. All three had their names tacked onto nightclubs, thanks to flattering scripts penned out by shameless wrestling boss Eddie Quinn. But not all wrestlers lived happy and complete lives. Eric "Yukon Eric" Holmback had an ear torn off by Killer Kowalski at the Forum in Oct. 1952 in front of 12,000 fans. He killed himself a dozen years later in Georgia. Mohawk wrestler Carl Donald Bell, aka Don Eagle, died of gunshot wounds in Kahnawake in March 1966. It was deemed a suicide. His wife Jean Eagle, who might have killed him, was murdered two years later. Adolfo "Dino Bravo" Bresciano was shot and killed at his home in Laval in

Giant Jean Ferré

March 1993, possibly in connection with a cigarette smuggling ring. Camillle "Tarzan Tyler" Tourville died at 58 on the highway back from Lac St. Jean in 1985 after his vehicle slammed into a truck in the Laurentian National Park. The most superhuman of all Montreal wrestlers was André René Roussimoff, known in Montreal rings as Giant Jean Ferré. The 7'4", 400-plus-pound French wrestler came on the advice of compatriot Édouard "The Aristocrat" Carpentier. He slept in a large bed at the Windsor Hotel 1971 to 1973 and later at 2155 Mackay. The massive André had an unlimited appetite, once drinking over 100 beers at one sitting before dying in 1993 at the age of 46. Regularly-scheduled wrestling left the Forum in 1976 but the most famous Montreal wrestling match took place in 1997, as the WWE packed the Molson Centre with fans who witnessed a real-life double-cross. Bret Hart, in his final match before defecting to a competing wrestling league, was duped into believing he would allowed to win but was instead beaten by Shawn Michaels, an infamous event known as The Montreal Screwjob.

Royalty on Delorimier

Many came to Montreal Royals games to drink, fight and gamble on upcoming plays, creating action in the stands often livelier than on the field. The

stadium at the northeast corner of Delorimier and Ontario opened in 1928 and contained a tavern, restaurant, printing press and Canada's largest roller skating rink. Slugger Dale Alexander became a legend by clobbering a homer 500 feet that first season, one of many bombs that flew over fences covered in ads for IGA, Buick, Molson, Coca Cola and British Consols cigarettes. Colour barrier-smashing legend Jackie Robinson (who lockered next to less famous Stan "Happy Rabbit" Rojek) starred, as did Carl Erskine, Don Newcombe, Carl Furillo, Junior Gilliam, Duke Snider and Don Drysdale. The Royals thrived between 1945 and 1950 when they attracted 600,00 fans and generated profits of over $300,000, with the 1946 and 1948 teams considered the greatest-ever minor league squads. Brooklyn Dodgers players snickered when manager Leo Durocher threatened to dispatch them to Montreal, realizing that great nightlife awaited. So the Dodgers tamed their wilder prospects by sending

Jackie Robinson

them to sleepy St. Paul, Minnesota. The Royals were enfeebled and many of the 20,000 seats went empty, with one game in 1957 attracting 265 fans. A dozen investors made a pitch to keep the team alive in 1960 but stadium landlord Sherburn Investments sought $60,000 in rent, a sum too rich. Appliance shop owner Roland Faucher purchased the land in 1962 and vowed to build a shopping centre and an indoor ski hill. None of it was built. The stadium was demolished in 1969 and a school was built.

Dam team didn't catch on Johnny Newman was dubbed Montreal's most-destructive man in an era when city officials practically issued more demolition permits than parking tickets, as Beaver Construction bagged upwards of $50 million a year to knock down buildings.

**BEAVERS
C.F.L.**

England-born Newman had suited up briefly for the Montreal Alouettes and yearned to purchase his former squad. But the team snubbed his $500,000 offer so the Westmount High grad instead purchased a team from the fledgling American rules Continental Football League and moved it to the newly-built Autostade. Newman, who once raised charity dollars by allowing donors to swing a wrecking ball on the doomed St. James Club, soon learned that the Autostade's unpaved parking lot turned to mud when it rained, forcing fans to trudge through the wet dirt.

Newman

The Beavers lost $1 million and Newman threw in the towel, as the CFL Alouettes moved in for eight years. The Autostade was a 33,000-seat collection of 19 modular prefab cement slabs set on beams that looked like a oblong daisy from above. Ford, Volvo, Chrysler, AMC and GM teamed up to build the stadium that was filled by such acts as Van Morrison, Jefferson Airplane, Pink Floyd and The Who. It was earmarked as home for the baseball Expos until baseball chief Warren Giles deemed it inadequate. Field jumpers and streakers were frequent and fans routinely pulled down the uprights after football games, a tradition that ended when security enlisted four German Shepherds to attack anybody who jumped on the field, with the hounds savaging one fan vigorously in 1975.

Old time rollerskating

Early Montrealers didn't only collect firewood, blast muskets and memorize Bible passages, they also roller-skated from at least 1862 when Canada's first

rollerskating facility opened at the Victoria Rink on Drummond. Another rink sat at St. Denis and St. Catherine, its existence making news when roller skating was forbidden during the 1885 smallpox epidemic.

Coliseum on Guy

The Montreal Forum began as a roller rink in 1888, featuring a race between an American roller-skater and a skateless sprinter from Toronto. The Valiquette Roller Skating Rink on St. Maurice (three doors east of Duke, south side) hosted roller skating shows of "Japanese fan entertainment" that same year and indeed roller skating was a popular spectator attraction, with The Skating Vanities revue hitting The Forum until the mid-1940s. Delorimier Downs ballpark came with a roller-rink and the barn-like Coliseum at 1005 Guy, ended its days with a spectacular fire that saw 60 skaters barely escape in May 1950. Rollerskating enjoyed a big uptick in the 1970s when it fused with disco at the Skadiu (4550 Metropolitan), Cezar's Palace, the Paladium (at The Show Mart) and the Disco Drome (4475 Ballantyne). And there was the roller derby. PR guru

Norman Olson

Norman Olson launched his *Fleur-de-Lys* of the sporadically-televised 12-team men's Roller Derby League franchise in January 1967. It rolled for 126-games at the Forum, Paul Sauvé Arena and elsewhere in Quebec. Roller derby stars Gwen "Skinny Minnie" Miller and part-time boxer Diane Syverson skated for Montreal's Canadian All Stars in the early 1970s before the teams folded, partly due to the high cost of transporting and assembling the track.

The cockiest rookie Eddie Dorohoy had plenty to say when he tried out for the Montreal Canadiens in 1948. The Great Gaboo, as he was later known, flaunted hierarchical custom by offering scoring tips to the legendary Maurice Richard. The Rocket, who led the league with 45 goals the season prior, hardly needed unsolicited advice from the 19-year-old rookie. Self-esteem was never an issue for Dorohoy, who told veteran Habs teammate Murph "Old Hardrock" Chamberlain, "When you were a rookie you weren't as good as I am." Dorohoy's fate was sealed when Coach Dick Irvin solemnly asked each player why he wasn't scoring, Dorohoy cracked up the room by explaining that he had zero points after 16 games for a perfectly valid reason. "I've been trying to score from too sharp an angle, the end of the bench." Dorohoy was dispatched to minor league Dallas and never returned to the NHL.

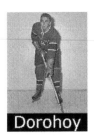

Dorohoy

Take me out to the blowpark Cocaine was so popular among the 1985 Montreal Expos that one player was both a user and a dealer according to St. Louis Cardinals Manager Whitey Herzog. Cardinals players were so eager to buy cocaine off the Expo that when a pitcher accidentally plunked the Expo with a pitch, the Cardinals admonished their hurler for his recklessness. "Hey! Be careful! Look what you did! Now he might not sell us any cocaine tonight!" The Cards skipper said that he always focused on winning the opening game of every Montreal road series because by the second game his players would be too debilitated by cocaine consumption to play well. Avid cocaine consumers on the Expos included Tim Raines, Ellis Valentine and Darrel Evans. Manager Dick Williams reported that four players were caught with drugs at the Canadian border and said he frequently worried players would stash their drugs in his luggage. Expo Warren Cromartie blamed high-profile activist Bobby White for supplying the cocaine.

Herzog

Was hockey fixed? For many years the Montreal Canadiens' Stanley Cup parade was a near-annual event, as the Habs won 14 of 24 championships between 1956 and 1979. And while the Canadiens teams were rife with talent, some suspect that organized crime might have had a hand to play in some of their good fortunes. Maurice Richard once expressed unease that

gambler Jim Norris had a controlling interest all four U.S.-based teams, the New York Rangers, Boston Bruins, Chicago Blackhawks and Detroit Red Wings. Norris owned the Blackhawks, while his father James Sr. owned the Red Wings. Federal investigators even investigated the father-son team for links to the gambling underworld. Only Toronto and Montreal were outside of the Norris influence and by some coincidence those two teams combined to win 13 of the 14 Stanley Cups between 1956 and 1969, leading some to suspect that the Norris family had arranged for their own teams to lose for their gambling gains.

Montreal's greatest Forget Maurice Richard, Mario Lemieux, Mike Bossy and Raymond Bourque, insurance

salesman Russell Bowie was the greatest hockey player from Montreal. Bowie attended Tucker High School across from the Victoria Rink on Drummond and was "almost frail" as an adult, weighing just 112 lbs. But Bowie could score eight goals a game while sipping champagne between periods. Bowie refused to take a cent for his efforts, refusing a grand piano, $3,000 and $4 per minute to switch from The Victorias to The Montreal Wanderers. Bowie was a jaw-dropping, eye-popping outlier, once bagging 39 goals in 10 games for the Montreal Victorias in 1906-07. Bowie played the rover position, used a short stick and had 42 stitches in his head when he retired to devote his energies to selling insurance and refereeing hockey games.

Bowie

Rocky of the running shoe Walter Young reckoned his employment woes might end if he won the 1937 Boston Marathon. But Young had never won a marathon and could not even afford the bus ride to Boston and pawning his runner's-up prize watch was only good for a one-way bus ticket. So he approached Verdun Mayor Hervé Ferland, who handed Young $50 and the promise of a job if he emerged victorious. Young found himself neck-and-neck with 1935 champ Johnny Kelley as the lead changed 16 times. Young eventually prevailed and Ferland hired the triumphant Young as a Verdun police officer. He later switched to firefighting and was known to fearlessly stroll into fierce blazes without wearing a mask. Young kept running as a hobby and walked a long distance to work daily, where he never missed a day until retiring in 1978. Young's coach Peter Gavuzzi, who recommended short strides, training in snowshoes and avoiding starchy foods, went on to train Gérard Côté of St. Hyacinthe, who won the Boston Marathon four times.

Young

Road hockey straight outta Westmount Road hockey was invented in Westmount, as the wealthy downtown-adjacent suburb was the first place in Montreal to get paved roads. The smooth asphalt permitted a young Art Ross to organize games, which he controlled because his parents bought the equipment. Friends Lester Patrick, brothers Sprague and Odie Cleghorn and other future stars joined in. The Patrick family went on to build the Westmount Arena at Wood and St. Catherine, the first rink specifically designed for hockey. The Wanderers and Canadiens played there until it burned down in 1917. Ross and Patrick made the Hockey Hall of Fame, as did Sprague Cleghorn, the last defenceman to lead the Canadiens in scoring. Odie Cleghorn played in the NHL and became the first coach to switch players during plays.

Ross & Patrick

Come back kid Goalie Charlie Hodge stopped many pucks for his hometown Habs but only after overcoming a misunderstanding that nearly derailed his dream.

Hodge

Montreal Junior Royals hockey coach Tag Miller invited a young Hodge to a tryout but Miller died in the off-season at age 37. As a result nobody recognized the tiny Hodge when he showed up. An assistant coach ordered Hodge home for being too small. The coach called and told Hodge to return the next day. Hodge complied but the assistant ordered him home again. The coach phoned yet again and Hodge finally came and won a spot. But his high school team threatened him with expulsion if he played on another team. Hodge dropped out at 16 and never returned to a classroom. Hodge, an only child from Lachine, later formed a tandem with Gump Worsley of Point St. Charles.

Habs boot superfan For a dozen years Dutchie Van

Van Eden

Eden led ear-punishing chants from the standing-room-only section, creating a tidal wave of noise that invigorated the entire building. Dutchie and trumpeter Michel Blanchard alternated megaphone cheers and brassy fanfare, inciting waves of *Go Habs Go!* and *Charge!* to echo through the old building from 1963. Dutchie fathered five children, worked at the port and drove a Pontiac Parisienne emblazoned with a Habs logo. He rented a $30-a-month telephone pager and charged fans $5 to join his fast-growing fan club, which had 1,300 members in 1975 and he trademarked the Go-Habs-Go! slogan. Dutchie even cheered the Habs at the airport, which led tough guy John Ferguson to grab and crush his megaphone. Dutchie's days as a superfan ended abruptly when a Forum security guard confiscated his megaphone that same year, citing noise complaints. Dutchie never watched another Habs game.

Shooting up the Main The high-pitched *ping-ping* of metal-on-metal was an ubiquitous component of the St. Lawrence Main Street soundscape in the early 1900s, part of a cacophony that included crowing roosters and gypsy fortune-tellers hawking palm readings. But the guns also provided tragedy. Amabile Baril shot Mary Bosco dead in September 1901 at Bosco's shooting gallery on the Main after she repeatedly rebuffed his amorous advances. A boastful sailor dropped into Joseph Bertrand's shooting gallery on the Main four doors up from Viger in 1926 and vowed that he could light a match with the gallery rifle. Bertrand turned his back and the sailor shot himself dead. Mengo Kerr—who had never held a firearm—accidentally shot and killed friend William Anterton, 26, at the same place four years later. Other arcade thrills included one where a model would sit on customer's lap. The timeless framed photo keepsake of the contrived amorous memory cost 75 cents in the 1920s.

A whole mess of chess For every belligerent drunk

hanging perilously onto a Montreal bar stool there's a thoughtful chess player sipping chamomile tea at a chess club. That formula might not be entirely precise but Montrealers have been sliding rooks, pawns and queens over squares since the European stuck clog in Montreal mud. The Montreal Chess Club launched in 1844, convening at Victoria Hall in Westmount, on Phillips Square in the 1880s, University and St. Catherine a decade later, where a brazen showoff named Mr. Pillsbury played 16 players at the same time while blindfolded. Then it was on to Guy and St. Catherine in the 1920s and back to Drummond Street later. Chess cafés became a 1970s fad with such places as the Downtown Chess Club (University and St. Catherine), Montreal Chess Club (1500 Stanley), Long Live the King (5017 St. Hubert) and the *En Passant Café* on St. Denis where a a 14-year-old once caused his 70-year-old opponent to suffer a heart attack. "Chess pieces danced around the board like Mexican jumping beans while the poor old Soviet clocks would get pounded like punching bags," read a description.

Superstar rides the bus Romanian gymnast Nadia Comaneci became a legendary sports goddess at 14 by earning perfect scores at the 1976 Montreal Olympics while also  hoarding packs of McDonald's condiments to haul back to her ketchup-starved Communist homeland. But circumstance later conspired to return her to live cheek-to-jowl among the Montreal masses that once adored her. Disastrous romantic flings with a Ceausescu in Romania and a married roofer in Florida led Comaneci to flee to Montreal in 1989 where she briefly lived at the Westmount mansion of eccentric billionaire cryogenics fan Robert Miller and his Romanian wife. She then moved downscale to countryman Alexandru Stefu's triplex on Louis Hebert near the delightful Cinéma Beaubien. The frumpy Comaneci humbly rode around Montreal on city buses and signed on as underwear model for Jockey Canada, even though her once-taut body hauled lumps of Soviet flab. Brighter times returned as Comaneci hosted *The Mystery and Majesty of Nadia* stage show in Reno, Nevada. She had an audience with Pope John Paul II and received a two-minute standing ovation at a Quebec gala. Comaneci settled deeper into Montreal life, becoming gym buddies with *vedette* Veronique Beliveau and committing to a book with author Georges-Hébert Germain. But romance swept Comaneci out of Montreal, as she fell for gymnast Bart Connor and followed him to the United States. Her friend Stefu, a rugby coach, drowned at the age of 47 while spearfishing alone in Lake St. Francis near Valleyfield on Labour Day 1991.

6

Odd moments

Spring in Montreal is like an autopsy, as a poet once remarked. Surprises abound under the frozen grounds we tread with frosty boot. Let us proceed to exhume Montreal's past for the unusual.

ANTONIO BARICHIEVICH

Pig parasite poisoning New Yorker Eric Kranz, 24, was studying Parasitology at McGill's Macdonald Campus when he feuded with his roommates over a $16 debt in 1970. Keith Fern,

Kranz

David Fisk, William Butler and Richard Davis then fell ill with a mystery ailment that an alert Dr. John Harrold diagnosed as a parasite never before found in humans. The roommates, all McGill post-grad students, had been infected with the *ascaris sum* porcine parasite, which grows into seven-inch worms that attack pig lungs and livers.

Davis and Butler came close to death but all recovered after ingesting around 400,000 larvae. Kranz's bedroom walls were adorned with slogans reading "Revolution Now" and one porcine reference: "The Police are Pigs." He was not charged with any crime. Macdonald College Dean Dr. George Dion said that "there is obviously a twisted mentality behind this thing."

Swinglers only Steamy encounters with sexy babes formed the unusual marketing strategy of a unique Montreal apartment complex in the free-love era, as The Royal Dixie

apartments sought to attract swingers and singles, or "swingles," as they called them in a 1970 ad. The building, near Trudeau Airport at 405 Bourque, became Crescent Street-west during the meet-market era, a time where bartenders would pair off any remaining singles and at 3 a.m. closing time.

Happy Hooker author Xaviera Hollander, the prima libertine of the era, attended parties at the complex, as did pro athletes and stewardesses. Management warned residents that they would be asked to leave if they made the mistake of settling down in committed couples and indeed attempted to follow through on the threats, although their legal right to evict tenants on the grounds of insufficient promiscuity might not have been solidly enshrined in law nor backed by legal precedent.

Cop launches religion Montreal cops come and go but only Eugène Richer Dit Laflèche started a religion that endures to this day. Richer Dit Laflèche was recruited to fight crime due to his tall, muscular physique but his law enforcing days ended when he was fired for operating a bordello. So he turned to religion, starting his *Mission de l'Esprit-Saint* in 1913 and hit the road to grow his flock, telling folks he was Jehova, Jesus Christ and the Holy Spirit. Richer had five concubines, gave sermons clad in translucent robes and asked followers to give him all their money. Authorities hounded him wherever he went, so he frequently switched towns and pseudonyms in the United States before dying in 1925. But his eugenics cult outlived him. Adherent Georges Haché took over and predicted that the world would end. It didn't and the group's 144,000 followers were a bit disappointed when the sun kept rising. Wilfrid Messier was jailed after defrauding 104 followers of their life savings by claiming to be Richer reincarnated. They sought a refund but Messier had already blown the cash on horse races. The Holy Spirit faithful then followed Eugene R. Robitaille, calling him "Prince Charming," even though he was rotund and bald. Robitaille was arrested in 1941 and charged with subversion after police seized literature and pornography from the temple at 6910 St. Hubert. Police accused the group of siding with the Nazis, who were also keen eugenicists. Leader Gustav Robitaille fathered at least 15 children before dying in 1965 and was replaced by a committee of 29 who concurred that the world would end in 1975. They all hunkered down at a special facility at Oka to greet the end but were once again disappointed. The group still maintains about 1,000 adherents near Joliette just outside of Montreal and a similar total divided between the Carolinas and Los Angeles. Kids are home-schooled, generally named after the founder and are usually not vaccinated.

Richer Dit Laflèche

Emergency clergy Priests were often first on the scene at Montreal accidents, as quick-moving holy men were known to speed to the aid of victims' souls. Those suffering grievous injury by speeding streetcar or flying quarry rock might be first assisted by priests more concerned with souls than gaping wounds. Such was the case when a woman was hit by a car while dashing for a trolley in 1929. The victim was rushed to a church where she was read her last rites before an ambulance finally came for her. Priests were Johnny-on-the-spot for an impressive number of such accidents, such as in 1932 when a 72-year-old woman was crushed by a streetcar on Maplewood and then again in 1947 when a construction worker fell 35 feet at Dorchester and Beaver Hall Hill. In later days priests mostly hung around hospitals to perform last rites.

St.   Urbain's   traumatized   men Mordecai
Richler was scandalized by his mother's brazen adulterous dalliances but it didn't prevent him from penning famous fiction.

Lily & Mordecai

Richler's mother Lily came from an esteemed family with a rabbi as patriarch but Mordecai's father Moses was of the vulgarian class, being the son of a junk dealer. Lily felt superior and consequently berated husband Moses endlessly until the winter of 1944 when she fell in love with a German Jew renting room at the back of their home at 5257 St. Urbain. That affair spelled the end for Lily and Moses. She turfed him out and coupled unashamedly with her new beau right in front of 12-year-old Mordecai, who later made mention of Lily and the man "humping together only 12 feet from a boy." Mordecai remained close with his mother for many years but fought—occasionally with fists—against his father. Mordecai forgave his mother for her sex stunts but could not pardon her unfriendliness towards his wife Florence. He wrote her a goodbye note in 1976 and never spoke to her again.

Actor collared American actor Thomas Placide and his troupe tread Montreal boards with great regularity from the 1830s, delighting countless crowds with dramatic flair during a period when plays were often performed by bored amateurs from the local military barracks. But Placide was not good with money and indeed he went so broke that he couldn't afford proper shirts. As one theatre observer from the 19th century noted: "He was the first man to wear paper collars in Montreal, not being in good credit standing with his laundry and set a fashion followed out some years later." Placide, who once had to convince his wife to put up with the sexually explicit paintings he purchased in Paris, contracted throat cancer and ended his own life in 1877.

Placide

Malcolm X of Montreal Black rights leader Malcolm X had roots in Montreal, thanks to mother Louise Norton, who came from Grenada during WWI to live with her nasty old uncle Edgerton Langdon at the now-demolished 150 St. Martin in St. Henri. Louise met her future husband Earl Little at a United Negro Improvement Association in 1918. The couple married in Montreal but moved to the United States, where they gave birth to seven children, including Malcolm. Earl went to court to defend the family's right to live in a white neighbourhood in Lansing, Michigan and their home was burnt down. He was later found run over by a streetcar. Louise was committed to a mental institution in 1939 and the children were sent to foster homes. Malcolm Little eventually became an academic and athletic star before running into troubles of his own, which he overcame to become the legendary civil rights leader Malcolm X. His cousin, the more conciliatory Henry Langdon (Edgerton's son) remained in Montreal where he also went on to become a prominent representative of the black population.

Norton & Little

Mini-royalty under microscope

Tourists were once invited into a home full of tiny appliances and furniture so they could stare at dwarfs like fish in an aquarium. The Midgets Palace was a heavily-publicized tourist attraction that began after miniature circus star Philippe Nicol Sr. met fellow small individual Rose Dufresne on the circus circuit in 1906. The

Rose & son

tiny couple moved to Montreal in 1913 and Nicol bargained with authorities to allow him to live in a specially-built home in Lafontaine Park. Instead they moved into 961 Rachel W. and opened their doors to all comers. The blinged-out Nicol was "the richest dwarf in the world," and was the seventh son of a seventh son, as the hype machine informed. The blissful duo gave birth to their miracle baby Phillipe Nicol on September 19, 1926 in a well-hyped media event. Great things were

expected of The Rare Baby and dad mused that he could one day become Prime Minister in spite of his tiny stature. "He will have a man's head and be charitable and courageous," said proud dad. The dwarf parents doted over their tiny child and even had a full-time nurse until mom fired her for getting along too well with her hubby. Philippe Sr. died in 1940 and instead of going on to greatness as planned, Junior became a thief. Philippe Nicol, 20, was caught breaking into a store across the street where he stole an electric drill and hunter's knife and five years later was nabbed for robbing a tobacco store and then a taxi driver with a nickel-plated toy gun. The easily-recognizable, tiny, drunk celebrity held a gun to the cabbie's head and took his cash and smokes. He later went on to do occasional pro wrestling gigs. The Midgets Palace continued until the early 1970s. A series of financial disputes preceded its eventual demise. The premises later became a gay bathhouse and then condos.

To hell with garbage Residents of about 30,000 Montreal apartment buildings could simply haul their garbage down the hallway, open a chute and watch it tumble into a fiery

incinerator below. No need to wait for garbage day, just feed the flames with your orange peels and old newspapers and watch plumes of smoke rise to the skies outside. A 100-unit apartment building could generate 800 pounds of garbage per day, as tenants dropped refuse that became air pollution. The not-so-environmentally-friendly

blazes plagued city air and the fiery fun ended when Montreal city council passed a ban in 1970. All that garbage then had to be picked up in trucks, leading to an often-frustrating new era of garbage collection. The fires led to occasional tragedy: in 1948 a dead newborn was found in an incinerator at 1248 Wolfe and in 1970 a janitor rescued a badly-burnt child from an incinerator.

Skeleton in the closet Someone opened a shed door at the Jacques Cartier Normal School near Lafontaine Park on Sherbrooke East in 1947 only to stumble on the gruesome

Victor Lord

discovery of a gnarly skeleton hanging from a rope. A suicide note welcomed the finder to use the corpse for scientific research. Montreal police sleuths couldn't identify the body, so they concluded that it must be that of the missing Victor Lord, a widowed veteran of both World Wars and a blacksmith by trade, who had

disappeared after living at Mrs. D'Aoust's rooming house. Before hitting the dusty trail, Lord handed his insurance papers to his landlady, presumably so she could pay for his funeral. Three years after being declared dead, Lord showed up at a government office to apply for his military pension. He was alive and well and and living in Pembroke, Ontario. He was confirmed undead and received his pension in 1950.

No vaccine for stupidity Smallpox was a nasty bit of pus-filled business that would blind, scar and kill one-in-three victims before it was finally eradicated. Luckily there was a

Smallpox riot

vaccine to combat it, so there was no need to worry when the variola virus returned to Montreal in 1885 after a four year absence. But misguided demagogues like Dr. A.M. Ross persuaded great swathes of Montrealers that hygiene issues were at the root of the condition and that the vaccine actually caused the disease. So when a pair of porters from Chicago brought smallpox back to town, many gullible souls—mostly francophones—refused inoculation. An epidemic ensued, as did pitched street battles, as authorities dragged the afflicted out of their homes into quarantine, from which roving thugs would frequently break them out. The Catholic clergy and Mayor Honoré Beaugrand pleaded with their French-speaking brethren to get vaccinated but others subverted their efforts by dispensing harmful medical advice, leading some parents to send their infected children to play with other kids. One afflicted woman responded to a side-eye glance by crossing the street at Notre Dame and Champlain and rubbing her blisters over another woman. Smallpox killed about 500 Montrealers annually before 1880 but earlier attempts to make vaccination mandatory proved a failure. Authorities tried again

Ross

in 1885, leading 2,000 anti-vaxxers to toss rocks and fire bullets at city hall. The vaccinations prevailed and the 1885 epidemic petered out after claiming 3,000 Montrealers. "From morning to night could be seen the burial-carts of the city standing in front of the door, as if waiting until the pestilence should claim another victim. They seldom waited in vain," as a home on McGill Street was described in *Montreal by Gas Light*.

Bros in trouble Nicholas Rossi was a university graduate who boxed and penned murder mysteries. His brother Robert  was a snappy-dressing transvestite who called herself Lana. The two were close companions and shared an Italian mother but had different African-American fathers. They left Montreal on a road trip and stayed at the home of Hedwig Wegner, 60, in Plainfield, Connecticut where Robert toiled as maid and half-brother Nicholas posed as her husband. All was fine until Wegner was found bludgeoned to death behind her home on September 22, 1943. The brothers were later found motoring around Missouri in her car. An officer pulled them over and yanked off Robert's wig. Nicholas was executed by electric chair in a state prison in Connecticut on July 17, 1945. Robert was sentenced to life in prison.

Nick & Robert

Beauty riot The Point St. Charles Beauty Pageant of May 10, 1958 was particularly violent, even by local standards. The mayhem began when Betty Simpkins edged out Joan Dwyer,  whose brother sparked the hostilities at the Polish Hall by screaming, "It's a set up man!" Usually-outgoing city councillor Frank Hanley refused to take the stage for the winning ceremony and a recount was made impossible, as 100 ballots had been stolen. Thirty thugs beat on a police officer, a publisher and a city councillor, who also had his glasses smashed as thieves stole his wife's fur coat. MP/Councillor Gerard Loiselle, who had previously had his car and home windows smashed, simply wept during the violence. Other dignitaries wisely skipped the event, after being threatened at home. "For 15 days my family and me have been living under threats. We have been getting phone calls night and day and it's almost impossible for me to go out unaccompanied," said Councillor André Lecourt. Hanley declined to comment.

Dwyer

Them's fightin' threads! Zoot Suits with high-waisted pleated trousers and knee-length jackets were like red rags to bulls when spotted by servicemen during World War II. The soldiers routinely attacked anybody seen sporting the flamboyant outfit, probably because they imagined Zoot Suiters partying with pretty girls while they were busy dodging German bullets.

Fights were usually sparked when a rumour spread that one of their own had been attacked by a Zoot Suiter. Staredowns and insults were mandatory when the two crossed paths and one major battle took place at the train station on Park in 1943. But it was just a precursor to the city-wide battle on June 1944, where 400 sailors scoured downtown just east of St. Denis for Zoot Suiters to beat on. Some attempted to ditch their fancy threads but sailors recognized them from their hairstyles. A young Jean Drapeau, then a little-known lawyer, argued that the attacks were inspired by French-English conflicts rather than sartorial differences.

Nice boys get rough Montreal's Jewish Defence League sprouted up in the early 1970s to patrol supposed hotbeds of antisemitism, such as the area around Jeanne Mance St. and Fairmount. The 300-member vigilante squad met regularly in an office above a Decarie Blvd. butcher shop and tried to organize protection for their co-religionists, even though chief Arnold Mintzberg confessed that there weren't a whole lot of attacks happening. Irv Rubin, who grew up in a Montreal that he claimed contained signs reading "No Dogs or Jews Allowed" and where epithets as "dirty Jew" were common, took over the JDL after moving to Los Angeles at age 15. Rubin sought to reopen a JDL chapter in Montreal in 1994 as an "insurance program" to protect the Jewish population. The effort quickly fizzled out and Rubin died eight years later in a Los Angeles prison, falling off a 20 foot balcony.

Ready, aim, fiasco! Sir John A. Macdonald would not have his curly mop and cardboard collar emblazoned on Canada's 10 dollar bill had his duel challenge ended differently.

Macdonald objected to fellow MP William Hume Blake's comments in 1849 at Parliament near McGill Street. He sent Blake a written invitation challenging him to a gunfight and the two slipped out to settle their differences with loaded pistols. Guards were dispatched. The battle fizzled out and neither was harmed. Sir Georges-Étienne Cartier challenged journalist Joseph Doutre after Doutre accused him of cowardice during the 1837 revolt. Police stopped it. But Doutre persisted with his insults, so both met at Chambly and fired and missed. Rodolphe Des

Macdonald and Blake

Rivières and Dr. Jones partook in another bloodless duel in 1836 after the much-larger physician sucker-punched the nationalist for refusing to stand during God Save the Queen before a play. Hotheaded Major John Richardson challenged a man to a duel following an argument on St. Lawrence Street in 1839. Richardson failed to organize a second, so his rival postered the city with insulting images of Richardson. Tragedy occurred in 1838 near what's now De l'Eglise and LaSalle when Robert Sweeny shot friend Major Henry John Warde dead in a duel after Sweeny wrongly accused Warde of sending flowers to his wife. Sweeny was inconsolable after learning of his error and died two years later. Captain Kirwan, irritated that he was refused entry to a dance, invited a party organizer to a gunfight in 1879 in what might be Montreal's final duel challenge. The two talked it out at Professor Richardson's gym on St. James, as police were secretly on hand to stop the gun battle.

Priests versus libraries

Libraries were "100,000 times more infinitely dangerous than the most malevolent smallpox virus," said Archbishop Paul Bruchési. Such Quebec clerical disapproval doomed a 1901 offer from American philanthropist Andrew Carnegie to build a $150,000 library in Montreal offered on condition authorities spend $15,000 a year to maintain it. Mayor Raymond

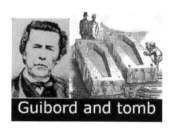

Guibord and tomb

Préfontaine was keen to accept the gift but the church nixed the initiative. Carnegie funded 100 libraries in Ontario, 1,600 in the United States and none in Quebec. The *Institut Canadien* opened Montreal's first French public library in December 1844 to promote patriotism and learning. But clergy objected to critical thinking and attacked the group. Nonetheless the *Institut Canadien* grew to 100 branches in Quebec within a decade, in spite of church refusing members Catholic burials. The widow of *Institut Canadien* member Joseph Guibord won a five-year court battle against the ban, forcing the Côte des Neiges cemetery to bury Guibord's tomb. His coffin was carried in a military convoy and encased it in cement to prevent vandalism in 1875. Tiny lending libraries later became common. They included The Mary Arden Lending Library on Park, The Patricia Circulating Library on Christophe Columb and The Golden Dog Lending Library on Sherbrooke. One major Montreal library collection was doomed, however,

Bruchesi

as New Yorker Guion Gest handed McGill University 100,000 Chinese books in 1926, instantly turning McGill into a leader for Chinese studies. But Gest later demanded compensation. When his ally McGill Principal Arthur Currie died suddenly in 1933, McGill closed its nascent Chinese Studies program and sold the books to Princeton. McGill relaunched a Chinese Studies program in 1968, with a much more modest collection.

Gadfly in white gets swatted Gilbert Croteau stood out in a crowd wherever he went when he campaigned for mayor in the 1960s, as the chiropractor's signature snowy apparel  attracted attention during his efforts to replace incumbent Jean Drapeau. Croteau wore white in tribute to Pope John XXIII, who died in 1963 and vowed to only to dress more conventionally after Montreal voters elected him mayor. Croteau had drawn Drapeau's ire in the late 1950s by organizing the Jeanne Mance subsidized housing slum clearance scheme that Drapeau so intensely reviled. So when Croteau later attacked such Drapeau projects as Place des Arts, the metro and Expo 67, Drapeau was entirely unamused. Drapeau trounced Croteau in 1962 and then crushed him with 117,000 votes to just 5,000 in 1966. Croteau was, nonetheless, resolved to challenge Drapeau again in 1970 but that dream died when Montreal police raided Croteau's chiropractor office and charged him with quackery. Croteau opted to dress in black during his court appearances. He was sentenced to 30 months.

The count who misbehaved Count Georges de Beaujeu was a legitimate nobleman from one of the most honoured Quebec families but he proved less gentlemanly than his title suggests. Beaujeu was arrested for drunk driving in Outremont after he killed Berthe Gisasson, 22, in 1929. Police arrested him in a downtown nightclub later. His ex-girlfriend Mrs. Herbert Feehan sued him the next year for gossiping about her, as Beaujeu had met up with her new beau and told him all of the unflattering stories. Beaujeu managed to scuttle his ex's new relationship and she was given $1,450 in an out-of-court settlement. Beaujeu was living in a hotel on Sherbrooke Street a decade later when he dressed up in riding clothes and started hitting restaurant diners with a blackjack, as if it were a riding crop. He was arrested and charged with disturbing the peace and assaulting an officer. Beaujeu was taken in for mental evaluation.

Candy for everybody! Fred Meilleur's grandchildren cost their poor old grandpa a large cash fortune in June, 1980, simply because they liked candy. The octogenarian lifelong welfare recipient had rented the ground floor apartment at 786 Greene Ave. for 40 years when his grandchildren stumbled onto something unusual in the crawl space. The kids found cash money and lots of it: $290,000, mostly in plastic-wrapped $100 bills. Police caught wind of the stash after the kids took to indiscreetly purchasing penny candy with the big bills at the corner store. Police dropped into Meilleur's apartment and seized the loot, which had been stolen from banks. Meilleur said that had no knowledge of the hidden treasure but noted that he sometimes allowed bank robber and suspected cop-killer John Slawvey to stay at his home.

Controlling brains through silence Leonard Cohen was 17 when he agreed to take part in psychological experiments at McGill University in 1951, as conducted under the infamous CIA-financed MK-ULTRA mind control program. Program leader Donald Hebb was given $10,000 to study sensory deprivation for the purposes of improving confession-extraction

techniques and possibly transforming subjects into assassin robots for the American military. Hundreds signed on to the sensory deprivation experiment, which paid an impressive $20 a day. But only 72 remained long enough to provide useful information and only a half dozen made it through the full six days. Cohen, unlike others, enjoyed the sensory deprivation experiments and participated on several occasions. Dr. Ewan Cameron would also aim to achieve the same results with his disastrous LSD experiments at the Allen Memorial Hospital. Cameron left Montreal in 1964 and died in the United States three years later. Cohen went on to become a famous musician and poet but also suffered from severe lifelong depression.

Muti-task snoozes Spooky footsteps have fallen nightly in Montreal since the dawn of human settlement and today about 150,000 sleepwalkers stroll unconsciously at night. No somnambulist went as far as Jean Rivard in 1939, as the 18-year-old sleepwalked for 17 hours, strolling 55 kilometres from Côte St. Paul to his old home on the South Shore. Rivard regained consciousness and walked right back home.

Rivard

Sixteen years later René Lessard, 26, sleepwalked 90 metres up to top of the Jacques Cartier Bridge and leaped from girder to girder before being woken and rescued. Lessard, who was afraid of heights, said that he never would have considered such a stunt. Not all sleepwalks had happy endings, as Bernard Panet Raymond, the brilliant assistant to developer Sir Rodolphe Forget, walked out to his death from a third floor window while on vacation in St. Irénée in 1913. Montreal researchers have been world leaders in sleepwalk research and believe the cause to be largely genetic. That information might have helped police drug squad chief Henri Marchessault, who blamed his drug thefts on sleepwalking caused by chronic overwork in 1983. He was still convicted.

Peg leg dancing The hottest Montreal dance of 1953 required imitating an amputee, as dance teachers and performers Rosita and Deno unveiled the peg leg dance at the Ritz Carlton Hotel.

The new dance had able-bodied participants strapping on a wooden leg and moving crazily around a dance floor, which led to mirth and merriment, except perhaps to amputee war veterans. While not employing prosthetic limbs to create new dance moves, the couple ran a dance school and did performances, teaching audience members how to samba without getting out of their seats. Deno was Bernie Dezwirek, who quit to sell insurance in 1952. Diane Auclair was one of the Rositas.

Self-flagellation

Jeanne Le Ber had wealth, youth and beauty when she turned 18 in 1690. But she shot down all suitors in favour of a cloistered life of prayer, self-flagellation and of sporting painful corn-husk shoes and hair-shirts. Le Ber was born at the top, her godparents being city founder Paul

Le Ber

Chomedey de Maisonneuve and religious leader Jeanne Mance, who urged Jeanne to work hard and pray less. Other girls derided Le Ber for vowing at a young age to remain a lifelong pious virgin but she stayed secluded in her parents' home before funding a three-room apartment inside the Congrégation de Notre-Dame in the middle of St. Lawrence Street, south of Notre Dame. Le Ber prayed six hours a day but cheated on the solitude, as she often had her chubby, industrious cousin Anna Barroy at her side. Le Ber refused to come out for her dying mother and skipped her father's funeral, possibly on the advice of Dollier de Casson, a soldier-turned-priest who planned Montreal's first roads. Le Ber donated her property to the church.

The human soundtrack

Early films came with silence, so theatre owners hired live pianists to bang out melodies, a process that made Billy Eckstein a star, as he improvised and composed countless tunes during his 20 years tickling ivories the Strand Theatre at Mansfield and St. Catherine. Eckstein's tunes included *Beautiful Thoughts*, which

Billy Eckstein

Montreal movie star Norma Shearer loved after hearing it at the theatre. Eckstein's drinking sometimes prevented him from performing, so back-up Harry Thomas was ready to grab his stool, the problem being that Thomas was his drinking partner. Eckstein owned five parrots that spoke different languages and a spoiled dog named Casey. He was feted at the closing of His Majesty's Theatre in 1963 and died soon after, his ashes spread over his beloved Mount Royal Park.

Accountant flees with fortune For five years Claude Phaneuf would rise every morning at his home in Repentigny and then motor to his office at Mount Royal Paving at the corner of Jarry and 17th, where he tended to the books. Company owner Leonard Franceschini, along with his brother James, had been interned in a war camp as Italians suspected of

disloyalty to Canada during World War II but they bounced back to create a lucrative paving company that snagged many municipal contracts. All things changed on April 15, 1965, however, when Phaneuf failed to show up to work. He did not return the next day either, for he had absconded with between $1 million and $6 million, up to $45 million in modern terms. Phaneuf stood 5'2" and weighed 146 lbs as noted on RCMP Most Wanted alert. That information and a $15,000 advertised reward did little to help track him down and he remains undetected to this day.

They loved him until the party ended Jack Ross was such a big-spending party animal that he burned through the equivalent of $250 million over 17 years with parties considered

the highlight of the Montreal social calendar. Yet all that celebration failed to buy him happiness. Ross inherited $10 million in 1910 and shared his bounty through grandiose blowouts at the Edwardian Baroque mansion that his railway baron father James built for him at Peel and Penfield. J.K.L., as he was called, also gave big donations to the Royal Victoria Hospital and various Canadian military causes. Ross owned race horses, which also helped the inheritance cash trot from his pocket. Ross depleted his fortune by 1927 and ruefully noted that many party pals who enjoyed his generosity would now cross the street to avoid him. Ross retired to Jamaica where he died in 1951.

Miracle statues

One day in October 1994 a family of West Island Catholics noticed a mysterious oily liquid emanating from a porcelain religious statue in their modest ground-floor apartment. Pakistan-born Maureen and Clayton Marolly eventually needed to rig a drain to catch the steady flow. Then they learned that their daughter, born with Down's Syndrome, cured illness when seen in visions. The Marollys welcomed busloads of miracle-seeking visitors and distributed religious loot bags with vials of oil, while refusing donations. Other local miracle statues included a Rosa Mystica Virgin Mary on 35th Ave. in Ste. Marthe that wept human blood and tears. Huge throngs came to witness it in 1986 until a judge ordered Maurice and Claudette Girouard to move it beyond city limits. Joseph Bergeron claimed that his Virgin Mary statue wept nightly at 10173 15th in Rivière des Prairies in the 1950s.

Maureen Marolly

Goodbye marriage, Hello Montreal!

Billy Rose had fame, fortune and money but he lacked peace of mind. Rose, a 4'11" songwriter, TV host, newspaper columnist and wealthy investor, decided to pop into Montreal for a discreet weekend in a hotel with someone other than his wife in 1951. Rose knew Montreal well, having celebrated the city in his Prohibition-era drinking anthem *Hello Montreal*. Montreal knew Rose too. Somebody recognized him and soon his dirty weekend became public knowledge. His mistress Joyce Mathews returned to New York and slashed her wrists but survived. Rose's wife Eleanor Holm (already in a bad mood after being booted from the Olympic swimming team for drinking) launched what media called the War of the Roses. Holm won a whopping $100-a-day divorce settlement for enduring the two-timing Rose for 13 years. Rose often wrote fondly about Montreal in his newspaper columns but likely banged out fewer words of praise thereafter.

Rose & Mathews

When doves cry Youth Day at Expo 67 aimed to be a big deal so organizers went to great lengths to get 100 endangered North American doves to fly out from pens in a spectacular  salute to peace and freedom on August 6, 1967. The doves were special creatures, as only an estimated 150 remained in the wild at the time. The crowd went crazy. The stands of Place des Nations shook with excitement. The birds flew triumphantly upwards. Except once free, the critters had no idea where to wing to, so they landed on makeshift perches all around the stadium. Days later, the birds were still haunting the stadium, swooping down on people in hopes of obtaining birdy num-nums. An SPCA director ordered the Youth Day organizers to round the birds up but the young folks proved uninclined to do so, as they now dismissed the rare birds as mere "light coloured pigeons."

Gay orgy shocker Five Dionne sisters became instant celebrities at birth by virtue of being born all in one shot and surviving. After a childhood in the media eye (and being sexually abused by their father, as some sisters later claimed), the  quintuplets mostly settled in Montreal. Cécile Dionne wed Radio Canada technician Philippe Langlois in Nov. 1957 in a big deal, splashy affair. Cécile sported a $10,000 white wedding gown that glittered in the flashbulbs of the many cameras recording the magic

Langlois & Dionne

moment. The couple settled in Dorval and Cécile swiftly learned that Philippe was a not only an alcoholic but he was also gay. Cécile caught Phil smooching with another man on the couch so the couple consulted their priest who urged them to get over the hurdle. It worked until she came downstairs again and saw him with having a full-blown orgy with nine other men in their kitchen. She shooed them out, moved her four kids to St. Bruno and became a cosmetician.

Father of God "Clapton is God," read a famous 1970s London graffiti honouring guitarist Eric Clapton. Yet Clapton's life had a major void, as he never knew who his father was and

Edward Fryer

even mused publicly about his sad quest for dad in the song *In My Father's Eyes*. His search was solved when an industrious genealogist determined that Clapton's father was a married Montreal pianist named Edward Walter Fryer, who fathered Ol' Slowhand with 16-year-old Patricia Molly Clapton while stationed in Britain during in World War II. Fryer returned home to the NDG district after the war and continued womanizing and drifting through piano lounges across the continent before dying of leukemia in Toronto in 1985. Clapton only learned of his Montreal ancestry in 2004.

Sex workers knit socks Friendless women was the oxymoronic description employed to describe the prostitutes that social workers aimed to rescue from the sex trade back in

Pinzer

1876. Officials at Montreal's Protestant Home for Friendless Women referred to their clientele as "disappointed in their endeavours" and women who are now "earning an honest livelihood" thanks to their "reformation under God." The rehabbing escorts lived in a facility on Upper St. Urbain (east side just south of Bagg) from 1876 to 1898, moving over to Vinet in 1887. Two dozen took in laundry and knitted socks at the donor-supported home, while resisting the temptation to perform erotic acts for cash compensation. One-eyed former Philadelphia hooker Maime Pinzer later came to Montreal to set up a similar establishment at Bleury and President Kennedy (near the future Bellevue Casino) during WWI and declined to employ the old-fashioned "friendless women" terminology, as it needlessly increased their shame. Pinzer disappeared into obscurity in 1922. The sex workers' lobby group Stella was named after a prostitute Pinzer admired.

That intimate mass wedding German jackboots echoed on a faraway European horizon on the sweltering summer afternoon of July 21, 1939, as 100 couples arrived at the Delorimier baseball stadium stadium to tie the knot in front of 20,000 onlookers. The ambitious mass wedding was the culmination of years of planning by Reverend Henri Roy who headed the JOC (*Jeunesse Ouvrières Catholiques* Young Catholic Workers) group. Roy considered the modern workplace to be vulgar and soul-crushing and his organization aimed to counter the growing godlessness it promoted. He selected the lucky 100 couples from among thousands of applicants who attended his mandatory marriage-preparation courses on morals, economics and medicine. The couples were aged between 17 and 25 and most were gainfully employed. Each bride and groom had a dedicated priest conducting their ceremony, while model couple Henri Seguin and Thérèse Seguin (presumably unrelated) were featured in front. Most of the sizable crowd was clad

Henri Roy

in the JOCist blue-and-white uniform and about 300 of those spectators fainted in the intense heat during the lengthy ceremony, which finished in darkness with the stadium

lights dimmed and each couple holding a lit torch, as they marched towards a cross at centre stage, as a young girl sang *Salve Regina*. One year later, 77 of the 105 couples were either parents or expecting a child, while one unlucky groom had died by then. The massive rush to the altar might have been partially inspired by the looming clouds of war, as married men were expected to be less likely to be conscripted than their bachelor brethren.

Lesbian outlaws Although legal today, same sex marriage was once a fast way to the slammer as Marie-Antoinette Arsenault, 34, learned when she dressed up as a man to marry Eugenie Ouellet, 25. The manly-looking Arsenault played the male role in a marriage "solemnized" by Rev. Paul Chodat of the Oratoire French Baptist Church on Jeanne Mance on Feb. 14, 1942. The two lived together as a couple in Ste. Thérèse for a month before the law got involved and a judge declared the marriage a "ridiculous conjugal farce." Arsenault was slapped with a 23-month jail sentence to be served at the Fullum Street jail for participating in the lesbian marriage. She did not serve her full sentence, however, as just 18 months later she was arrested for shoplifting. Officers were convinced that Arsenault was a man when they took her into custody.

Missionary in a tricky position Drunks, gamblers and other lowlifes did their best to make St. Dominique south of St. Catherine a godless place during the last century. So where

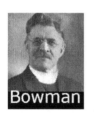
Bowman

better for a unconventional street preacher to win souls? Aging Englishman W. Tucker Bowman opened his Montreal City Mission at 287 Cadieux (De Bullion near Charlotte) in 1910 where he aimed to rehabilitate the wicked and convert Jewish kids with ice cream, candy and movies.

Tucker was arrested for handing out Romanian-language pamphlets designed to convert Jews but charges were dropped, as religious material was exempt from the pamphlet ban. Jews sought revenge by disrupting Tucker's sermons for years after, while Rabbi Glazer threatened to fine anybody in his flock seen in Tucker's church. Tucker was frequently assaulted and harassed by fake inspectors, while noisy gamblers on the street outside kept the girls upstairs and boys downstairs awake at night. Tucker suffered an accident that "lamed him" in 1933 and he died the next year while visiting England. His All People's Mission continued until a July 1965 demolition silenced the bell that tolled for five decades.

Toothless en vogue Almost half of all Montrealers had no teeth problems for much of the last century, mostly because they had no teeth. Forty percent of Quebecers popped fake chompers into bedside glasses at night in the 1970s, as the province long topped all provinces for the rate of edentulous people, as the dentally-extracted are called. It was once common for Quebecers to get all of their teeth pulled out in full mouth extractions on their 16th birthday but as Quebecers started living longer, the dentures became problematic. Those surviving into middle age found their jaw bones reduced to almost nothing by years of denture wearing, which made chewing difficult, leading to severe malnutrition among the elderly. The rate of toothlessness has since been whittled down to about 15 percent, partly because full-body anesthetic for such extractions became less common after three patients died in gas-related dental mishaps in 1973.

Monopedal monument A generation of Montrealers knew the waterfront statue of Neptune as a monopedal sea god after its left leg mysteriously disappeared in 1940. Some claimed that a drunken brawler tore the leg off the 1908 statue to use as a weapon, while others claimed that the leg was knocked off by a  truck swerving to avoid bales of clothing. British sailors were overheard at nearby Joe Beef tavern confessing to removing the leg as a prank, according to another explanation. But the real culprit was young Griffintown resident Denis Delaney, who was playing with his friends near the statue. One of the boys tripped over Neptune's ill-fated limb, causing it to snap off, as Delaney confessed six decades later. The terrified youngster disposed of the incriminating evidence by selling it to a scrap metal dealer for a pittance. The city placed a wooden replacement leg on the statue in 1942 but it broke off six years later. Cash was finally earmarked to fix the statue in 1957 but the repair was only completed five years later.

Smoking saved his life
Réal Gilbert, 37, hallucinated that intruders were invading his spaceship one Sunday morning in 1978. So he went to the window of his apartment at 336

Delvecchio

Ontario E. and shot at a police officer parked beneath his window. The bullet smashed through a window and hit patrolman Mario Delvecchio in the chest. The officer was not wearing a bulletproof vest he but was protected by another item. The projectile was deflected away by a metal lighter nestled in the officer's shirt pocket. Delvecchio's smoking habit allowed him live to see another day. Sadly, Gilbert's shot his 27-year-old landlord Pierre Thibodeau dead in the hallway.

Drama sparks dynasty
Reine Johnson became the wife of a Quebec premier and the mother of two other premiers but only after narrowly surviving a murder-suicide attempt.

Reine Johnson

Johnson left her home on Oxford Ave. in NDG on January 10, 1953 to visit her secret lover Bertrand Dussault, a 28-year-old CBC employee, at his rooming house at 4041 Dorchester. (Later removed as part of the Westmount Square demolitions, even though it was blocks away). Dussault asked Johnson to leave her husband but she refused. The distraught Dussault aimed five shots at his clandestine lover, blasting her twice. He then turned the pistol on himself and ended his days. Johnson managed to flee to nearby Tupper Street where she hopped a cab to the hospital. Reine's cuckolded husband Daniel, then a 37-year-old Union National backbencher, offered his resignation following the distressing event but Premier Maurice Duplessis, who had endured his own share of lady troubles, instead had newspapers hush the story up. Johnson was promoted and succeeded Duplessis after his death. His son Daniel Johnson Jr. later served as premier for the Liberal Party and his other son Pierre-Marc also served as Quebec premier for the Parti Québécois.

A headless historian Gustave Lanctôt was a soldier, Rhodes scholar, lawyer, historian, journalist, federal minister and chief archivist of Canada as well as an accomplished hockey player. His history texts were revered and his influence put an end to an initiative to remove Amherst Street from Montreal map in 1964, as nationalists sought to rename it Christophe Colomb. After a full life of impressive accomplishments, Lanctôt was awarded the Order of Canada before dying in 1975. For reasons unknown, vandals dug up his grave and mutilated his body a dozen years after he was buried. One of the young vandals removed Lanctôt's head and stored it in a shed next to his home in Dolbeau, Lac St. Jean. It was not to be Lanctôt's only postmortem indignity, as in 2006 a vendor put Lanctôt's Order of Canada medal on sale on eBay.

Gustave Lanctôt

Lunatics streetfight Veteran hippie rocker Serge Fiori racked up the 1970s soft-rock hits as head of Harmonium and was living a low-key existence in August 1997 when he had a fateful sidewalk encounter with four strangers. Fiori was leaving a bistro near Rachel and St. Denis when he encountered Haddi Doyle, Suelynn Taylor, Jennifer Holmes and Joanne Zergiotis, friends from Park Extension aged 18-21, who had just left the Jungle nightclub. A diminished willingness to share the sidewalk in the late summer 3:30 a.m. glow caused a shouting match, then a streetfight that left Fiori, 44, and his girlfriend Marie-Jocelyne Dion with minor scrapes. Police arrested the girls and a government fund handed Fiori and Dion $27,000 annually in victim-of-crime compensation. Fiori and Dion were astonished when their psychologist slammed them in court as "narcissist, hysterical, lunatics" before a jury acquitted the young women of assault two years later.

Who needs kitchens? Roswell Fisher felt that slicing carrots and frying steaks was too lowly for chic dwellers of Montreal's first apartments, so he included no kitchens in his

pioneering structure and instead equipped each apartment with a dumb waiter to transport cooked meals up from a downstairs kitchen. Downtown bachelors and fashionable female tenants, he figured, should shun the drudgery of kitchen duties. The

First apartments

Sherbrooke Apartments opened in 1891 at the SW corner of Crescent and Sherbrooke but Fisher failed to get a restaurant organized downstairs, so he improvised and hired an Englishwoman to send cooked meals up the shaft. Instead all 16 tenants—mostly Roswell's friends and relatives—installed kitchens in their apartments. Roswell, undaunted, built another kitchenless apartment building a few doors down. Fisher's first building was demolished after a 1978 conflagration.

Weeping policemen Families were routinely shattered when a husband walked out, lost his job or hit the bottle, as the chief of a dedicated family tragedy police unit often noted. Montreal's Squad of Tears tackled everything from suicide to drunken disasters and its boss Det. Onésime Lemieux urged lawmakers to make home-wrecking a criminal offence, as he argued that anybody who lured a someone away from their spouse deserved to be jailed. Suicide, Lemieux noted in 1948, was often prompted by alcoholism, as drunks and insurance salesmen frequently took their own lives. Lemieux described a woman who relentlessly encouraged her son-in-law to go drown himself. The man eventually complied. "There is no state of mental depression, degeneracy or wickedness of which human beings are capable that I have not come across," said Lemieux. He believed that many problems sprouted from girls marrying young. "They quickly become discontented and when temptation comes along they grab at it. After all, a girl of 23 is still a child, although there seems to be no age limit to childishness."

Unwilling model A teenager perched on stairs on downtown St. Catherine Street in 1988 became the fulcrum of a legal battle that ended up making street photography uniquely contentious in Quebec. Photographer Gilbert Duclos snapped a picture of Pascale-Claude Aubry, 17, sitting on the steps of a

Scotiabank, and the portrait went on the cover of tiny *Vice-Versa* magazine, which sold 700 copies that month. But Aubry pointed out that she was not a model and never okayed the shot. She sued for $10,000, telling a court the photo caused schoolmates to mock her. Top Supreme Court Justice Antonio Lamer rejected her claim but the majority sided with Aubry, who was awarded $2,000. As a result, Quebecers can sue for appearing in non-newsworthy photos taken without their permission. Duclos led a public campaign against the ruling.

Aggressive campaigning Federal Progressive Conservative candidate Paschal Hayes was glad-handing on a vote blitz in Lower NDG when he popped into the Edward

Restaurant at 1089 Girouard (now a corner store) to buy some smokes in March 1963. The ill-fated quest would become Canada's most epic episode of bad campaign etiquette, as Hayes, a fiery-tempered Irishman, asked restaurateur Gilda Nittolo why she had a rival Liberal Party poster in her window. The question exposed a difference of philosophies that led Hayes to slug the woman in the face, costing her two teeth. Subsequent headlines referred to the Tory hopeful as "The Fat Guy Who Hit Me." The Progressive Conservatives, who won the seat with a comfortable majority just five years earlier, lost the seat by 22,000 votes and have never won it back. Hayes vigorously protested his innocence but was fined $25. Prime Minister Brian Mulroney mirthfully referenced the incident in a memoir, speculating that gin was to blame. Hayes later moved back to Ireland.

Pill pusher in pith helmet

Herb doctor Francis Tumblety, 24, arrived in Montreal in 1857 clad in war medals, a pith helmet and an outlandish handlebar mustache, accompanied by a valet and two greyhounds. He booked into a posh hotel and announced that he would not be running for public office, in case anybody had their hopes up. Tumblety advertised his medical services on the front page of the *Montreal Pilot* newspaper, attracting the attention of authorities who arrested him after he sold a $20 abortion pill to police informant Philomène Dumas. Tumblety's high-powered team of Irish-Catholic lawyers eventually got him cleared of charges and Tumblety called the failed prosecution a "foul and criminal conspiracy by which it was sought to ruin my character and degrade me in your esteem." Chemist John Birks sniffed Tumblety's potion and declared it to be "black hellebore." His abortion pill included "cayenne peppers, aloes, oil of savine and cantharides." Tumblety left town soon after and later became a suspect in the Jack the Ripper investigation (as did McGill grad Dr. Neill Cream). Tumblety despised women and often showed off his collection of female reproductive organs, which he boasted came from women all social classes.

Tumblety

Poisoned appetites

Accidental poisoning claimed more Montreal lives than one might care to remember. Michael Flaherty and Edward Hawkey stole a bottle of wine from a pharmacists' cart in the ramshackle area known as Tabb's Yard near St. Patrick's Church in 1873 and then rushed home to share it with family, never suspecting that the wine contained extracts of the colchicum root, employed in small doses to treat gout. Flaherty's wife Jane and 13-year-old Benjamin Thayer were among seven who died after drinking the medicinal beverage. Alexandre Godin, 16, came out to Montreal West to shoot birds with friends in April, 1908. Godin neglected to bring lunch, so he pulled some parsnips out of the soil and gobbled them down.

His friends sampled as well but spat it out due to the bitter taste. Godin soon learned that he had eaten *conium maculatum*, a poisonous plant in the carrot family otherwise known as hemlock. He was transported downtown by train for emergency medical assistance. But like Plato, young Godin died of hemlock poisoning. In May 1932, a pair of Russian immigrants in their mid-forties ambled to the dump at the foot of Charron Street in Point St. Charles where they and about 100 other men salvaged old rags. Times were tough during The Great Depression and Fred Filipov and his friend Frank Yoka survived on the 30 cents a day they earned reselling scavenged items. Filipov found a fresh box of oatmeal and prepared and ate it without realizing that someone had placed rat poison in the oats to slay vermin. Filipov died a rapid and painful death.

A giant display Montrealers loved giant Édouard Beaupré so much that his embalmed corpse was put on display for all to admire at a university for decades after his death. A 20-year-old Édouard Beaupré came to Montreal in 1901, his 8'2" frame turning heads by towering 32 inches over the then-average 5'6" adult male. The 360-lb Beaupré took part  in a staged battle with celebrity strongman Louis Cyr. He lost. Beaupré—one of 20 kids from a family in Willow Bunch, Saskwatchewan—was known to visit Sohmer Park, where he enjoyed the thrills and cold beer. Sadly, the Ringling Bros Circus star died in 1904, aged 23. Nobody would pay for his funeral, so promoters embalmed his corpse and placed it on display at the Eden Wax Museum on the Main for six months in 1907. Promoters then misplaced his body in a box on the waterfront, where children discovered it. The *Université de Montréal* anatomy department purchased it for $25 and displayed it on campus for eight decades until it was returned to his relatives in Saskatchewan in 1990. His ashes were spread around his hometown.

Buddhist booty Sex cult leader who fathered 20 kids with his female followers: so must read the CV of Tyndale Martin, who scored funding from the Catholic Church to open The Greatheart Monastery in 1969. Martin promised to get young people interested in Christianity but no Bibles were cracked open at 3664 Mountain. Serious-looking newspaper ads attracted spiritual searchers and soon an emboldened Martin declared himself the Panchem Lama, one of the chosen people of Buddhism. "I don't enjoy seeing myself as the Panchem Lama. For me it's a very serious responsibility," he told a reporter. His practices included coupling with female devotees and urging them to perform lesbian acts. A TV news ambush saw Martin implausibly deny his sexual activities. The damage was done, alas. Funding dried up and most male followers left the group. The cult moved to 3474 Mountain and then to the town of Dorion, where Martin retained 11 followers. Its final embers were doused in 1991 when Martin was sentenced to six months for fondling two underaged girls three years earlier. Many of Martin's 12 sons and eight daughters now live in Montreal, although few boast of their Buddhist cult lineage. Years earlier Martin's father Harold George Martin headed the Christian Homes for Children at spooky Singer Castle on Dark Island in Ontario. The organization was slammed in a 1961 article "How to Make a Million in the Charity Game."

Tyndale Martin

Peace and Love Who brought peace and love to Montreal? In spite of his claims, it was not your pot-smoking hippie uncle. The peace and love mantra arrived courtesy positive-thinking, Georgia-born George Baker, who reinvented himself as cult leader Father Divine in the 1930s. Father Divine's Montreal followers included Rudolph Clark and James Scott of the Peace Tailor shop at 1196 St. Antoine across from what's now the Bell Centre. The group also held thrice-weekly meetings at a home on Coursol near Atwater. One shoe-shiner showed his

Hitchings & Divine

devotion to the international cause with a sign reading: "Don't give to me. Give to Father Divine." Divine's female followers lived in a rooming house at 471 Prince Arthur W. and included a Miss Peaceful and Miss Blessed Heart. Divine denounced alcohol, gambling and sex and at age 71, the chubby, bald leader married his Montreal-based secretary Edna Rose Hitchings, 21. He described her as "the lamb's wife, a spotless virgin bride." Divine's final Montreal heaven, as he called his places, closed at Mountain and St. James in 1951. He died in 1965.

Nude lobby Miss Nude World 1973, Nancy Sellers, 22, strode into Montreal's city hall on January 3, 1974, sporting only a fur coat and boots, in hopes of scoring a sit-down with Mayor

Jean Drapeau. She came with Norman Flinkman, clad only in silver shoes, a raincoat and sunglasses. The duo strolled around city hall unashamedly as they sought to persuade the notoriously-prude mayor to give his blessings to their show at Motel Diplomate (4645 Metropolitain. E) which consisted of Novak cavorting nude and Flinkman doing some naked stand-up. A security guard smiled and tipped his cap at the nude Americans but the mayor was nowhere to be found. Police in Halifax, Quebec City in Ottawa had allowed the show to go on but Montreal cops busted the duo on stage five days later. They completed their week of shows wearing only the flimsiest of costumes and later fought the obscenity charge, as a jammed courtroom watched their act on a small TV. Flinkman, an army vet who had penned a hit pop song as a teen, spoke from the heart. "Our nudity is beautiful and uplifting both for us and our fans. Why is the mayor so scared of bodies?" They were find $200 each for appearing naked on Jan 5, 1974. They opened a strip club in Alabama and divorced in 1979.

Vagrants and other martyrs Montreal police have long tossed harmless vagrants into jail cells, often for years, without requiring much justification. Police arrested Lui On at  least 25 times for quietly meditating cross-legged next to his two leather suitcases on the ledge of a building on St. James Street during World War II. One-legged Arthur Williams was jailed for two years in 1909 for pretending to be deaf and handing out cards claiming that he needed money to return to school to learn a vocation. Williams attempted to appear handicapped by keeping his arm contorted, while jamming donations into a hole he had drilled into his cork leg. Not all vagrants were pathetic and weak: a dozen officers were required to hold down feisty 135-lb vagrant Jacob Iseman when police apprehended him in 1913. In 1938, hearty misfit Yvan Vernchuck, a 53-year-old Russian, became known for sleeping in freezing caves on Mount Royal, clad only in his underwear. Vagrants could even be children, or at least technically, as police once charged a six-day-old abandoned newborn with vagrancy in 1915 as a means of separating the infant from a woman attempting to claim it as her own. Police got the baby and the charges were dropped, as kids under seven could not be charged with adult crimes.

Cops and bikers roll together Biker gangs were simply misunderstood red-blooded males who just liked riding motorcycles. Or so some authorities wanted to believe. Montreal police officer John Dalzell naively spearheaded the *Motocyclists Unis de Quebec*, which sought to allow bikers to practice their riding maneuvers at a space donated by British Petroleum on Henri Bourassa near Highway 13. Riders from such clubs as the Sundowners, Hot Pistons, Satan's Choice, Popeyes, Death Riders, Dead Men, Cave Men, Outsiders, Les Gorilles, Playboys, Arch Angels, Phantoms were welcome, as were a dozen police officers.

Bikers suspected the officers of spying on their activities and simply stopped coming. The federal government then tried to tame 25 bikers by handing St. Henri's Dead Men MC a generous

Brian Powers

LIP grant to carve wooden bolo bats, cars and tractors in hopes that the toys could help stem Canada's trade imbalance. Authorities later lost patience with bad boy bikers, as police routinely hauled motorcycles off of Crescent Street whenever bikers were unable to provide vehicle registrations. Many bikers could not show their registration because a previous cop had taken them away to examine. Legislation from 2001 outlawed membership in criminal gangs.

Need for tweed Sprinting on icy downtown sidewalks is never an easy task, but doing it while chased by store detectives was adrenaline-pumping hell for Parti Québécois House Leader

Charron

Claude Charron on Jan. 30, 1982 as he fled Eaton's department store after stealing a $120 tweed sports jacket. Charron, 35, paid for a jacket but wore another one out without paying. "I was testing something that seemed idiotically easy," he later said. It turned out to be difficult. The highly-recognizable Charron dashed with his bodyguard to McGill College Ave., then south at Place Ville Marie and then down University before Charron slipped on the steep hill. He pleaded with a store detective to allow him to pay double the price of the stolen jacket. Charron was charged and fined $300. The theft, combined with a drunk driving charge, ended Charron's political career. Many PQ supporters burned their Eaton's credit cards in protest, with some noting that only one-in-five apprehended shoplifters was prosecuted at the time. One arsonist attempted to torch the store, leading a judge to sentence him to 14-years in prison. Charron's autobiography became a hot seller the next year and he went on to become a popular TV personality. Eaton's department store closed in 1999.

Crazy bans Dancing after midnight and on Sundays was long forbidden in Montreal under a sporadically-applied, fun-hating bylaw. The ban was propelled by the *Ligue du dimanche*, a religious group that sought to keep bums in church benches. The dancing ban was only rescinded in 1957 after Belmont Park management challenged it in court. City council returned three

years later with another outlandish ban, this time outlawing candles employed "for lighting or decorative purpose in a public hall." Pool rooms and bowling alleys were, however, exempt. Council forbade bar employees from socializing with customers in a 1967 bylaw, making it unlawful for "any entertainer, to mingle with customers...to drink, dance or sit at the same table or counter with a customer." Police spent two years jailing dozens of young women for talking to men at bars likes the Casa Del Sol on Drummond, Pal's near the Main and the Silver Slipper on Metcalfe. The clumsy attempt to crack down on watered-down drink scams and prostitution was widely denounced but survived court challenge. Police enforced the bylaw until owners got proof of Morality Squad boss Paul Boisvert committing an undisclosed compromising act in a downtown bar in 1969. Boisvert quit the force and the bylaw faded out into obscurity.

Fiery domestic cleaning Gasoline was once routinely employed to clean household items. This turned out to be a disastrous practice for those who burned to death while scrubbing away. The most notable gasoline cleaner disaster claimed Montreal's top mobster Louis Greco, who ran the local Mafia in a duopoly with Vic Cotroni. Greco was using gasoline as a solvent to lay tiles at his brother Tony's Gina's Pizzeria at 3212 Jarry E. when he became a human torch, dying on Dec. 3, 1972. Flames killed a couple at 5760 St. Dominique two years later when Serge Méthot, 25, accidentally lit $1 of gasoline he had hauled home in a styrofoam cooler in order to clean his bicycle. Earlier gasoline cleaner tragedies included the dreadful deaths of Steve Horvath, 32, and Theresa Jekkel, 26, killed in a blast at 3493 Hutchison. They were fixing up the apartment they were to share as a wedded couple but the five-gallon tub of gasoline in the bathtub exploded on Sept. 29, 1957. Mrs. Miron was set ablaze while using gasoline to clean a bed at 9 p.m. on a Saturday night in 1937 at 7632 Drolet. She ran outside and her fireman neighbour wrapped her in a blanket but she died nonetheless. By 1948 authorities were still urging people to "be careful" when cleaning with gasoline, four years later they were recommending people avoid using gas to clean their homes altogether.

Montreal flag snubs French
Montreal's flag offers few hints of its majority French population, with its English rose, Scottish thistle, Irish clover and French *fleur-de-lys*. The flag was adopted by Mayor Camillien Houde in 1939 as an adaptation of Montreal's coat of arms, created under Montreal's first mayor Jacques Viger in 1833. Few nationalist groups complained, although early critic P. J. Leduc found the flag so offensive that he said he would have preferred the Union Jack, "until the day another revolution places us under a domination other than English or until we got an independent political regime." Mayor

Houde turned out to be not much of a fan of the British Empire, as he was arrested and interned a few months later for discouraging Quebecers from fighting for Canada in the World War II. Mayor Jean Drapeau spent $300,000 for the cookie cutter city logo in 1981, a shape meant to represent a flower in which each of the petals contains a V and a M, for *Ville de Montréal*. Mayor Gérald Tremblay rejigged that flag at the cost of $12,000 in 2003, erasing the words "Ville de" in an effort to persuade the newly-merged English-speaking municipalities from demerging from the brief one-island-one-city project.

Ponzi scheming

A parking lot just west of the Place Bonaventure loading ramp offers no hint of the drama, lies and greed that reigned at the spot after 1907. Luigi Zarossi hired  fraud artist and gambler Charles Ponzi to work at his bank and the ingeniously devious duo, along with pal Antonio Salviati, solicited deposits and then waited months to credit accounts while they pocketed interest on the money entrusted to them. Their Banco Zarossi, three doors east of Inspector, offered eye-catching returns and soon deposits flooded in from Canada, the United States and Italy. The bank hit a snag and so the desperate gang improvised the pyramid scheme that later bore Ponzi's name. Customers were rewarded extravagant returns not, as they claimed, from shrewd investments but rather from the mountains of cash that kept snowballing in following enthusiastic word-of-mouth. Zarossi felt the heat and fled to Mexico while Ponzi kept the operation going, meanwhile falling in love with Zarossi's 17-year-old daughter. Ponzi was jailed in Montreal for forging a $400 cheque, which he claimed that he selflessly wrote to take the fall for his boss. Ponzi served 20 months in prison and then earned greater infamy in the United States.

Decapitated chatterbox

A thick head of long hair can be a source of pride but early settler Jean Saint-Père paid a terrible price for his handsome flowing mane. Saint Père, a  notary and faithful assistant of Paul de Chomedey, sieur de Maisonneuve, received a visit from hostile Iroquois posing as friends in October 1657. The natives proved not-so-friendly, as they scalped and killed two Frenchmen. But they liked Saint-Père's hair so much that they decapitated him and kept his head. But Saint-Pere's decapitated dome started speaking to them in perfect Iroquois, a language that the victim could not speak while alive. The disembodied head kept on talking to them no matter where they placed it, saying things like, "You believe you have hurt us but you have sent us to heaven instead!" The Iroquois told the French of the troubling head and the tale was retold by Marguerite Bourgeoys, Dollier and Vachon. Chattering severed heads were not as rare of as one might imagine. Scoundrel priest and devotee of poverty St. Vincent de Paul, also a friend of the *Société Notre Dame de Montréal*, claimed that while enslaved in Tunisia a Muslim named Montorio taught him how to make, "a dead man's head talk by some artificial means to seduce and trick people to believe that Mohamed was speaking his will to them."

Undercover teen battles Reds Authorities felt so

threatened by Communism that Montreal launched a dedicated anti-subversive squad in 1930. The Red Squad did not start

Maurice Boyzcum

smoothly, as overenthusiastic second-in-command John Boyzcum shot a Polish immigrant to death two years later. He was acquitted of manslaughter after claiming that he had been drugged. Boyzcum was then tasked with busting softball fundraisers and attempting to determine whether Lili St. Cyr's

stripteases were subversive. He decided that they were not. The anti-Communist squad enjoyed its triumphant moment when Boyzcum's 15-year-old son Maurice infiltrated *The Daily Tribune* newspaper in 1946, presenting himself as Morris Taylor. The youngster dropped out of school, quit the Boy Scouts, shunned his friends and became a delivery boy for the paper. He won the trust of his new Communist friends by claiming that that he had been fired from a previous job for standing up for workers' rights. "It was a slim chance but with luck on my side I succeeded in slowly climbing the ladder of the Red movement in Montreal," he later said. His cover was eventually blown but police raided four locations on Dec. 5, 1951, carting off many piles of pamphlets. The meeting places were shuttered under the provincial Padlock Law, later ruled unconstitutional.

Mail order extortion Montreal's first wave of Mafia thugs relied on penmanship and drawing skills to earn their keep. Black Hand Society members were adept at writing threatening notes complete with drawings of dripping daggers, skulls and cross bones, scary snakes and coffins. If the drawings were sufficiently terrifying, the recipient—usually an Italian immigrant—might pay to avoid injury or death. Vincenzo Marino led the sinister illustrators until he was shot dead by his own crew at St. Felix and St. James in June 1908 as punishment for pocketing money from the legal fund. The Black Hand killed an informant named Poplander at the Vitre Street Gateway three years later and the assassins took time to nail a cross over the

body to symbolize the betrayal. Black Hand gang member Carlo di Battista was sentenced to hang for killing the proprietor of Manford's Grocery at St. Genevieve and Latour and spent three hours on the stand in 1909, shedding light on the gang's activities, which included running white slavery prostitution rings across Canada. The Black Hand was best known for pinning their scary illustrations to would-be victims' doors, thus saving on postage stamps. The epistolary intimidation endured at least another two decades, as musician Vincenzo Indeluca and movie theatre manager Philip Hazza complained of receiving extortion notes while someone named D. Weinberg grumbled that a Black Hand attacker hit him on the head with a nail-embedded stick.

Censors protect tender eyes Anybody can watch endless hours of debauchery these days but authorities long went to great lengths to prevent Montrealers from seeing even the tamest of films. Audiences were prevented from viewing a film of boxer Jack Johnson's heavyweight victory over James J. Jeffries in 1910, as theatre owners believed audiences could not cope with watching a black fighter beating a white opponent. (Yet nobody bothered Johnson when he came to town three years later to canoodle with white girlfriend Lucille Cameron). Then in 1953 provincial authorities kept Protestant leader Martin Luther's bio-pic out of Quebec theatres, as they deemed the film to contain historical inaccuracies. The ban was a source of pride for some Quebecers who chanted *Vive le Québec!* in a Winnipeg movie theatre when it played there. A new Quebec censor overturned the ban in 1962, calling it "incomprehensible."

Censors pulled Marlon Brando's biker flick *The Wild Ones* from theatres in 1956 after leather-jacketed youth proved unruly during the Rocket Richard and bus ticket riots. Days after the October Crisis of 1970, Mayor Jean Drapeau focused on getting *Quiet Days in Clichy* out of theatres, as he urged provincial inspectors ban the libertine film, as it might corrupt minds.

Fugitives among us The Boodle Gang, five aldermen who defrauded New York City by signing a crooked 999-year streetcar contract, proved the gaudiest of Montreal-bound fugitives. Journalist Joseph Pulitzer gained fame by accusing the

five even without much evidence. The group fled to Montreal in 1886 where they lived lavishly in costly homes and hotels. Fugitive John Keenan built the Boodle Block apartments, as it became known, somewhere on Sherbrooke Street. New York reporters were avid for constant news of the group but Montrealers shrugged at the bored politicians who sat around hotel lobbies smoking cigars. They eventually returned to New York to face justice. Other Montreal-bound scofflaws included John C. Eno, who stole $4 million from the Second National Bank, George Bartholomew defrauded the Charter Oak Life, Cincinnati's Amadeus Ebert who stole $150,000, and Manhattan poisoned-liquor dealer Carmini Licenziato, who came in 1919.

A lock on Communism Quebec's 1937 Padlock Law

Red Squad raid

allowed police to barricade any premises they thought might be used to promote Communism, an ideology Premier Maurice Duplessis deemed "worse than smallpox." Places barricaded under the Padlock Law included offices of *La Clarté* newspaper, dress-cutter Muni Taub's home, the Hebrew Consumptive Hall, the Jewish Cultural Centre Library, the UJPO Cultural Centre at Esplanade and Laurier and *Le Combat* newspaper. Duplessis even attacked mainstream *Le Devoir* as a "Bolshevik newspaper" in 1954 but did not lock it up. Critics abounded but a court upheld the law, which was inspired by a Montreal bylaw that permitted police to padlock doors at gambling halls and bordellos. That bylaw was struck down in 1955, opening the door for a reversal of the provincial legislation. A phony rental dispute finally felled the law. Max Bailey sought to cede his apartment at 5321 Park Ave. to John Switzman, a known Communist. Landlady Freda Elbling went to court to block the transfer on the grounds that the likely padlocking was a threat to her income. Landlady Elbling was, in fact, friends with the duo and shared their political leanings. Lawyer Frank Scott had the law struck down at the Supreme Court in 1957.

Toronto won't do The event that most cemented

Montreal's reputation as a romantic destination for lovey-dovey tourists was originally meant to take place in Toronto. Superstar screen icons Richard Burton, 38, and Elizabeth Taylor,

32, landed in a Trans-Canada Airlines charter and settled into the Ritz Carlton Hotel for the purpose of becoming man and wife, an event that left stargazers in paroxysms of fascination and joy. A trio of black limos ferried the wedding party, with Taylor sporting a yellow daffodil chiffon

Irene Sharaff dress and hair adorned with hyacinth and lily of the valley in a coil bun, as hardened reporters dutifully informed. Burton ideally would have married Taylor in Toronto where he was performing *Hamlet*, but Ontario religious authorities were not fully convinced that the couple's Mexican divorces were legal. Rev. Leonard Mason of the Unitarian Church of the Messiah had no qualms performing the high-profile ceremony because Quebec marriages operate under the Napoleonic, rather than the Civil Code. The couple divorced seven years later, remarried in 1975 and divorced again one year after that.

Crucifixion cult hits rough times

Religious services at Ovila Girard's Sect of the Crucified Ones featured semi-clad adherents worshiping an actor reciting theatrical sermons while flanked by four attractive young maidens. A dead

Ovila Girard

girl named Aurore Brière provided Girard his healing powers and that magic proved strong enough to attract five dozen faithful, mostly women, who attended sessions at a home on Visitation Street in the early 1930s. Worshiper Eugene Cazeault abandoned wife Lucienne, who then complained to a judge of lacking financial support. The neglected wife disapprovingly denounced the services as, "no place for a husband" and where "women prayed in scandalous attire" and "offend God in scanty clothes." The cult staged plays around Quebec until they were shut down by Montreal censor J.P. Filion. Girard was then jailed for conducting illegal wedding ceremonies and resettled with 20 followers in the rural Quebec town of Namur. Girard hoped to heal his psychopath brother Omer, who instead raped a 15-year-old devotee and killed three elderly townsfolk, then spending the loot on the Lower Main. Omer was hanged in Hull in 1937. Ovila then showed his more noble side as he shelved his cult and raised his orphaned nephew, the child born of his brother's sexual assault, as his own son.

Romance delayed Two lovers came from Paris in March 1975 to pen the next chapter of their storybook romance but not all went smoothly for Dalila Zeghar and her French-born husband Denis Maschino after they were handed keys to an apartment at 4850 Cote des Neiges. For three years Maschino taught French while Zeghar worked as a waitress but Zeghar's brother Messaoud Zeghar, a billionaire with ties to the CIA, refused to accept the relationship. Messaoud incessantly urged his sister to return to Algeria and marry a man of his choosing. She refused. So he dispatched their three sisters to visit her. The sororal conspirators knocked Dalila out with poisoned tea, wheeled her through an airport and boarded her onto a Boeing airplane using a fake passport. Maschino, shocked at his wife's abduction, rushed to Algeria and converted to Islam in hopes of reversing his fortunes. Protesters urged her return. She finally sneaked away from captors in Switzerland and returned to Montreal in 1981. The couple was reunited at Mirabel Airport in a teary scene attended by three-dozen. Messaoud Zeghar was imprisoned after a regime change in 1978 and ordered to pay a hefty fine from his estimated $2 billion fortune. He died in 1987.

Dalila Zeghar

Abortion disasters Abortion doctors are now considered respected professionals but such specialists long risked being jailed for murder. Dr. Paul Émile LaLanne charged $1,000 for the procedure (multiply by 15 to get today's equivalent) offering abortions at his clinic at 2009 Sherbrooke E. in the 1930s, while his home on Devil's Island (now Beaubien Island near Valleyfield) allowed women to recover while admiring his portraits of Hitler. LaLanne, who once gave a speech entitled "Why We Should Oppose the Jews," sold the island to a priest and died in 1951, at the age of 68. Other Montreal abortionists were dealt with more harshly, including

Sadik Bey, a "Turkish military adventurer, crystal gazer and fortune teller" who was accused of aborting Emelienne Raymond's fetus in 1913. Neither party would confess. Dr. Oscar Dunn Duckett was charged with murder when a patient died at 4152 St. Hubert in 1928 and patient died in 1937 after a backroom abortionist injected her with bleach. Other victims of botched abortions include Rita Pallo, 21, Emilienne Leclerc, 23, (1947) and Simone Joncas, 21, (1961), whose boyfriend committed suicide upon news of her death. Bagel baker Jack Seligman, 41, was charged with manslaughter in 1955 after dumping patient Dora Blackburn's body into an alleyway. One year earlier the very same Seligman made news in another gruesome way after he he let 12 inner-city kids ride on his boat. The vessel capsized and they all drowned.

Booze cops frolic Quebec's Liquor Police blazed a trail of fraud, theft and corruption—none of it a secret to longtime premier Maurice Duplessis—before the force was disbanded in disgrace. Quebec was one of the few places that gave an emphatic

thumbs-down to Prohibition in 1919, although for a time the province limited liquor sales to beer, wine and cider. The resulting booze stampede inspired Quebec to set up a 35-agent liquor squad that soon grew to 250 agents. Duplessis once ordered them to revoke the liquor license of Frank Roncarelli's Roma Restaurant at 1429 Crescent as punishment for constantly bailing his fellow Jehova's Witnesses out of jail. Roncarelli, who had four years remaining on his license, went broke and later won a personal $33,000 lawsuit against Duplessis. Officials plundered the liquor police budget and an auditor pointed out the rampant fraud but was told to shush up. Another whistle-blower was beaten, shunned and suspended. Duplessis died in 1959 and liquor police chef Rosario Lemire, 73, was sentenced to three months in prison for fraud soon after. The booze cops were disbanded in 1961.

Hanging Art Arthur B. English (pseudonym John Ellis) not only went unpunished for killing hundreds of Canadians, the government paid him for his lethal enterprise. Canada's official hangman put the noose to 300 Canadian prisoners from 1914, after hanging a similar total abroad. English was a man-about-town who would tell strangers of how he would always smile while attaching a noose because his was the last face a condemned convict would see before death. But Ellis had a dark side, as he was once accused of beating his wife and his reputation took a further fall at the Bordeaux Prison gallows on March 8, 1935 when he put the noose to Thomasina Sorao, a woman condemned for having her street-cleaner husband killed for his $4,500 insurance payout. English, then 71, miscalculated her weight and the rope ripped her head clean off. Her co-conspirators Leone Gagliardi, 30, and Angelo Donofrio, 19, had been executed earlier, so they did not witness the decapitation. English retired and pleaded for hangings to be abolished, describing the practice as "cruel and antiquated." He argued that "nobody suffered more than I have." English separated from his wife and died penniless and starving in July 1938 at a rooming house at 3452 Lebrun. He never wrote his promised autobiography but the Arthur Ellis crime writers' award is now named in his honour.

English

From lambs to rocks Every pious Quebec mother dreamed of getting her rosy-cheeked son chosed to carry the lamb in front of Montreal's St. Jean Baptiste Parade. The parade was such a big deal that in the 1950s Montrealers would occupy the route days in advance to sell their seats to the highest bidder. But nationalists grumbled that the sweet boy carrying a harmless lamb constituted a pathetic symbolic of weakness, only proving that Quebec's biggest celebration was a display of the defeated held for the amusement of the oppressor. Someone anonymously threatened to kidnap the lamb in 1964 and the fluffy beast was sidelined from then on. The parade degenerated into riots in 1968 after nationalist leader Pierre Bourgault refused to sit on the reviewing stand with Prime Minister Pierre Trudeau. Crafty undercover agents disguised themselves as nationalists and carried Bourgault in celebration all the way to the police van,

where he was hauled off into custody. Others tossed rocks at Trudeau, who brazenly stood his ground on the review stand as 234 protesters were arrested. Similar chaos struck the next year and the parade was cancelled until 1981 when organizers compromised by featuring powerful-looking, 18-foot-tall puppets of children. The 1990 parade saw a return of the lamb, as nationalists irritated by the failure of the Meech Lake Accord fallout showcased a giant wooden Lamb of Troy.

Huguenot discipline Dreams of gold inspired French
Calvinist Jean de la Rocque de Roberval to sail to Quebec with a crew of between 70 and 200, a group that included many

Roberval

prisoners. The prospectors hit no pay dirt, so Roberval hanged seven. Roberval favoured Batman villain-like execution methods, placing his victims in leg shackles and leaving them to die slowly on remote islands. One was hanged for stealing during a time of rationing and six others for performing their work in an unsatisfactory manner, likely meaning insubordination or mutiny. Roberval left Marie de la Rocque (his sister, or niece) along with her lover, child and servant on an island to die. Only Marie survived and eventually moved back to France. A Catholic mob finally killed the Huguenot Roberval in France in 1560. Protestants like Roberval and other non-Catholics were later banned from settling in Quebec with the Revocation of the Edict of Nantes in 1685. Non-Catholics already in Quebec were forced to participate in Catholic rites. Many secretly kept their Protestant faith. Religious freedom returned with the British conquest. By 1764

Huguenots began being accepted and promoted in government circles.

A lonely millionaire One day he was an oddball outsider, the next he was one of the world's most desirable millionaire bachelors. Such was the narrative of McGill Geology professor John Williamson who grew up in the Laurentians, studied Geology at McGill and then found himself kicking around a copper mine in Africa. Williamson believed that diamonds were sometimes pushed to the surface through gem-rich underground tunnels. So when the diamond company

Williamson toiled for abandoned its search in Tanzania in 1939, Williamson took it over on a shoestring budget. He was on his last nickel and coping with malaria when he found a diamond in an unexpected spot. His mine went on to produce many other gems, including the flawless 54-carat rough pink diamond he gave to Queen Elizabeth as a wedding gift in 1947. Williamson donated to African schools and hospitals and also helped train many Canadian geologists. But the public mostly fixated on his rugged good looks and unmarried status, not to mention his fortune, said to be worth up to $80 million. The handsome bachelor died unmarried in 1958, felled by disease at the age of 51. His three siblings inherited his estate and sold off his mines to De Beers and the Tanzanian government.

Teens in coffins Black-clad teenage girls were whipped, made to sleep in coffins and worship a shroud of Jesus at Dr. Louis Jacques' Sister of the Holy Face Convent on Amherst, just

south of St. Catherine. The physician took care of five Aubin sisters during the smallpox outbreak of 1885 and soon they were among 14 girls dedicated to a life of religious rigor in a home decorated by skulls, chains and scourges. Each month hundreds of visitors would worship alongside the girls, who were forbidden to even visit the backyard. Their Mother Superior, a young woman in her early twenties, would usher them to pray at dawn at the nearby St. Jacques church on St. Denis. Dr. Jacques—who also slept in a coffin but did not get whipped—traveled repeatedly to Rome in futile attempts to obtain

Coffin bed on Amherst

papal blessing for the cult. The girls were lashed on Fridays and would occasionally sport gowns emblazoned with an image of the Veil of Veronica, a mystical shroud of Jesus. In spite of the morbid atmosphere, the girls were a joyous lot, prone to laughter and giggles. The cult appeared in local listings from 1894 to 1904 and doc Jacques remained at the house for another decade after.

War hero blasted Roland Haumont joined the French Resistance and helped beat Hitler before moving to Montreal, where many intellectuals had discretely supported France's

Haumont

Nazi-approved Vichy puppet government. Haumont irked many powerful people his loud denunciations of Nazi collaborators in Quebec. One Sunday morning in October 1963, a mysterious explosion rocked Haumont's home at 3430 Beaconsfield in NDG, as a natural gas line blew, killing his wife Sheila and daughters Nicole and Leslie. Haumont and his son Marc, 13, survived with serious injuries. Prosecutors convinced a five-man coroner's jury that Haumont should be charged with the blast, which occurred days before the family was to move to the United States. Prosecutors suggested that Haumont sought to kill his family so he could be with his mistress. But a month later Justice Claude Wagner exonerated the embattled Haumont, who later remarried.

Petty imprisonment Johnny Young grappled hard to win a handful of Greco-Roman wrestling titles before hamming it up as a pro wrestler. By age 27 he had saved enough money to open a menswear store with a dozen employees. But The Depression forced the store to close after seven years. Young

then operated a gym and an an illegal after-hours blind pig joint, while toiling as a bouncer for future Mafia boss Vic Cotroni's nightclub and as a part-time bodyguard for Premier Maurice Duplessis. Young was convicted of series of minor crimes before getting in real hot water by harbouring two bank robbers from the Perrault gang after they killed a pair of cops in an East End bank robbery. While awaiting trial in 1949 Young sold heroin, reviving an appetite that had been starved in Montreal since the start of World War II. Police raided Young's place at 1061 St. Denis later that year and seized 55 ounces of heroin and a Schmeizer machine gun, then tackling Young as he fled down the street. He was sentenced to five years in prison but prosecutors hit him with a newly-created punishment originally designed to keep sex offenders behind bars indefinitely. Prosecutor John Bumbray, who was close to Premier Duplessis, convinced a jury that "dealing drugs is worse than murder" and Young became and remained Canada's first and only habitual criminal for many years. Once in prison Young complained about everything, especially his old pal Duplessis. High-profile author and journalist Mavis Gallant pleaded for his release but her efforts proved fruitless. Young became increasingly embittered and obese, occasionally fighting with guards and inmates. He served 21 years longer than his sentence when he was released in 1975. The chunky Young died of a stroke two years later, after eating a load of hot dogs and marching up the hill to Sherbrooke Street.

Telltale heart thieves Young Peter Fryer was hanging around outside a tavern in Point St. Charles drinking beer from a paper bag one evening in March 1973 when Bobby McGee came up with the wild notion of stealing Brother André's heart from its coveted marble pedestal at St. Joseph's Oratory. He thought the venerated organ could serve as a bargaining chip to negotiate a reduced charge in his impending armed robbery sentence. So Fryer and Addlin drove to the massive house of worship, walked past the display of abandoned crutches and picked the two small locks on the iron gate guarding the treasure. They escaped unseen and the robbery made headlines around the world, with many suspecting that

Heart on display

the theft was a college kids' prank. Many expected its swift return. Instead, the duo threatened to incinerate the heart unless given $50,000, with lawyer Frank Shoofey leading the negotiations. Father Marcel Lalonde of the Catholic Holy Cross

Fathers rejected the demand, even though many worshipers offered to pay the ransom for the glass-encased relic of André Bessette, now a saint since 2010. The thieves started fearing for their lives and grew increasingly anxious about the telltale heart. "Every time I heard a loud bang, I would just about crap my pants," Fryer wrote decades later. Meanwhile a group of artists, including Frank "Montreal Main" Vitale, Stephen Lack and Alan "Bozo" Moyle saw levity in the standoff, lampooning the panic in an exhibit at Véhicule Gallery, that featured a fast-rotting cow's heart in a baseball glove and a crucifix with a vibrating erection. The thieves anonymously directed police to the heart just before Christmas, 1974. It was returned after 645 days.

Cranking out the tunes Hand-cranked machines supplied the first recorded music in Montreal, as licensed organ grinders generated tips by rotating handles on delicate and costly machines. Many organ grinders were Italian immigrants, leading one to describe his brethren as "a shame for our nationality," while a Montreal mayor once indelicately urged two young women to split from their lowly organ-grinder husbands. Grinders peaked in the 1930s when 150 cranked flowery Italian folk music, including Belgian-Italian Canadian Arthur Lachapelle, who followed in his fathers' trade and turned handle downtown until his death in 1970.

Lachapelle

Lachappelle was a small man with long black (later grey) hair who provided tunes for five hours each afternoon at Phillips Square, then hauled his machine to his electricity-less apartment on Grubert Street (later demolished for the Jeanne Mance housing project) where his five kids would occasionally express shame at his line of work. Procuring a new set of songs required sending the beastly contraption to a company California that charged $500 for a half-dozen tunes. Organ grinders competed with buskers like Joseph "One Man Band" Panette, who died in 1931 aged 76, and a former British Army captain who sported a black mask while playing his saxophone. One-legged Gaspard Petit, who lost his limb to a train, attracted handouts by hauling a gramophone. Not all loved the busking DJ. A man named Martineau attacked Petit with a knife in 1905. Petit defended himself by smacking Martineau in the head with a crutch, killing him. Police did not charge Petit with any crime. He kept playing records around town until his death in 1924. Nowadays, many buskers prefer to play their tunes inside metro stations but their efforts are sometimes curtailed by cranky ticket attendants who tire of hearing the same tunes repeatedly and then force the musician out.

Loving the smokes Montrealers long embraced tobacco with a lusty fervor in their quest to out-chainsmoke all other Canadian urban counterparts. Old school parents routinely wrote principals notes requesting permission for their 10-year-old kids to smoke in the schoolyard, while tobacco industry officials relentlessly insisted that smoking was harmless. Even Dr. Hans Selye, the world-famous Montreal academic who invented the term "stress," became a well-paid apologist for the relaxing benefits of tobacco. Imperial Tobacco official Leo Laporte spent 40 years denying the link between smoking and lung cancer. "Many eminent scientists publicly question the cause and effect relationship of cigarette smoking and health," he noted in 1963. Canadian research into a link between cigarettes and cancer decreased in the mid-1950s and McGill pocketed $300,000 from the Canadian Tobacco Manufacturers' Council to study breathing problems in 1972, a time when 40 percent of Montrealers lit up. "It is not practical to expect the public at large to give up smoking," said Dr. Peter Macklem. "The role of research is to find the 'high risk person' who is likely to develop lung disease and get him to give up smoking." For decades Montreal homes, schools and public places were full of malodorous cigarette smoke. Smokers would light up in CEGEP classes, airplanes and offices until the late 1980s, as clothing would require frequent washing just to lose the stink. Meanwhile many non-smokers died of lung and throat cancer from second-hand fumes. Air Canada started experimenting with non-smoking flights only in 1987, while a study seven years later recommended that Quebec should not discourage smoking, reasoning that taxpayers save pension money when people die prematurely; 84 percent of Quebecers surveyed in 2004 felt that smoking should be permitted in nightclubs. Smoking was banned in Quebec public indoor places in 2006, in spite of massive support to keep cigarettes burning.

McGill smoking lab

The pension pest Jules Crépeau's lavish pension deal presented a conundrum for City Hall, as his bloated payments strained the municipal budget, leading to what might have been a nefarious plot to put an end to his cheques as well as his life. Crépeau wielded big power as head of the City Services department but he was scapegoated for a financial scandal as well

Houde & Crepeau

as The Laurier Palace theatre fire, which killed 78 children near Prefontaine and St. Catherine on January 9, 1927. Mayor Camillien Houde wanted him gone at all costs and agreed to a lavish pension in 1930, which left him as the highest-paid bureaucrat in administration, even after retirement. The Great Depression made it more difficult to pay Crépeau's pension, at a time when mayors brazenly bribed journalists $1,000 a year for favourable coverage. Mayor Houde failed to convince a judge to rescind the pension in 1931 and a half dozen years later he was still trying to persuade the province to pass legislation axing the pension. Then in 1937 undercover Montreal police officer L.P. Coulson slammed a police car into Crépeau at Royal and NDG Ave., leaving the 63-year-old badly injured. Was it an accident or an attempted vehicular homicide? The question became moot after Crépeau died the next summer.

Folksy Finn found Psychedelic folk singer Simon Finn was bummed out with his efforts to make a breakthrough in swinging London, so he moved to Montreal in 1973 and shelved his musical ambitions. Finn lived as a Plateau bohemian in an $75 apartment on Mentana and enjoyed it so much he obtained Canadian citizenship. He then rented a loft at 3810 St. Lawrence where he taught karate and then moved on to 5295 Esplanade (near Fairmount), making some money repairing and flipping homes, all the while feeding his non-musical artistic tendencies. "Montreal was right up with Berlin as a utopia for artists in the 80s but without the pig's feet stew," he said. But his life changed when he Googled his name for the first time in 2003. "A female

friend was telling me about Googling a man who'd invited her out. I asked her what it involved. I ended up Googling myself." Finn was shocked to find that the obscure album had forgotten about, featuring a song where he wails repeatedly "Jerusalem," had reached cult status. People had been speculating as to his possible demise, disappearance or changed identity. Finn dashed those rumours and went headlong onto any stage that would have him and has been performing his music ever since. He is now based in the U.K. once again.

Sex for sale Montreal street walkers were once more numerous than phone poles and more tenacious than mosquitoes. The bucolic Priests Farm on Sherbrooke and Fort was a hot spot for commercial sex in the early 1800s, as prostitutes could feast on ample vegetation growing around the seminary while also meeting sex-hungry clients, who often

included wayward soldiers. Musicians accompanied the ambulatory black-robed religious crews, so hookers and clients would hear the oncoming procession and hide away before being seen. Streetwalkers were often destitute and homeless and further embattled not only by threat of arrest, assault and ripoff but also by alcoholism, hypothermia, unwanted pregnancy, as well as tuberculosis and venereal disease. Many women sought painful mercury cures for sexually transmitted infections and Montreal doctors were incapable of differentiating between gonorrhea and syphilis until 1860, long after the difference was known elsewhere. Women were sometimes happy to be sent to the awful Montreal jail where city hall now stands, as it was better than freezing to death on the streets. About three dozen women found a rehab opportunity at the Magdalene Asylum (where Place Bonaventure now sits) until it closed in 1836 when its boss got married. Streetwalkers would share resources, sometimes squatting together in abandoned houses. At other times they were at each other's throats, such as when Margaret McGinniss fought Elizabeth Reid, who ended up getting smacked on the head with a shovel. Some turned to armed robbery, such as Eliza Martin, who came across one-legged William O'Brien sitting on a bridge on the Lachine Canal and stole the $30 he had saved to move back to Ireland. Operating a brothel in the early 1800s was an offense punishable by pillory, as at least 10 brothel operators

were taunted and pelted near Nelson's Monument, while Marie Deguire and Angelique Godin were publicly shamed by being carted around town for all to see. Most brothel owners were sentenced to about three months in prison but former convict and hangman, the African-American Benjamin Field, was given much-harsher sentences of two and four years, in what seems like a blatant case of racism. Field's landlord Sheriff Ermatinger avoided punishment by claiming ignorance about the existence of the brothel in his building, as did Montreal High Constable Jacob Marsten when caught in a similar situation. Brothels were often owned by women in spite of their husbands' objections. James Davison even denounced his wife brothel-operating wife Mary Ann Crawford in a published advertisement in the *Montreal Transcript* renouncing financial responsibility for her. Montreal street prostitution has practically gone extinct in the 21st century, ending a tradition as old as the city itself.

7

Retail

Come browse budget memories from our aisle displays but beware the screaming shoe store owner and trigger-happy pharmacist. Line up at the sweetest cashier. Cash only.

Hawking like a boss Selling newspapers on sidewalks was as heroic as leaping on hand grenades, or that's what newspapers inferred when they covered the street hawkers who generated their profits. Little Pete Murphy was dubbed The King of Newspaper Boys, after starting in 1856 at the age of six, eventually taking charge of a buzzing kiosk on St. James. Murphy launched a protective association that clad the lads—mostly

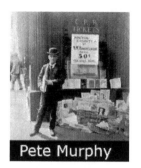
Pete Murphy

Sam Rosenberg in 1966

young Jewish boys—in nifty knickerbocker suits for workers parades and held Christmas dinners. He gifted fellow vendors with musical instruments and pleas to quit smoking. The rickety kiosks played a central role in the information pipeline and Murphy even mused about launching his own newspaper in 1904 after the *Sunday Sun* went on strike. Murphy died in Ste. Agathe in 1917. His son took over his stand, which lasted until 2000. Other kiosk inhabitants included Sam Rosenberg, an illiterate who never missed a day in 49 years selling papers at Mountain and St. Catherine. His brother-in-law Max was such a fixture at the southwest corner of Mackay and St. Catherine that Ogilvy's gave him a raccoon coat when he retired. Then there was Morris Tenser who sported a deep-pocketed news vendor bib daily from 1926 to 1976. Spoken word poet Ken Hertz—who Bob Dylan opened for on Stanley Street in 1962—ran the ramshackle booth at Pine and the Main in 1976 and cursed rainstorms that left him chasing wet papers around "like an Indonesian peasant." Vendors hawked news on Montreal streets from 1778. Coin-operated newspaper boxes were banned in 1948 and again in 1970, making Montreal the first North American city with such a restriction.

Gun shop disasters William Sucher received a Lee-Enfield rifle as payment for a typewriter repair and was so beset by purchase offers for it that he opened International Firearms at

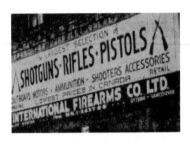

1011 Bleury. Sucher's wares included refurbished World War II Italian army rifles, one of which Kennedy assassin Lee Harvey Oswald, who came to Montreal in 1963, purchased through the mail and employed to killed President Kennedy. Sucher sold the machine gun used by Santa Claus bank robber Georges Marcotte, who was disguised as St. Nick when he shot two St. Laurent police officers dead in a bank heist in December 1962. Anne Kanner, 21, bought a rifle from Sucher and shot her mother dead in 1972. She later asked for a refund. Hungarian-born FLQ terrorist François Schirm, 33, came to rob weapons in August 1964, killing manager Leslie McWilliams, 56. Police shot employee Albert Pinisch, 37, dead by mistake. The store closed soon after. Sucher moved to Florida and died in 1976. Other gun stores had regrettable moments. Teenagers Frank Shafer and Joe Abramowitz shot gun store owner Williams Haynes dead in a botched hold-up at

Sucher

1221 Hotel de Ville in 1936. Shafer fled to a nearby gas station and shot himself dead. Abramovich's death sentence was eventually commuted. The Haynes Gun Shop survived many more years at 610 St. James W. (where the Quebecor building now stands). A Romanian entered T.W. Boyd & Son on Notre Dame, seven doors west of St. Lawrence in 1914. The man, who stood 5'7", was despondent after being rejected for a post on the Montreal police force on the basis of being too short. He borrowed a pistol from a salesman and calmly inserted his own bullet. His last words were, "Well, here goes. I am going to kill myself."

Spectacular signage

The 1948-lit Farine Five Roses Flour illuminated sign reigns as the most celebrated Montreal sign, in spite of language laws killing its English-language final word in 1977. But a larger elevated radiant monument once outshone all others. The "world's largest illuminated rooftop sign" was lit atop the Dawes Brewery at the still-standing 740 St. Maurice on the now long-gone Haymarket Square in July 1930. The 45-by-28 metre sign featured a black horse and the words *Bière Black Horse Ale* all lit by 1,700 metres of neon tubing. Neon lights soon transformed Montreal's commercial signage, as massive illuminated marquees hovered over almost every door on such strips as St. Catherine and St. Hubert. The eye-catching, brightly-lit oversized signs started slowly disappearing after a Feb. 1959 disaster in which the massive 90-metre Pollock's department store sign tumbled down in Quebec City, killing two and injuring 10. Montreal's heritage of neon has since largely been eradicated and even the Five Roses sign narrowly avoided obliteration in 2006. Signage custom dates back to 1688 when lawmakers chose discreet symbols to represent every variety of commercial outlet. Judge Migeon de Bransat cited an ancient Roman custom by ordering every Montreal tavern to display a bough, tree or bush outside rather than a sign. Similarly, sheep tails were hung over tannery doors but most other shops were recognizable by their wooden signs overhanging the sidewalks, a drawing of a boot would mark a boot store, a barrel represented a brewery and hardware stores were recognizable by a depiction of a hammer.

St. Hubert St.

Black Horse sign

Nyet to Soviet vodka What kind of awful, repressive dictatorship would ban vodka? Look no further than Duplessis-era Quebec where the heavenly joy of fermented potatoes was

Duplessis

kept from lips by the Soviet-hating premier. Not only were bars not permitted to sell vodka, anybody caught sneaking bottles in faced harsh punishment, including Adrien Dulude who was fined $200 for bringing a dozen bottles to town on a train from Toronto on Nov. 6, 1959. Premier Duplessis banned vodka during the Cold War as punishment for being a Communist export and hoped that the ban might encourage Quebec-made *whisky blanc*. Vodka was finally allowed back in on December 28, 1960, during a time when social reformers helped put an end to the repressive Duplessis-era *Grand Noirceur*, or Great Darkness.

Radioactive shoes Shoe-shoppers were once delighted by X-Ray radiation technology that allowed them to see right through their feet. X-Ray Fitting machines, or fluoroscopes,

offered the shoe shopper a chance to look through a porthole at a green X-Ray image of their toes. The machine purportedly gave shoppers a precise notion of whether a shoe fit, although it was ultimately pointless because the machine did not reveal the flesh around the bones. At various times between 1930 to 1960 shoppers could watch their toe bones wiggle in such stores as Jerry's on Queen Mary, J. Walter Cross on Sherbrooke near Claremont, D'Aoust's department store in Ste. Anne de Bellevue as well as Eaton's department store. Radiation became a serious concern after studies shed light on damage afflicted to those exposed to nuclear bomb fallout. But the tiny amount of radiation emitted during a 20-second foot viewing was ultimately considered benign. Store employees, on the other hand, were more significantly threatened by the rays due to prolonged and repeated exposure.

Bottle at city hall Alcohol was the demon's drink to be banned at all costs, or so argued abstentionists who incessantly railed against liquor intoxicants. So it came as no surprise that

Cognac bottle at City Hall

the anti-liquor lobby reviled the gaudy 15-foot ornamental brandy bottle that towered prominently for 17 years near the front door of City Hall. The gold-labelled, super-bottle became a Montreal landmark, as it dwarfed an adjacent newspaper kiosk from 1895. Nobody admitted to knowing how the giant advertising prop found itself implanted on such prominent real estate. The city had allowed news hawker Mondou to occupy the newsstand for free since 1877. But who, if anybody, okayed the prop brandy bottle remained a mystery. Montreal Sheriff Lemieux campaigned to remove what he described as a "disgraceful object" in 1911. Officials said they made all efforts to locate any contract or permission given to permit the landmark vessel on the grounds. They gave it a one-year notice and finally hauled it off in 1912. The newsstand was permitted to remain but the giant advertisement for drinking was never to return.

Food budget freezer flop Putting food on the table was a big challenge for many in the 1970s when the cost of groceries gobbled up about one quarter of the average family income, about double the current portion. Price-watching was a high-priority practice and vigilant coupon clippers would pressure stores with boycotts and demands to justify their price hikes. Dominion Provisions at 9009 Park Avenue attempted to harness that thrifty shopping demographic by launching a food subscription service in 1973. The company delivered an Amana home freezer to members, who would mail in a check-list of desired items, which the company delivered for a fee of $20. The effort failed, as have all subsequent attempts to make remote grocery shopping work.

Tattoo Gods of the Main Tattoo artists hold inky needle at the ready at over 40 dedicated Montreal parlors these days but such specialized venues were rare until recently. Boston's Ted Liberty was one of Montreal's earliest tattoo specialists, as he inked sailors at a pool hall on the Main near Viger in the early 1900s and continued decades later at a billiard hall at 1204 St. Lawrence. By the 1950s the best-known Montreal tattoo artist was Vivian "Sailor Joe" Simmons (1885-1965) who only inked in red and black, also from the back of a pool room after arriving in 1910. Simmons, deemed by the Guinness Book of World records to be the world's most tattooed man, mainly worked in Toronto and saw business explode during the fake beauty mark fad. Simmons once inked a legal will and testament on the back of a 65-year-old Newfoundlander, slept on his parlour floor and died of blood poisoning in 1965, possibly from black ink he made from lamp oil and molasses. Other skin scribblers included meticulously-clean Fred Baldwin, a Boer War vet who turned many on to tattooing from 1910 to 1920. Professor Paul inked loads of lovers' initials onto the skin of World War II conscripts and their girlfriends, while Joe Lavoie ran a tattoo shop at 997 St. Lawrence from 1939 to 1955. World War II veteran "Professor" Clément Demers (1916-1977) raised a family behind his International Tattoo Studio, Montreal's only dedicated tattoo parlour in the 1960s, at 1011 St. Lawrence. He drew many rose tattoos, popularized in the film of the same name but styles got nastier, as he noted in 1959. "Young people want more violent motifs, warriors, Nazi eagles, death skulls, daggers. A few years ago they were getting crosses or tributes to their moms. Right now the most popular are the cobra head and the German helmet," said Clement, who had 217 tattoos and worked until his death in 1976. More recently inker Frank Lewis helped transform Montreal street kid Rick "Zombie Boy" Genest into the world's most famous tattooed model.

Clément Demers

Poultry liberation

Nobody minded that Louis Tucker arrived early to kill chickens, ducks, pigeons, rabbits, geese and turkeys at his shop at the southwest corner of Roy and St.

Dominique until hippies Juergen Dankwort and Kevin Cohalan moved upstairs in 1970. The Chicken House Gang tolerated rodents and a tub in the living room but they could not abide the sound of animal death slaughter, which started at 6 a.m. So artist Maurice Spira drew up a Free The Chicken sign and posted it next to Tucker's commercial signage. A newspaper described the image as a "a heroic spread-eagled chicken leaping a brick wall and breaking its chains as the long awaited sunrise bursts forth from behind." "We are trapped poultry all," Spira pithily explained. The sign lasted a few months. Tucker's closed five years later.

Get your shine box

Polished shoes were an essential element of style that created the need for an army of professional brush boys in guilds like The Shoe Shine Parlour Operators of

Montreal and The Catholic Union of Shoe Shine Workers, which won its members minimum pay of $8 for a 69-hour work week in 1938. Montreal was home to 130 dedicated shoe shine parlours in 1930, including Fabien Biondi's, who raised 18 children with his earnings on the Main just north of St. Antoine from 1896 to 1964, employing lifelongers Louis Fusco, Sangolia Nicola and Salvatore Guadagno. Biondi liked his days lengthy, as the shoe-shining patriarch fought against early closing laws. Noted shoeshiner Joe Rizzo made mirrors on Montreal footwear for 16-hours a day at Phillips Square from 1922 to 1975, earning well enough to put a son through medical school.

The shouting shoe salesman

"So-o-o?! Are you going to buy those shoes!?" shoe store owner Ludy Karls would routinely bark at bemused footwear shoppers who dropped into 4259 St. Lawrence. If it was any consolation, Karls kept his harshest verbal abuse for employees at his perpetual jamboree of sonic punishment. If a shopper requested a different colour,

Karls would dispatch a salesperson to spray-paint the shoes and present the still-wet footwear to the customer. Karls bickered with firefighters who eventually ordered his unstable building evacuated, depriving Plateau bargain hunters a chance to access his unruly piles of shoes. Karls took to a lawn chair in front of his shuttered store and would furtively sneak in to fetch footwear for customers. A judge then ordered Karls to pay a contractor five times the amount of the bill he sought to reduce. Karls reopened but a knife-wielding maniac torched the building in February 2002. The combative Karls said that firefighters didn't try very hard to save his building.

Pharmacy freak out

Architect François Dallegret disliked his hometown so intensely that he ditched Paris in 1964 and created a swinging, avant-garde, op-art Montreal utopia of

modular plastic tables perched under phallic plaster stalactite lamps. Those undaunted by Robert Roussil's forbidding chain link sculpture at the entrance to 2125 Mountain could enter Le Drug pharmacy and the freaky downstairs restaurant that served up Scandinavian and Caribbean fare, as well hot dogs. The narrow building had room for an art gallery and Caty Lullier's fashion boutique that sold suits with fur collars and pyjamas designed to be worn to dance clubs. Perfume manufacturer and art sophisticate William Sofin and his well-heeled wife Beverly bankrolled the futuristic shopping project, which also included a disco operated by DJ Alfie Wade who lived upstairs for a time. But it all proved too rad and closed within a few years. Sculptor Roussil, who countered Dallegret by moving from Montreal to France, later complained bitterly that his landmark chain sculpture was sold for scrap.

Barber shops in freefall Rotating tricolor barber poles swirled colours proudly on about every Montreal street, avenue, boulevard and alley in the mid-1930s, as men had well over 1,000 barber shops to choose from at a time when the city was home only about one-third as many people. Men could hit Eddie's, Eddy's or Edrick's, or drop in on Godon, Golding, Gosselin or one of four Goulets for a shave and trim. But two-thirds of those barber shops disappeared within two decades, partially because competition was fierce. Montreal was home to

eight barber associations and—unlike cities like Toronto, New York and Ottawa where barbers charged $1.50 a cut—Montrealers could get snipped for as little as 35 cents. Barber shops went into freefall after 1967 when the twice-monthly barber visits became twice yearly visits for many newly-longhaired men. One Montreal barber was such an important historical figure that he was featured in a serious academic biography. Shadrack Minkins (aka Shadrach Minkens) was a freed slave who moved to Montreal after being busted out of custody by Bostonians outraged that authorities were attempting to return him to slavery. Minkins launched a restaurant called Uncle Tom's Cabin in the 1850s before opening his barber shop on Mountain between St. Antoine and St. James. He fathered two daughters with an Irish immigrant before dying in 1875.

Bank bans men If a man stumbled into the lone Montreal bank decorated with elegant drapes, lawns of broadloom, satin chairs, *Vogue* magazines and antique tables serving as counters, he would get promptly ushered out. The Bank of Montreal Ladies Branch served as Montreal's only gender-exclusive banking institution when it stood at the northeast corner of Mountain and Sherbrooke from 1967 to

1979. Customers were required to maintain a balance of $2,000 at the branch, where only the most charming tellers were recruited to work. The Bank of Montreal also unwrinkled another variation to the traditional bricks-and-mortar banking set-up when it opened what it called a Semi-Automatic Teller Machine at the Galeries d'Anjou in August 1968. There wasn't much automatic about the bank by current standards, which was placed in a retail island in the middle of a wide hallway. The CIBC opened Montreal's first automated bank machines in 1975. Customers were permitted to withdraw up to $30 cash at its 19 machines.

Frogs and bees protest Shoppers were forced to navigate bargain bins amid frogs and bees during an unconventional workers protest at the Dupuis Frères department store on May 17, 1954. Members of the Communist-

inspired National Federation of Labour Youth released the creatures into the crowded store at St. André and St. Catherine while shoppers snapped up discount hats, hosiery and lipstick at the 20 percent off sale. Sarah Tatigian and Gaby Dionne were arrested for their part in the stunt, with one report later noting that Dionne was such a promising Communist that she had been sent for special training in North

Korea one year earlier. About one-third of the store's 2,000 shop assistants had gone on strike two years prior, leading the store to replace them with security guards and store detectives. It became the first Montreal store to encourage shoppers to locate their own items in return for lower prices, a practice that soon become standard everywhere. In 1868 Nazaire Dupuis founded what would become the most-important department store for French-speaking Montrealers. It remained in family hands until 1961 and had 700 employees when it closed in 1978.

Catalogue shopping thrills Shoppers overwhelmed by the sensory stimulation of browsing through aisles favoured Consumers Distributing, where purchasing goods required grabbing a stubby pencil and scribbling a set of digits onto a form, then waiting as an attendant disappeared to fetch it, often returning with news that it was out of stock. Consumers Distributing launched in September 1971 with a 10-store Montreal roll-out advertised exclusively via home-delivered catalogue. The fat book of consumer items created an appetite

for cutting-edge Ronco Smokeless Ashtrays and easily-breakable electronic doodads made by companies like Yorx, Candle, Citizen and Sanyo. Jewelry and vibrators were big sellers in the 22 Montreal outlets while telephones sold well after 1979, when the government no longer required people to rent phones from Bell Canada. Consumers purchased the Steinberg's-owned Cardinal catalogue stores in 1978 while the Woolco catalogue shops closed the same year, with management blaming Quebec's language law for forcing them to send French-only catalogues to the anglo West Island. Shoppers could purchase items via home computer through Telidon, "the federal government's two-way television system" in 1983 but they still had to come to a Consumers outlet to collect their purchase. Provigo bought the Montreal outlets but the final stores were gone by 1996.

Old bottled water Bottled water has recently become the must-drink trendy consumer aquatic accessory but Montrealers have embraced it for over a century, as many imagined tap water to be rife with poison and disease. One pure water well was located downtown beneath a tannery at Montcalm and Notre Dame where management eventually valued water over leather, so they opened a public bath on the site and advertised it as a cure for typhoid. But then a bather drowned, leading the Wells and White families to transform the business into the Laurentian Water Company, while also opening a mail-order booze business during the Prohibition years. For decades, muscular deliverymen would haul a pair of 30-kg glass bottles of Laurentian water into homes and offices, occasionally leading to splashy accidents involving large puddles and broken glass. The huge glass bottles also frequently exploded at the factory when sterilized with boiling water. Laurentian eventually sold out to Labrador, which considered itself the inheritors of Laurentian's "over 100 years in business" title.

Fries to Italian toothpaste A million 1983 bucks were devoted to creating the 24-hour Lux, where shoppers could get a drink, munch fries, peer at magazines and tilt heads at oddball items. The multi-purpose emporium, bankrolled by thirtysomething physician Dr. Jean-Marie Labrousse and whipped into shape by designer Luc Laporte, was hampered by slow-arriving waiters with a low tolerance for night-owl spendthrifts arriving after the evening had sputtered out. The cavernous interior featured a pair

of industrial, curved staircases but 4 a.m visitors had little reverence for the magnificence, as they thumbed through low-cost menu options after blowing their wads in bars down the road. Curious offerings like toothpaste from Italy, toast with Cheez Whiz and a 50-cent vitamins didn't prove hot sellers but Lux offered a place to pose under halogen lamps while flipping through *Vogue* and *Details* without cashier disapproval. The copper-green bazaar at 5220 St Lawrence was a remote circus at a time when nightclub poles were anchored by Business and Di Salvio's close to Sherbrooke. The end was near when poetry reading sessions started in the bar upstairs during the endless 1990s recession. Lux closed in 1993 and is now an arty office space but it remains remembered for injecting imagination into a building where generations of workers at Kiddies Togs Manufacturing, Grand Cloak Manufacturing and Lyon Textiles once dripped blood from needle-pierced thumbs.

Hitting the dep Montreal's corner stores have been so central to the fabric of daily existence that even English-speakers call them by their French name: *dépanneurs*. Montrealers purchased 40 percent of their groceries from such stores as  recently as the early 1980s but the trusty and convenient mom-and-pop shops have since seen a steep decline. Quebec was home to 11,500 depanneurs in 1988, a total that decreased by half, as grocery store competitors were permitted sell beer and wine while sales of corner store staples such as newspapers, cigarettes and lottery tickets have declined. Government regulations have also punished the handy deps, forcing them to prove that a majority of their revenue does not come from beer and wine, while also banning video lottery terminals and cigarettes power wall displays, thus eliminating many revenue streams. Larger chains such as Couche-Tard have also purchased many of the family-run stores, removing the neighbourhood connection that made the depanneur experience exceptional.

The battle on the boards

Commercial signs have fought on the front lines of Montreal's war between sin and virtue since at least 1924 when priests denounced movie posters for undermining morality, with a cleric denouncing the poster for *Queen of Sheeba* as a "serious evil."

Mayor Jean Drapeau was so outraged by a poster of singer Muriel Millard's midriff and frilly panties that he ordered it removed in 1967, making it a collectors' item now worth over $500. Mayor Jean Doré's MCM administration also took aim at sexy signage, handing councillor Léa Cousineau a blank cheque to tame the gaudiness. She was emboldened by a 4,500-signature petition urging the city to eradicate smutty imagery. But Montreal free-speech advocates were no pushovers, as witnessed in 1986 when an art gallery won the right to display a picture of a woman holding an erect penis. And strip club owners were ready to dig in to defend their signs. Montreal backed down. But lurid signage diminished, partly as strip clubs stopped inviting performers whose seductive likenesses were placed at eye level.

From horse to java

Horse importing proved a lousy business in the early days of the automobile, so French immigrant Albert-Louis Van Houtte sought a new line of work

after he arrived in 1911. Van Houtte met an older Frenchman at a meeting of ex-pats and agreed to take over his little imported foods store at 321 Ontario E. Van Houtte continued the owner's tradition of roasting green coffee beans on site, which filled the shop with a rich and enticing aroma that encouraged shoppers to empty wallets. Van Houtte died in 1944 and his heirs moved to the southwest corner of Berri and St. Catherine. By the mid-1970s three Van Houtte sons Pierre, Gerard and Christophe had their own cafés. The family, which had four outlets in 1980, sold half of its shares and new management dealt franchises for $40,000 a pop. Within six years, 50 Van Houtte cafés dotted the Montreal area. It became a publicly-traded company in 1987 and gobbled up other coffee chains before returning to private ownership under an American fund two decades later. The company remains headquartered in Montreal and Van Houtte's face still adorns the company logo.

Hat tricking Scoring a hat-trick is a mandatory aspiration for any red-blooded Canadian but the three-goal dream would not have existed without Montreal's last-remaining men's hat store. Henri Henri at 189 St. Catherine E., has been selling derbies, top hats and workers' caps since Honorius Henri and Jean-Maurice Lefebvre launched it in 1932. The original cash

register and cabinets are still in use, while an ancient rotary phone is almost as old. The elk head mounted above the cash has not missed a sale of a Greek worker cap, top hat or derby since 1939. Henri Henri brass transported the hat trick concept to hockey from cricket by offering a free item to any NHL player who netted a trio of goals in Montreal. Bobby Orr, Gordie Howe, Stan Mikita and Maurice Richard earned free hats by notching three goals, but they all had to pose for photos in order to get the lid. Competitor Joe Solomon's Vogue Hats further west at McGill College took another approach to selling men's hats, as his clever quips ran in newspaper ads. They included such knee-slappers as: "I know a gal who went out with a guy and she said 'he may not be handsome but his money is so good looking.'" The bar was low, ladies and germs. Solomon's closed around 1960.

Juicy days of joy Heaven in Montreal was leaping off the banana bike to lay a nickel down for a bag of orange or purple liquid sugar sustenance. Connoisseurs would stab the clear plastic sip-sack with a narrow pointy straw and suck it back greedily. Those more gregarious might tear it open with their teeth and forgo the straw, while other  insolent souls would complete the ritual by blowing the emptied bag full of air and exploding it underfoot. Perrette's became an icon of urban ubiquity after Robert Bazos opened  his maiden outlet on Côte Vertu in 1961, growing the chain to 195 stores a dozen years later. Milk cartons featured a throwback "Perrette and the milk jug" verse that implied that a husband was justified for beating his wife as punishment for dropping items. Perrette's dangling blue-and-white sign became so deeply emblazoned on the Montreal psyche that former outlets still don't look right minus the sign. Couche Tard purchased and rebranded the stores in 1985.

Dying for head Quebec nationalism was on the rise in 1963 and Dow Brewery sought to milk the growing demographic by introducing Kébec Beer, complete with a label that imitated t  he provincial *fleur-de-lys* flag. But consumers proved surprisingly hostile to the new brand and expressed displeasure that their cherished symbol was being slapped on a stubby. Kébec Beer was quickly discontinued. The flop might have saved lives, as Dow had been secretly adding cobalt to their beer to give their brew a frothier head. Up to 20 heavy Dow drinkers died in Quebec City in 1965 and the once-powerful brewery rushed to dump its supply away before it could be analyzed. Dow shut down soon after.

Shoot-out in aisle four Montreal merchants routinely kept loaded handguns hidden under counters, ready to take aim at would-be stick-up men. None was more prepared for a shootout than pharmacist Wilfrid Gagnon, whose maiden gun battle happened in 1928 at his store at Villeray and St. Hubert when he came downstairs at night and shot an intruder dead. Then in 1960 a man armed with a starter's pistol attempted to rob the aging pharmacist, now in St. Henri. Gagnon calmly reached for his pistol and ended the man's life. A decade later

Gagnon

Gagnon, then 70, tried to shoot a thief but—much to his frustration—missed. Pharmacist Ben Nudelman offered a similar welcome to would-be thieves, wounding a knife-wielding robber in 1967 at Dale's Pharmacy at 5350 Sherbrooke W. and two years later pulling a .22 calibre pistol from his pocket when pretending to be getting cash to give the thief. Both fired at each other and missed. Police also favoured shooting at robbers for many years as proven by officer Robert Ménard who boasted that he gunned down many, explaining that it costs much less taxpayer cash to kill a robber than to put him in prison. Three Montreal corner stores were robbed daily on average in the 1980s and the bodies piled up. Dépanneur boss Guy Guilbault pulled out his .357 Magnum outside his depanneur at Logan and DeSève in 1986 and pointed it at a robber who begged for mercy. Guilbault shot him dead and was not charged with a crime, one of a long series of such incidents from that bloody era. Robbers frequently toted fake pistols, with one notable toy gun spree being orchestrated by David Darwin, 27, who was from a wealthy family but still felt compelled to undertake a half-dozen payroll heists using a fake gun and duct tape in 1953. The longstanding Wild West tradition of retail gunplay came to an end after prosecutors became increasingly less forgiving of vigilante merchants, once filing assault charges against a pair of South Shore corner store owners after they camped out and ambushed and beat on a 45-year-old cigarette thief in 2003.

Who needs doors? Shoppers couldn't find the door at the 24-hour Montreal Pharmacy at 916 St. Catherine Street E. after an heir to Charles Duquette's pioneering drug store

removed a set of expensive automatic doors in 1958. In their place was a big empty doorway, or what management described as a specially-designed air conveyance system that supposedly kept the store toasty even on the coldest of winter nights. So celebrated was the drug store that tourists were offered guided tours of the multi-level facility loaded with drawers full of mysterious powders and tablets. Brass vowed to undercut competitors when it first opened in 1923 and the strategy worked, as it grew to employ 175 workers, with a fleet of 57 cars delivering to customers up to 25 kilometres away. The pharmacy sold butter and

other non-medicinal items, leading rivals to sue for breaking pharmacy rules but the Montreal Pharmacy prevailed against two dozen lawsuits. Notable customers included the mobbed-up Cotroni clan, Mayor Camillien Houde and Bellevue Casino customers seeking perfume for their favourite dancers, who would often return the bottles for a discounted

price, allowing the store to sell the same bottle twice. The pharmacy became the first Jean Coutu franchise in 1973 and started closing at night for the first time in its 50 year history. The Jean Coutu chain repurchased the store a dozen years later and sold the building, ending a longstanding family business that began at a time when nuns grew strawberries in nearby fields, the mayor sported striped suspenders and saloons poured Gurd's root beer and sarsaparilla soda.

Beauty sells drugs Pharmacy king Jean Coutu made his fortune on physical beauty. No, the hamster-face, pill-pushing drug store god did not attract people with his gnarly chipmunk mug. Rather it was a heartthrob Montreal acting celebrity namesake who drove many curious customers into the Jean Coutu pharmacy. Though shoppers were disappointed in their quest to bump into hunky actor Jean Coutu, they left the pharmacy with arms full of aspirin, cigarettes and shoe insoles. Pharmacist Coutu played the beauty card at his first humble store in the East End where he hiked sales by adopting a gimmick employed in American stores. Coutu invited shoppers to submit photos of their kids for a vote to see

Jean Coutu
pharmacist and actor

which was the cutest. The more a shopper spent, the more they could vote, so items flew off the shelves as shoppers attempted to tilt the deck in their child's favour. Coutu went on to launch a chain of mid-sized stores which he called Pharmaterias, but a visit to Toronto taught him that big stores were the future so he opened the much-larger Pharm-Escompte on Mont Royal which was so packed with diapers, shoe polish and shampoo that the floor required reinforcement. Actor-director Xavier Dolan appeared on many Jean Coutu commercials as a child and later bizarre TV ads encouraged a cult-like adoration of the bland pharmacist. In one TV ad a waitress is paralyzed with awe in the old man's presence. In another, boys list their idols. One chooses Jean Coutu, "no that's too powerful," they agree.

Money in laundering Washing underwear 18 hours a day in steamy rooms before catching a couple a few hours of sleep on ironing boards was the fate of many Montreal Chinese after 1887. Hand laundry long remained almost the only game in town for Chinese at a time when Montreal had seven Chinese laundries for every Chinese restaurant. The first appeared in Montreal listings in 1877 as the Song Long Laundry, on what's now St. Antoine across from the courthouse. Others sprouted up nearby as Chinese laundries, many recognizable by their green doors, spread through the city, peaking at over 400 in the 1920s and city dwellers became accustomed to the sight of men clad in traditional Chinese clothing pulling wagons full of paper-wrapped clothing. Many Canadians viewed the earliest Chinese laundries with irrational suspicion, as Montreal labour activist Gus Franq denounced them at every opportunity. City Hall slammed them with a $100 annual tax in 1896 and white-run competitors schemed to undermine the Chinese grip on the laundry market by lobbying for higher license fees. The city threatened Montreal's 2,000 Chinese laundry workers again in 1926 with a bylaw that would have forced such laundries to make costly upgrades, as Father Roméo Caillié fought hard to quell the requirement. And yet many Chinese laundries outlasted the politicians, with the longest-lasting laundry being Sam Hing's at 2412 Centre, which closed in 1972 after 78 years. The last ones standing (notwithstanding a sporadically-opened place on Decarie) included gruff Charlie Chin's at 1235 Crescent where paper-wrapped clothing sat on a wall waiting for a ticket. Tom Lee's at 2114 St. Catherine W. also lasted until the early 1980s, its namesake owner heartbroken in 1959 when one son stabbed another to death.

Donkey vendetta murder

L'Echange is now a spot to purchase used CDs and paperbacks but in the early 1970s that exact location opposite the Mount Royal metro hosted a Mafia vendetta killing of the cruelest variety. Michel Gurreri fled to Montreal from Italy after testifying against Mafia friends who killed leftist politician Giuseppe Spagnolo of Bassina, Sicily in 1955. The assassins brought a mule to the killing and Italian police cleverly followed the beast as it ambled home to Gurreri's residence. He was jailed but was freed after rolling over on his three accomplices, including Leonardo Cammalleri, who moved to Canada, as did Guerreri in 1962. Gurreri was found tortured and beaten to death at his Miss Mont-Royal Restaurant in 1972, surely as punishment for ratting out his pals. The restaurant closed in 1975 and later became L'Echange. Cammalleri's daughter later wed Montreal Mafia capo Vito Rizzuto.

Spagnolo

Chubby wraps Miracle weight-loss clinics such as Therma-Slim, Lady Stauffer and Figure Magic blitzed into Montreal after 1971 with promises of instant slimming. "Lose undesired fat in only 90 minutes without strenuous exercise, strict diet, without expensive pills. You sit on a comfortable couch while the Figure Magic Method does the work for you. Results guaranteed in writing." Customers would have a mystery chemical applied to their bodies and were then wrapped in plastic. It didn't work and many complained, including one who was duped of $300. "I don't like to be taken for a fool. I used the slimming cream they sold me for $30 a jar and I only ended up smelling like a snail." The outlets, including 10 Figure Magic joints, disappeared in 1973 as suddenly as they sprouted up two years earlier, their owners fined and one, an Australian, deported.

8

Geography

Settlers couldn't resist messing with the snow-covered natural perfection of Montreal and so they filled the once-virgin landscape with roads, homes and skyscrapers that mostly outlived their creators. Come stroll through some memorable places.

Municipality of madness

A secretive Montreal mental health facility long formed a separate municipality that answered to no one. Gamelin consisted solely of the St. Jean de

Dieu mental hospital (later the Louis Hippolyte Lafontaine) and operated its own fire squad and train line that traveled both outside and inside the hospital. The chief doc of the Longue Pointe Insane Asylum (as it was originally known) sought to lower the head count, pointing out in 1879 that every Catholic saint would have been hospitalized for having religious visions. Editorials accused him of seeking to empty the asylum to lower costs, with an article outing patient Eliza Ackhurst as "apathetic and unable to attend to her personal needs" and Michael Row for being a "wicked and quarrelsome madman." The overpopulation was settled a decade later when 81 female and five male patients died in a fire that saw some patients dash into the flames. "We could see the flesh and skin peeling off them in the terrible heat, roasted before our eyes," read a report. Poet Émile Nelligan was

later treated at the facility, as was Premier Maurice Duplessis, who checked in to beat the bottle. Many healthy orphans were raised at the facility as part of the Duplessis Orphans scam to score federal funding while Dr. Heinz Lehmann's largytil, known as the chemical straitjacket, flowed

freely. The 1962 Bédard Report exposed tales of a child being chained to a radiator and a a staffer stabbing a patient in the eye. Gamelin municipality disappeared and the hospital was modernized.

Artwork at the cemetery Ethereal bronze angels offer wistful tribute to the dead at Montreal's stunning *Notre Dame des Neiges*, (aka Côte des Neiges) cemetery, thanks to artists

like Joseph Brunet, whose crew of 20 created monuments at a workshop on Remembrance Road. Some consider sculptor Alfred Laliberté's Broken Wings monument to be the most alluring art in the Catholic boneyard, although the sculptor's own 1953 marker was vandalized by thieves who made off with its bronze bust. Prudent Beaudry, who served as mayor of Los Angeles from 1874 to 1876, is also

commemorated with a particularly eye-catching memorial while newer works, including those remembering Robert Bourassa, Maurice Richard and Jean Drapeau have met with mixed reviews. One snazzy new-era exception can be found at the top of the hill, where a towering interlaced metal body reaches out from the grave of Pierre-Luc Dorsonnens, who died in 2002. Other notable Montreal headstones include John Laird McCaffrey's sneaky 1995 acrostic, as the 54-year-old offered the world an inspiring poem, with the first letters of each line offering the world an indelicate downward-reading F-You. Other unusual Montreal cemetery monuments include one proposed at the St. Francis of Assisi cemetery, which declined to allow a grocery cart manufacturer to celebrate his life with a lit-up rotating cart. He was honoured with a discreet grocery cart etched on his headstone. Another customer ordered his own headstone, complete with date of his own death. The perplexed manufacturer complied and chiseled the gravestone. When the day came the man died by his own hand.

Royal thugs of The Main

Montreal's defining roadway came with royalty that ascended throne not via regal bloodline but through violence and intimidation. The self-crowned King of the Main reigned over St. Lawrence Main Street with fists and threats before typically being deposed in swift underworld regicide. Tough guy Eddy Sauvageau offered bar owners legit protection from bandits when he became the first *Roi du Main* in 1957 but his relatively-benign rule ended after he beat his assistant Bruno Marinelli for $20,000 in a card game. Marinelli suspected that

Sauvageau

Sauvageau had cheated, so he shot the king dead, taxied to the police station and then killed himself at Bordeaux Prison. Peace returned to St. Lawrence, so successor Guy St. Onge had to justify his service to proprietors by providing the threat as well as the protection. His reign also lasted just a few months, as a rival plugged a pair of bullets in his chest as he ate a smoked meat sandwich at Frank's Deli. The next King of the Main ascended the blood-stained throne in 1959, controlling drugs and prostitution in the bars of the strip, extorting not just bar owners but also their busboys and waiters. Midway bar employee Yvon Verbile failed to pay his protection fee and when his debt rose to $50, new king Jean-Paul Servant ordered his boss to fire him. The frustrated and newly-unemployed Verbile got drunk at the Rialto bar and stabbed Servant and henchman Michaud dead. Later Kings of the Main included André Giorgetti, shot dead at his bar by an calm Italian assassin in 1963, the Poirier brothers, who were later nailed for murder, the bloodthirsty Dubois gang, early FLQ pioneer bomb-maker Gabriel Hudon, and more recently Joseph Ducarme who collected a tax from drug dealers in the various establishments on the boulevard before being felled by bullets in 2014. Around four-dozen people were killed on the Lower Main between 1960 and 1990.

Sun Life's hidden treasure Ask the one million square foot Sun Life Insurance building what it did during the war and it will spin a heroic tale of guarding a secret fortune.

After France fell to the Germans, British Prime Minister Winston Churchill tossed the dice on the riskiest cash gamble ever taken by a head of state when he evacuated $5 billion in treasury notes and gold and had it stuffed into 900 crates emblazoned with the label Fish.

Britain's massive fortune was loaded onto ships that braved enemy submarines en route to Halifax in 1941. The treasure landed in Halifax, was transported by train to Bonaventure Station and was then hauled to a massive vault in the third level basement of the Sun Life building where it was hidden in 9,000 four-drawer filing cabinets. Two dozen RCMP officers guarded the loot until the Brits spent it all on wartime debts. Not a cent was stolen and the stash remained a secret until it was dispersed. Drama returned to the Sun Life building on Jan. 6, 1978 when company president Thomas Galt informed workers that they would have to move to Toronto to keep their jobs, in a relocation

initiative later dubbed the worst public relations disaster in recent history. Only 500 of the 2,200 employees ended up following the company down Highway 401. The Sun Life building was the largest commercial building in the British Empire when it went up on two acres of land previously occupied by the YMCA's five-storey 1891 redstone facility. Granite for the Sun Life monolith was hauled from the Eastern Townships and includes two 15,000-kilogram blocks and 900 more weighing one third that size. The ornate interior is souped up with syenite, a dark green stone notoriously difficult to manipulate. Peregrine falcons nested on the roof between 1936 and 1953, once terrifying rooftop maintenance workers.

Beauty blamed on Protestants

Marguerite d'Youville's husband was a high-profile bootlegger, so when haters shamed her organization by calling them the *soeurs grise*, (drunk nuns) she let the name stick. The Grey Nuns set up at Dorchester and Guy near a red cross that has stood at the northwest corner since 1752, marking a grisly murder committed by the thief Bélisle, who was executed by "breaking

alive." The nuns complained that their Protestant neighbours insisted that their building be extra-posh in order to fit in with the area. So the humble sisters created an architectural gem with massive doors, neo-Roman chapel and stunning works of art, many donated by wealthy patrons when built between 1872-1902. The structure also housed d'Youville's tomb and basement catacombs containing the remains of 361 nuns from as long ago as 1752, causing some to worry that smallpox might spread if the remains were ever displaced. Their darkest moment took place on Valentines Day 1918  when an electrical fire spread up the curtains in the upper floors of the west wing, killing 65 of 170 orphans, many of them newborns, while wounded soldiers one floor below managed to get out. The nuns saw many of their charity endeavors taken over by government agencies and sought to downsize by selling the property to Swiss developers, a plan that would have seen much of the property demolished for an office tower in 1975. The plan was nixed and nuns steadily dwindled, with the 800-nun facility sitting over two-thirds empty in 2002, the youngest sister being aged 53. Concordia University now uses part of the facility for student dorms in an ongoing academic takeover to be completed in 2022.

Osborne obliterated Grass in front of Chateau Champlain once housed an epic downtown strip until it was eradicated by a doomed and misguided road plan carried out by

one-term mayor Sarto Fournier. Osborne Street was once home to landmarks Drury's Restaurant and the Alberta Lounge, where legendary jazz pianist Oscar Petersen played nightly. The buildings were sacrificed as part of a half-baked plan to connect De la

Gauchetière to Overdale and beyond to create an east-west route south of Dorchester. The plan was was abandoned in 1962, long after Osborne was needlessly wiped out. The surviving section of Osborne west of Peel—now Des Canadiens Street—fared little better, as its entire north side became parking. Osborne was where Protestant moms got help at the Diet Dispensary, Italians visited their consulate and shoppers bought horse-pulled vehicles and motorized REO Speedwagons. Lilian Gertrude Horsfinger introduced the 15-cent meal at her rooming house, feeding budget diners until 1929. The Roncarellis—later persecuted as Jehova's Witnesses—ran their first restaurant on Osborne Street and hundreds mobbed returning Spanish Civil War combatants on

Peterson

the street outside Windsor Station in 1939. The Khaki Club soldiers' canteen served meals around the clock during World War II. The all-night Casablanca blind pig had a role in the murderous 1946 Louis Bercovitch-Harry Davis gambling dispute. The fancy plan to hook the street up west became impossible when Oldfield Place was wiped from the map after 16 died in a blaze that wiped out its main building in November 1958.

Hippies vs. developers A motley cluster of hippie underdogs heroically saved the Milton Park district from greedy developers. Sadly, that uplifting narrative is only half-accurate, as 252 buildings were torn down in 1972 for the La Cité apartment complex. The battle started when self-proclaimed Communist-sympathizing developers from Concordia Estates promised to create something progressive by demolishing the venerable old properties. The Company of Young Canadians, a government make-work project embraced by fledgling radicals, teamed up

with others from the University Settlement community centre to mobilize against the expulsions. The developers responded by hiring veteran Communist Gerry Fortin, who later called himself "a sucker" for lobbying for the developers. Norman Nerenberg, one of the trio of developers, described his project as "the kernel of the future" and "a salute to life." The planned $250-million Cité Concordia would have laid waste to six downtown blocks. Tenants demanded to see the developers' plans but were rebuffed until a young resident obtained the documents from her father, an employee of the Ford Foundation, which was a major investor. In the documents the developers described the venerable old buildings as being full of roaches, bedbugs and vermin. Concordia Estates stormed back by placing a spy in the residents' committee but a disgruntled employee exposed the ruse. Hippies, radicals and draft dodgers held sit-ins, demonstrations and hunger strikes and hauled placards with such slogans as "Milton Park and Vietnam: It's the same War!" The protesters lobbied investors until they divested and also guilted chief architect Ray Affleck into quitting the project but not before wrecking ball did its damage and La Cité became a concrete beast towering over Park Avenue.

Bikers and their bunkers Bulletproof protection formed a must-have component of biker home décor, as motorcycle gangs souped up their bunkers with every protection device short of a moat. Hells Angels-

affiliated Rockers moved into an Angus Yards-adjacent Rosemont bunker at 2887 Gilford in 1993 where André "Toots" Tousignant told a reporter that bikers spent their time listening to classical music. He neglected to mention the cash-weighing, cocaine cutting and beatings that also took place in the home, or the time he picked up a bomb left outside, defused

Huron Street biker bunker

it and tossed it into a field. Police routinely inspected the home and harassed bikers entering and exiting. But the law was unable to do more and neighbours were not amused when a bomb exploded outside in March 1995. Two Rock Machine bikers were killed delivering a bomb at a rival Jokers bunker in rural Quebec later that summer and the intended victims kept some of their rivals' bones in a jar as a keepsake. Hells Angels bikers bombed a Rock Machine bunker on Huron Street in October 1995, leading the fire

Tousignant

department to padlock it as a safety hazard, as well as a bunker on Gilford. The province later allowed municipalities to ban steel doors, bulletproof windows and video cameras. Montreal expropriated the Rock Machine's Huron Street quarters (south of Ontario and Delorimier) and demolished it in 2001 for a park. The bunker on Gilford became condos. An Outlaws gang clubhouse at 4805 Cazelais was felled by fire and is now a vacant space known locally as Bikers Garden. About 165 people were killed and 180 injured in the biker war between 1994 to 2001. Legislation outlawed the gangs, although the Montreal Hells Angels still maintain a haven in Sorel, well upriver from where they represent.

Killer maidens

Four majestic stone canephorae—Greek maiden statues—towered high overhead on a 22-metre high perch at the Provincial Bank of Canada building at 221 St. James Street W. in 1908. For eight decades New York sculptor H.

Augustus Lukeman's massive stone statues representing Industry, Agriculture and Fishing peered down benignly on the business district, but the fourth statue, Transportation, proved less harmless when it dropped a detached arm while being cleaned by a sandblasting machine in 1978, killing the son of a board member. Developers Mario and Brian Cytrynbaum removed the landmark statues for repairs in 1990 and deposited them at Entreposage Beloeil Inc. The Cytrynbaums planned to house the statues inside their $100-million hotel project a few blocks west. But the hotel was never built and the warehouse owner sued the Cytrynbaums for $27,000 in unpaid storage bills. The province of Quebec acquired the statues and placed them inside the archives on Viger near Berri where they now stand sheltered in a hallway.

Bridge over nothing

No Montreal spot offered more majestic rust belt grandeur than the Guy St. bridge over nowhere, a 60-metre overpass built in 1931 and demolished in 1987. The

bridge initially offered a view of Montreal's fast-growing skyline and of steam trains barreling to and from the Grand Trunk Railway's Bonaventure Station below. After the tracks were removed, the structure pointlessly spanned a barren expanse of of mud, rocks, dandelions, strewn cans and candy wrappers, as lofty wanderers crossing between St. Antoine and Notre Dame were left to wonder why a bridge hovered over such barren scrubland. Pedestrians withstood piercing winds on ambulatory passage under yellow-lit winter sunsets, ambling towards the shiny Golden Square Mile from a down-at-the-heels St. Henri full of forlorn spots like Bar Victoire and the Salvation Army. A span four blocks east at Mountain offered a similar but less-breathtaking view of downtown. The muddy grounds below were eventually built up with affordable condos, leaving neither trace nor fragment of the elevated crossing that long sparkled pointlessly overhead.

Folly on the Main The gas station at the corner of the Main and Sherbrooke was once home to an eccentric mansion nicknamed Torrance's Folly, a title critics devised to mock its

unreasonably remote location, as it sat amid babbling brooks and fields of wildflowers far from the buzzing St. James Street. Steamship magnate Thomas Torrance moved into 1 Sherbrooke W. with his seven daughters in a home that contained a magnificent spiral staircase and mysterious tunnels. Torrance remained only seven years before selling the home to beer tycoon John Molson in 1825. Four generations of Molsons occupied the home until John Molson III died in 1907. It then went mostly vacant until United Automobile Supplies started selling gas at the site in 1924. Every spot needs it

Torrance

tragedy and so that same year Mrs. Henri Lavallée became the first woman to be charged with manslaughter in a car accident after crushing Abraham Finger at the gas station. Finger, 38, had just sold his bakery and bought his train ticket out of town. The mansion burned in 1935, its remains demolished two years later and its mysterious tunnels sealed off. The Torrance family went on to own another impressive-but-doomed mansion near the now-barren downtown street that still bears their family name.

Tanning riots The Plage Laval—or the Plage Beach as some anglos redundantly called the sandy spot in northwest Laval—was a hotspot for sun worshipers until it was overrun by

violence. The Plage Laval district was home to just 300 residents in 1930 but almost 20 times that total would hit the sands on hot summer days. The area grew to 1,500 residents in 1950, split almost evenly between French and non-French. Local thugs disliked the newcomers and bullied them at the Cosy Corner Restaurant one day in July 1943. Tensions grew as the same troublemakers showed up a week later and started a massive 75-combatant free-for-all brawl. Among the injured was Moe Herscovitch, a Romanian-born former Canadian Olympic boxer and war veteran. Moe was sipping on a soda pop along with his wife and another couple when he was punched and kicked so savagely that he lost an eye. René Bolduc, the son of the Laval police chief, was behind the assaults and was eventually jailed for two days as a draft dodger. The incident sparked probes and worried editorials. Regulars stopped showing up at the beach. Jewish homeowners reported that they feared for their lives. Pollution forced the beach to close after WWII.

Invisible taunting borders Smart alecks seeking to ridicule police officers could start their excessive consumption listening to Johnson the black banjo player at Omer Vallières'

hotel on the south side of Mount Royal at St. Lawrence, a hotel that sat in the Saint Jean Baptiste municipality, which joined Montreal in the 1840s. The Wiseman Hotel, right across the street, sat in the separate municipality of Saint Louis du Mile End, a town with its own police force. Drunken rowdies could cause a ruckus in Montreal and then flee across Mount Royal Ave. into Saint Louis de Mile End, where Montreal police had no jurisdiction. One day Montreal cop John Spedding tired of dodging projectiles launched from across the street, so he rushed to his home next to the police station at Laurier and St. Denis, changed into civilian clothing and gave his tormentor, now sleeping on a bench, a serious beat-down. Speeding was fined $8 for the assault. There were no hard feelings between the two, however, as the man later showed up to help Spedding in an altercation with rowdy dock workers. The Vallierès and Wiseman hotels are long gone but history notes that Robert Wiseman of the hotel-owning family was "considerably injured" when tossed from his horse at the nearby Exhibition Grounds in 1870 and his arm amputated five years later after he was bitten by a dog.

Mill the thrill Mill Street is now known as a barren industrial wasteland that drivers endure as a shortcut form Old Montreal to the Victoria Bridge. But under the thin veneer of melancholy echoes a thousand jubilant moments, as the street was where one would check into the stately Exchange Hotel while bidding on a horse in the 1880s. Mill was home to The

Exchange Hotel Mill Street

Driving Grounds, where Buffalo Bill and his team of 150 performed before 8,000 spectators for a week in August 1885. The stadium also hosted Montreal's earliest pro baseball games, creating a furor in 1888 when the visiting Clippers complained that the hometown Montreal Beavers cheated by hiring ringers from Albany. The area is accessible from Old Montreal via Black's Bridge over the Lachine Canal, a storied span that once rose upwards for ships seeking passage. From 1819 Thomas McCord, who developed Griffintown, lived in a spooky house next to the bridge called The Grange. Mill Street gradually lost its charm, becoming home to a collection of stockyards and other commercial facilities.

From bones to passports The Guy Favreau Complex is where Canadian would-be travelers get their people-watching fix while waiting to get passports issued and renewed. But before 1847 the same spot was a gateway for a final visit to the afterlife. A verdant oasis full of wild roses, daisies and lush green grass sat

alongside somber headstones at what was alternately called The Dorchester Cemetery, Dufferin Square Cemetery, St. Lawrence Burial Grounds and The Protestant Cemetery. Dorchester Boulevard was widened in 1860 and many coffins were unearthed, one exposing a corpse that still had "beautiful, long flaxen hair." Authorities feared the downtown corpses might cause a cholera outbreak, so they ignored some save-the-cemetery opposition and moved the skeletal remains to Mount Royal in 1871. Bodies transported included that of typhus shed hero Rev. Mark Willoughby, who selflessly tended to Irish immigrants at the cost of his own life and Jane Davidson, originally buried in the first Protestant cemetery near St. James and St. Peter way back in 1790. The emptied cemetery became Dufferin Square and could be a sad spot, according to Dorothy Livesay's 1933 poem: "Hardly anyone plays there. Along the benches, sitting near the sand-piles men with unchildlike, wrinkled faces are huddled together. In small groups they dominate the playground. Solidly round the square they watch the wind." Modernity killed much of adjacent Chenneville Street, home to a first wave of Irish immigrants. The street also housed Montreal's second synagogue, which lasted from 1838-1890, while nearby food pioneer Arthur Lee later baked Montreal's first bilingual fortune cookie. Robert Campeau built the Complexe Guy Favreau in 1984 but bricks mysteriously tumbled down from the structure, requiring $8 million in repairs.

Lenny's creative cauldron Artists are the shock troops of gentrification, as a Montreal graffiti noted and a span of St. Dominique north of Rachel, supports the notion. Its artsy  transformation began after people spotted playwright Raymond Garneau banging out scripts all day on a manual typewriter at a window, with sign reading *Do Not Disturb: Artist at Work.* Sculptor Morton Rosengarten saw that it was a good place to create, so he purchased the ramshackle cold water duplex at 4307 St. Dominique, which still has an old bathtub retrofitted in a common area. Musician Leonard Cohen followed, purchasing the building at 28 Valliers in 1971, embracing the same rundown area his parent's generation was so anxious to flee. Soon the street became what photographer George Gurd called a cauldron of creativity, as rocker Michel Pagliaro and filmmakers Derek May and George Unger and others moved to the street derisively dubbed St. Dump. They lived cheek-to-jowl with new immigrants on a street so intimate that pedestrians could hear snoring from the sidewalk. Cohen once serenaded an elderly Polish neighbour with an early-version of his classic *Hallelujah* and knew it was special when the babushka-clad woman started singing along. Cohen eventually said farewell to Marie-Anne and left for Los Angeles and the tribe dispersed. Cohen grew up at 599 Belmont in Westmount where, at the age of nine, he sewed a note to his deceased father into a bow tie and buried it the garden. He spent the rest of his life metaphorically "digging in the garden. Maybe that's all I'm doing, looking for the note." Cohen later met a Spaniard playing flamenco guitar at the Murray Hill tennis court about 10 metres from the garden. The Spaniard gave teenager three guitar lessons and but failed to show up for the fourth session. Cohen learned that the mystery guitarist had killed himself. He credited the stranger with teaching him the "guitar pattern that has been the basis of all my songs and music."

Mount Royal dreaming Montreal could have boasted an epic cable car line from the mountain to St. Helen's Island had somebody acted on a brilliant plan forwarded in 1895, one of countless proposals for Mount Royal park that never went forward. The next year dreamers proposed a tower atop the mountain, with a railway, theatres, hotels, balloon rides and parachute jumping. Some of the seemingly-unlikely plans came to being, however, as 5-km mountain tunnel was completed in 1913, allowing trains to pass between the Town of Mount Royal

and downtown. Eleven years later kids raised enough cash to fund the giant cross that stands atop the mountain. (Its horizontal arms were originally designed to be used as observation decks but nobody got to sit on them except for separatist protester Hans Marotte, who camped out on the cross several decades later). The chalet and lookout were built in 1932 and Beaver Lake was filled in 1938. Mayor Camillien Houde sought to build a nine-story tower on the mountain, while another wartime proposal would have placed a metro station beneath Mount Royal with an elevator rising to the top of the mountain. The tunnels would have doubled as an air raid shelter that could protect 60,000 Montrealers from enemy bombs. After the war many lobbied to build roads over the mountain, an idea opposed by English leaders but viewed more favourably by French-speakers. Mayor Jean Drapeau sought to extend University Street over the mountain while adding another zig-zag mountain road to Park and Mount Royal. That never happened but Drapeau ordered thousands of trees chopped in order to dissuade perverts from using the space for outdoor hook-ups. Other facilities were carefully considered, such as a museum, indoor skating rink and indoor horseback riding facility. The plans were all shot down except for a police station, which opened in 1960.

Pink pill mansion George Taylor Fulford bought a patent for Pink Pills for Pale People from McGill-trained Dr. William Jackson in 1890 and made a fortune selling the coloured iron supplements before becoming the first Canadian to perish in a car crash, in 1905. Daughter Martha inherited the fortune but her husband died of cancer, so she remarried the sturdier Charlie Maclean, a poor-but-athletic Scot from Point St. Charles. Alas Martha was the next to go, succumbing in childbirth. Their baby died soon after as well.

Maclean

MacLean suddenly controlled the vast Fulford iron supplement fortune. He remarried and built the impressive Stewart Hall on Lakeshore Boulevard in Pointe Claire. MacLean complained that the municipality of Pointe Claire charged him too much in taxes, so he got vengeance by transferring the property to the tax-exempt Fathers of St. Croix, who used it as a farm. Pointe Claire acquired the property in 1962 and eventually transformed it into its current vocation as a library and community centre.

Oops! Wrong house Thousands of Montrealers were so ruined by the Great Depression that many homes were seized by banks and municipalities after loans and taxes went unpaid. Towns suddenly became large-scale landlords and managed great swathes of property. Lachine couldn't find buyers, so the riverside municipality rented the homes out, lowering prices annually to maintain good tenants. Occasionally Lachine was forced to demolish buildings and in 1936 a crew knocked down a building on St. Joseph between 6th and 7th Ave. The wrecking crews did a sterling job and returned home with the satisfaction that comes from demolishing the wrong house. Homeowner Louis Clement demanded $800 in compensation. The land still sits empty.

Weather reports in the sky

A 31-metre weather beacon atop the Canada Life building near St. Alexander reigned for almost a decade as the highest-reaching structure on Dorchester Boulevard. The luminescent

electric obelisk beamed weather tips from on high, as green lighting promised good climes, while red meant grab the umbrella or scarf or just leave town. Concentric white rings moved up or down, depending on which was the mercury was headed, although many observers were likely obelisk-illiterate, without the slightest clue what it all meant, although those on LSD said they could appreciate it on a deep level. The tower imitated Canada Life's still-standing Toronto beacon and contained 2,500 bulbs and 200 metres of neon tubing, which kept a repairman busy. Mayor Jean Drapeau attended the April 1956 ribbon-cutting and was still in power when it was removed far less ceremoniously 20 years later.

Early adopting

The Redpath sugar clan were avid early adopters, as proven at 3457 Du Musée, which became the Montreal's first home with electric lighting fueled by gas

generator. The 1886 redstone Queen Anne-style home was also the first with a telephone, allowing Redpaths to better pick up the device and gossip about the smallpox epidemic and Louis Riel's treatment. Francis Redpath was the second Montrealer to own an automobile at a time when street parking was a breeze and parallel parking skills largely unnecessary. The mansion went empty 1928 to 1969, as Francis Redpath chose to live elsewhere. The Sochaczevski family purchased it and long lobbied for permission to raze the uninhabited gem. They eventually obtained provincial permission to demolish the historic mansion in 2014.

Scattered geese Goose Village residents complained that the deathly stench emanating from the nearby tanneries and stockyards was so bad that they needed to keep their windows

closed at all times. "Blood runs out into the street and people can't pass and it stinks badly. Americans hold their noses when they pass over Victoria Bridge," one 1961 resident told reporter Bruce Garvey, a hard-drinking scribe with a reputation for polishing up quotes. People and cattle could not co-exist, so authorities sided with the beasts and expropriated and demolished the homes in 1964. The isolated neighbourhood was home to the Matticks family of West End Gang fame and saw occasional tensions, such as when Thomas Matticks, a father of 14, irritated a store owner by playing dice

out front, leading the merchant to attack him with a knife. Bulls occasionally escaped from the stockyards and stomped free in the area, while a resident desperate for beer shot his neighbour in 1945. Guides derisively referred to the area as Hobo

Town in 1948, causing some outrage. The 1964 demolition was seen as a costly waste, possibly motivated by Mayor Jean Drapeau's dislike for gadfly councillor Frank Hanley. Some speculated that Drapeau ordered Goose Village demolished because he feared it might give a negative impression to tourists arriving on the Victoria Bridge to get to Expo 67. After the demolition, city planners renounced the slum clearance philosophy, denouncing it as a "bulldozer complex" and vowed to approach things differently in the future. Former residents met in 1981 in a futile effort to rebuild.

McGill kills Prince of Wales Terrace

Potato patches flourished and cold springs flowed at now-busy corner of Peel and Sherbrooke before it became a chic place to live for

bigwigs like McGill President William Peterson and tobacco magnate William MacDonald, who moved into the Prince of Wales Terrace after it went up in 1859. Peterson dropped in on his pal

MacDonald's place one day, walking past an elegant porch, tall front door, statue-filled alcoves and up a graceful staircase. Peterson was hauling a brand new contraption, a record player. MacDonald got spooked. "I don't like it at all! It's uncanny!" he said before storming out. MacDonald had reason to be cranky, weeks earlier in 1895 his tobacco plant on Ontario Street was hit by a fire that killed four female employees. He had recently cancelled his insurance, convinced that his structure was fireproof. The Prince of Wales Terrace was doomed by a 1962 provincial law that gave McGill University the right of expropriation over the area bounded by Sherbrooke, University, McGregor and Peel as well as homes on McGregor, McTavish, Pine and Mountain. McGill chief Stanley Frost exploited the law to demolish the row of buildings. "We thought of restoring it but it would have cost a million and a quarter dollars. But what would we have done with it? People aren't interested in old buildings anymore," he said. So the building went down in 1971 and the cement poured for the Bronfman

MacDonald & Peterson

Building. McGill also razed some 19th century homes on University and McTavish, as well as three Victorian mansions on Redpath.

Gurus of Ridgewood Ridgewood Avenue emerged from the trees after World War II to snake up Mount Royal's eastern flank and offer thousands of affordable apartments on a meandering streetscape. The newly-built road, featuring many buildings shaped to look like crosses from above, was home to a 1950s rivalry between two eccentrics who sought to mentor young beatniks. Colin Gravenor, a developer, wartime anti-Nazi leader and writer for the *Midnight* scandal tabloid, offered odd jobs to young men like Alfie Wade and Billy Georgette and plied

them with unlimited customized Freudian inspirational bootstrapping speeches and dietary advice, all guaranteeing shortcuts to success. Meanwhile Stafford Harriman, a one-armed, diabetic, alcoholic, electroshock therapy patient, mystic and seller of shares in salted asbestos mines also vied for influence. So brazen was Harriman about his stock market swindles that he penned a *Saturday Evening Post* article entitled "How to Sell Phony Stocks To American Suckers" in 1952 and yet he still never got caught.

Wade described Harriman as a "crazy wisdom master with flashes of deep metaphysical insight." Harriman enjoyed peyote, marijuana and loads of booze and walked away from a massive swindle opportunity, choosing to devote his later years to

Gravenor & Harriman

rooftop meditation. Ridgewood was also home to poet Irving Layton who lived on the curly avenue from 1958 to 1960, while Premier Maurice Duplessis' Montreal girlfriend Mrs. Massey hosted the premier's late-night booty calls on Ridgewood until he died in Sept-Îles in September 1959. Some pious, elderly residents of the serpentine street believed that Duplessis died while making love in the apartment and would solemnly make the sign of the cross while passing the building.

Brutality beneath the hill Griffintown supplied infinitely more mayhem than shown in the go-to tale of Mary "The Headless Hooker" Gallagher, a prostitute decapitated by

2 kids freeze on Young 1879

rivals in 1879. Police feared to tread in the area thanks to drunks like boxer Cornelius Dear who smashed Constable Baique over the head with a spade in 1874. Young Street, or Kempt as it was first known, was the nastiest spot of all. Young St. was where Mary Denvers tossed Sarah Sheedy off a third floor balcony, earning herself six months in jail. Drunks Eliza Doran and Thomas McCaffrey allowed their two children to freeze to death at an unheated, unfurnished home on Young 1879. Young residents pelted rocks at police when they came to arrest Alexander Thomson for having his bulldog attack a butcher's dog on Young in 1874. Mrs. Wiggins, 40, drank herself to death on Young in June 1875 as did a neighbour woman eight months later. Lloyd Chapman, who moved to Young from London, England in 1907, starved to death six years later, as he was too ill to work, leaving two sick children and a pregnant widow. Griffitown bullies would, "attack individuals alone–grossly insulting women and terrifying children, kicking at the doors of residences of Protestants and demanding young men supposed to belong to the Orange Order be brought out so they might reek vengeance upon them," read a 1878 description. Ne'er-do-well Johnny "Get Your Gun" Henratty was so disliked that he'd seek protection at the police station at 217 Young, where he died in a jail cell in 1913. The station, one of the few old buildings left standing on the street, closed in 1935. Reformist city councillor Herbert Ames detailed the difficult living conditions in the neighbourhood in highly detailed and moderately depressing report in the 1890s.

Quarrymen with dirty feet Des Carrières Street alone spurns the Plateau street grid, as it follows quarries that coughed up rock for such landmarks as the Notre Dame Cathedral and the Bonsecours Market. Quarrymen earned the nickname Pieds Noirs, Blackfeet, because they would prop up

Blackfeet party

their dirty feet up on their balcony railings after 12 hours of break-breaking work. The hard-drinking workers feuded with the Yellow Bellies east of the Main and the Silk Stocking Irish of Griffintown, so-named for their too-short pants. The Blackfeet also feuded with the Cleric-Doctors student gang, who controlled turf near Ontario and St. Denis. One rock-tossing battle between the rivals was only quelled after firemen doused the combatants with hoses. Blackfeet were enthusiastic francophiles, once providing a rousing welcome to a French politician who returned to France and raved about their Herculean strength. The Blackfeet were avid boxers and an 1890 fight between 265-lb Édouard Perrault and stocky James Haney saw both combatants suffer serious injury. Blackfoot Joseph Prud'homme was so swift-of-foot that hotelier Tom Wiseman brought him to United States where he outran all challengers. Blackfeet brawls at the nearby Exhibition Grounds prompted authorities to build a new courthouse and jail cells in the area. Police arrested 300 in 1897 and six times that total the next year, as rowdies were incarcerated for up to six months in the new facility. The Blackfeet intimidated voters uninclined to vote Liberal and broke many out of smallpox quarantine in 1885. The group eventually disappeared as quarries gradually closed, after extraction grew too costly, often requiring dynamite. A French politician gave a speech at Lafontaine Park in 1934 wistfully asking whatever became of the Blackfeet gang.

Staircase immunity

An exoskeletal vertical transport system attached to the front of houses has made Montreal immediately recognizable around the world and supplied proof that its residents are sufficiently well-balanced to navigate icy staircases.

The British-inspired outdoor staircase design was favoured because it maximized indoor space and served as a space-saving architectural response to a setback bylaw that forced homes to be built further from sidewalks. Legend suggests that clergy favoured the design because it eliminated indoor stairs, seen as a covert place for people to commit sinful acts, in a time when the Catholic Church also denounced tobogganing because of the way it got riders straddling each other. The outdoor staircase brought dignity and pride to tenants by giving them their own dedicated doorways, as under 10 percent of Montrealers owned their own homes in 1925 compared to about 55 percent in Toronto. Some city councillors led a campaign against the stairs in 1928 saying that the stairs "disfigured" parts of town, claiming they looked like ladders, are dangerous in the winter, require more repairs and make properties more difficult to sell. Jean Chauvin and Dr. Romeo Boucher wrote a book slamming the outdoor stairs but a city sanitary

engineer credited the exterior steps with saving many buildings that might have been demolished, as homes with stairs indoors were often seen as "breeders of disease," while buildings with outdoor staircases were believed to be better-ventilated.

Fairies of Old Montreal Montrealers might wonder why the words Fairy Land are etched in stone at 480 St. Francois Xavier, a whimsical inscription that many assumed to be a

reference to Ponton Costumes, which until recently occupied the premises for 30 of its 150 years in Old Montreal. The stony signage was created by and for property owner James Fairie, who had similarly named his previous home at University and Dorchester (a site later occupied by the St. James Club and then Place Ville Marie). When Fairie purchased the building in Old Montreal, he etched the same words in the stone facade to mark his turf and celebrate his specialness. Combined with the early-era flickering gas lights, the promise of fairies gave the location a surreal air for several decades. A plywood sign then covered the letters until 1956.

A movable palace Montreal's Crystal Palace was as original as a knock-knock joke when built at Peel and St. Catherine, where the Dominion Square building now occupies

the signature intersection. The glass-and-steel, greenhouse-like structure was rushed together in time for a royal visit in 1860 and builders had a pretty good idea how to assemble it, as it was a knockoff of models in London, Toronto and New York. Its pre-fab modular design proved useful after a land dispute forced it from its downtown perch. Before moving, it served as a hotel, a playhouse and meeting place where over 1,000 revelers feasted and slept in celebration of St. Jean Baptiste Day in 1875. It was transported to the Exhibition Grounds at what's now Jeanne Mance Park in 1877, where it served as a smallpox isolation clinic during the 1885 epidemic. It later burned to the ground.

Swastika and other streets

Swastika Avenue sat in the heart of downtown Montreal from around 1915 to 1934, when the ancient symbol was seen as a good luck charm. The

Former Swastika Ave.

half-dozen residents of Swastika lived behind what is now the high rise apartment tower at Ste. Famille and Sherbrooke but things got awkward when the swastika was appropriated by German Nazis. Alderman Schwartz quipped, "The name suits it, it's full of rats." Swastika was renamed Place Ste. Famille soon after. Other lost Montreal streets include Amity, Busby, Cadieux, Chaboillez Square, Conway, Evereta, Fulford, Glackmeyer, Gonzague, Hanotaux, Hays, Hood, Hopper, Josephat, Joslin, Jubilee Court, Judge, Jurors, Kedleston, Kelly, Lannes, Latin Terrace, Leon XIII, Lauretta, Little Manufacturers, Longueuil Ferry Lane, Lymburner Lane, Marlborough, Market Square, Martel Lane, Meanie, Mullarkey, Nepigon, Ney, Oller, Oxenden, Kinkora, Painchaud Lane, Pea Lane, Peck, Plateau, Prenoveau, Suzanne, Shuter and Swiss Lane.

Circle jerks aim for upgrade

It's hard to keep up with the wealthy Jonses but residents of Circle Road attempted nonetheless, as they made a bid to join Westmount even though

the two areas are not contiguous. That inconvenient geography failed to deter 98 percent of Circle Road residents from signing Richard Simon's petition to join Westmount in 2000. Their quest was shared also by residents of streets such as Mira, Iona, Glencairn, Meridian and Ponsard and was inspired by a quest for better snow removal, lower taxes, a cuter library, more English services and increased home values. The failed proposal would have created an unprecedented, separate enclave of Westmountness, a sort of Beemer-driving municipal equivalent of Cold War West Berlin.

Westmount rock'n'roll heaven

The promoter genius behind The Spice Girls was once saved from Montreal homelessness by Martin Melhuish of 7 Burton Ave in Westmount, who provided a stranded Simon Fuller and his The

Teen Beats a roof after they ran out of cash while touring their *I Can't Control Myself* album in 1979. Singer Patsy Gallant previously lived in the home when her song *Sugar Daddy* charted and singer Nanette Workman also inhabited in it for a time before music journalist Melhuish took it over after moving from Toronto in 1976. The house became a jamming space for musicians ranging from rocker Frank Marino to synth pop stars Men Without Hats. Assorted party animals enjoyed the basement sauna after evenings of nightclub bacchanalia and radio host Doug Pringle regularly interviewed big name rock stars from the home before Melhuish returned to Toronto in 1983.

Collapsing homes

The green space at Liverpool and Coleraine was once inhabited by a dilapidated duplex that fell into disrepair after George Yates' inheritors disclaimed ownership. The abandoned structure became a place for neighbours to pilfer wood and bricks. Years of Jenga-like pillaging led to disaster one Wednesday afternoon in 1936 when kids playing inside heard the building shift. The house collapsed on nine-year-old Douglas Norman, who was crushed by a beam

to the forehead. His father Arthur Norman was told the bad news after returning from his work as a welder at the nearby CNR shops. Two other kids escaped unharmed. The dead boy's father sued the city for $848 and was awarded $639, as had Montreal neglected to demolish the unsteady structure. The City of Montreal attempted to appeal the ruling.

Drapeau's housing battle The sprawling *Habitations Jeanne Mance* social housing project south of Ontario from The Main to near St. Denis created a vicious political battle that

almost curtailed the career of a young Mayor Jean Drapeau, who despised the plan and dramatically warned it would "present a psychological block between east and west and its two great races." Drapeau made it a prime issue and lost to Senator Sarto Fournier in a mob-assisted ballot-stuffing municipal election affair of 1957. When Drapeau returned, the 4,000 residents were gone and the new subsidized housing was built. Previous residents included Romeo Proietti who lost four children to a 1958 fire. Surviving daughter Monica "Machine Gun Molly" Proietti joined the bank robbing industry and was gunned down by police in 1967. The project cost twice as much low-cost housing as it created.

Tunneling a lobby The 288-unit Drummond Court was the Commonwealth's largest apartment building when it opened in 1923 but as Montreal grew, it found itself stuck in middle of

traffic, as the blockage on Burnside denied what's now De Maisonneuve its destiny as a legit east-west artery. Demolition was out of the question, so the city purchased it and excavated a $1 million hole through the first floor in 1956. For four decades Montrealers enjoyed the shadowy thrill of strolling through a lobby-turned-roadway, which contained a couple of well-sheltered locales like the John Bull Pub. Slumlord Guenter Kaussen made it part of his dilapidated housing portfolio until he hanged himself from the pipes of his German condo in 1985. The YMCA purchased it four years later but balked at the $7 million in required repairs and eventually received permission to evict the last tenants and demolish in 1998, creating a much airier look at the corner.

Nazis on Drummond Straight armed salutes, heel clicks and lusty cries of *Seig Heil!* reigned at The Harmonia Club at 1173 Drummond, a German cultural centre which started as a sleepy place for leisurely chess matches. But after Adolf Hitler came to power it was suddenly packed with Nazis who sang the *Horst Wessel Lied* to celebrate Hitler's National Labour Day in May 1935 and local Nazi leader Karl Gerhard led a sing-a-long the next year. Swastika flags formed an element of decoration at the same time that the symbol was being used to deface Jewish-runs shops in Montreal, leading McGill students to attack the building after the 1938 Kristallnacht attacks on German Jews. Many convened at The Harmonia to celebrate Adolf Hitler's 50th birthday in 1939, as Karl Dannenberg urged others to "put their hands in the hands of Adolf Hitler, the hand of the most sincere man who ever guided a nation." Hitler's foreign minister Joachim von Ribbentrop, by some coincidence, lived and worked on Stanley Street, just a stone's throw east of the spot from 1910 to 1914. The Harmonia was rechristened Preston Hall during World War II. The Sheraton Centre Hotel now stands at the spot.

Red spy in Verdun David Soboloff operated a photo studio at 5381 Bannantyne but in reality he was Soviet spy Yevgeni Vladimirovitch Brik, who entered Canada in 1952 with the aim of ferrying Soviets through the porous border United States Border. But the plan went awry when the heavy-drinking Soboloff fell for a married woman. He blew his cover and ended up begging to to defect to Canada. The RCMP was keen on cultivating a double agent, so they code-named him Gideon and sent him to Moscow. Sadly, his driver Corporal James Morrison had tipped off the Soviets and Soboloff disappeared and was presumed dead in Russia until the Soviets freed him from prison in the mid-1980s. Once released, Brik dialled the emergency number that he had memorized three decades earlier. Canada smuggled Brik out of the Soviet Union and he lived out his life in Canada, paranoid and bitter. Morrison confessed to his betrayal in the mid-1980s and was sentenced to 18-months in prison.

Bell's first home Bell Telephone's hello girls, as operators were first known, enjoyed Canada's first air conditioned offices at the now-verdant southeast corner of

Notre Dame and St. Jean, at a time when Bell had 200 phone customers. Operators memorized most telephone numbers and Lachine, The Back River and Longue Pointe were long distance calls from downtown, with long distance lines extended to the Eastern Townships and Ottawa much later. The building carried Montreal's phone traffic until 1929 and housed recreational rooms, lockers, a room where "clothes could be dried out if necessary," and "a number of baths placed in the most modern fashion." The Bank of Halifax rented space on the ground floor of A. Maxwell's nifty structure, which was demolished in 1935 as Bell moved to Beaver Hall Hill.

Mussolini divides Montreal Italian-Montrealers were emotionally split over fascist leader Benito Mussolini, with detractors led by Antonio Spada and his *Il Risveglio* newspaper while Dieni Gentile cheered him on. Both leaders were intense to

a fault, as Gentile once attacked a doctor with a knife for renouncing Mussolini and Spada ungenerously slammed Italian hero Giovanni Caboto as a "comic-book colonialist" after Montreal honoured him with a statue at Atwater. Many Montrealers were pleased when Mussolini handed Vatican City to the pope in the Lateran Treaty of 1929 and Guido Nincheri's ceiling scene at the Madonna Della Difessa Church on Dante tips a hat to Il Duce, while the Casa D'Italia also pays its respects, as Mussolini's government help pay for the structure, with support from Mayor Houde. Alas, many of those who stayed loyal to Mussolini after he inked the Pact of Steel with Hitler risked a stint in wartime internment camps alongside Houde. Canada temporarily seized the Casa d'Italia and a similar Mussolini-funded Italian centre on Springland near Hurteau in 1941.

Stolen house Historic Fendall House at 5333 Decelles was the lifelong home of Gertrude Fendall and her handyman Yvan

Chaput, who was long on bad luck and short on education. Chaput was a Duplessis Orphan whose youth was robbed by provincial bureaucrats who forced him to grow up in insane asylums as part of a fraudulent scheme to grab more federal cash. Fendall pledged Chaput her home in her 1986 will but the province declared her a ward of the state four years later and emptied the house, including the desk containing the codicil the promise was written on. The bureaucrats neglected the building and pipes froze and burst, ruining the interior. Chaput lost the house and didn't have the heart to tell Fendall that it was wrecked by neglect. Quebec sold it to developer David Owen for $200,000 in 1995. Owen's attempts to demolish it were rebuffed, so he had it moved a few feet over.

Lost for arts Much was sacrificed for the Place des Arts concert hall, as 32 addresses were expropriated and razed, costing $4.5 million in 1963, one third of the entire budget. The

International Ladies Garment Workers Union fought its expulsion from its seven-year-old building and then bitterly denounced tax hikes at their new home at 405 Concord (demolished 2010). The Catholic School Commission building at the northeast corner, as well as the Nazareth building and its gorgeous chapel at St. Catherine at Jeanne Mance were razed, while tiny Plateau Street was wiped off the map. The elegant seven-storey Woodhouse furniture building at the southeast corner was to be integrated into the new project but that plan sputtered after its annex across the street was hit by a blaze that killed two firemen and left another with a broken neck in April 1963.

Mystical roots What does a 400-year-old Knights Templars' cross emblazoned on a rock in Old Montreal have in common with a 1984 portrait of a newborn wearing a red

necklace? Both suggest that Montreal's founders aimed to launch a new ideal society where God is a woman. Or so argued author Francine Bernier, who points to physical clues—including an unconventional inscription on an old church soundboard and a family crest celebrating Jeanne Mance—that show Montreal was designed as a paradise where people could live to live pristine lives as The Primitive Church of Jesus. Other mystic historians suggest that Catholics celebrate Saint Kateri Tekakwitha because she was a direct descendant of Jesus. Author Michael Bradley claims that Samuel de Champlain moved The Holy Grail to Montreal. The Solar Temple cult served up similar historical mysticism until scuttled by murder and mass suicide.

St. Henri hospital tease For years St. Henri residents wanted a nearby hospital as desperately as a person being strangled seeks oxygen. Residents of The Hen were sicker and died earlier than people in other areas so Liberal MNA Philippe Lalonde promised a $6 million, 250-bed hospital for St. Henri in 1960 but soon realized that there was no land to build on. He proposed placing it on the other side of the Lachine Canal, where land was plentiful and cheap but voters booted him out of his safe seat in favour of Union National's Camille Martellani. But the new provincial representative proved no more able to move the project forward, brazenly telling reporters that he wouldn't put a hospital in any place that rival Frank Hanley might claim credit for. Martellani suggested building it at Irwin and Newman in vote-rich Ville Émard. The location was not in St. Henri and was already well-served by other hospitals. Voters returned the Liberals in 1970 and the hospital dream was shelved.

LaSalle explodes Gas lines were buried a mere 18-inches below the ground in LaSalle and, no, that was not a good thing, it turned out, as construction worker Lucien Paquette drove a bulldozer in the area on March 1, 1965, leading to a massive explosion that killed 28 people in 36 apartments. Eighteen of the deceased were children at the decade-old apartment buildings at

365 and 367 Bergevin. The blast hit at 8 a.m. when many husbands had departed early to pay the rent before going off to work. The explosion left a six metre-deep crater and countless psychological scars. A firefighter picked up a blackened doll lying on the ground only to realize it was the calcified remains of a dead child, while a Dorval cop rushed to the scene, only to smash into his brother's car, killing him instantly. A massive fundraising effort collected $600,000 for the victims, as Montrealers coped with the shock with an outpouring of public sympathy. The blast inspired many Montrealers to switch from gas to electric baseboard heating. It was not the only fatal explosion in LaSalle. Seven were killed just around the corner in 1956 and 11 killed a decade later in an explosion at the Monsanto factory. Natural gas was later injected with a strong scent to allow for easier detection.

Quarries were the pits Builders mined Montreal rock until the island became pockmarked with craters ranging from a cute hole on posh Stanton in Westmount to the massive Miron Quarry. The land supplied rocks for greystones, mud for bricks

and cement but it also served up heartbreak.The holes beckoned the suicidal, including Marie Louise Marion, found dead in a quarry in 1911, her body recovered on instructions from a clairvoyant. Two years later a woman tried suing Montreal for $11,000, claiming the city should have fenced off a quarry where her husband fell nine metres to his death. Noise and dust and the occasional flying rock were common as populations grew around the pits. Many were filled in the 1950s land boom but quarry disasters did not end. A 13-year-old boy fell 100 feet into the Francon pit where he was searching for pigeon eggs in 1983. He was unhurt as his fall was cushioned by snow. A pair of male strippers fell to their deaths in a Laval quarry in 2005 after attempting to flee without paying a taxi driver outside of the Red Lite after-hours club.

Chaos in little China Chinatown was a forbidding place full of gambling and opium dens, including one where Caucasian "Crooked Neck" Smith shot another white man to

death in 1908. Chinese Tong Wars were frequent and in one incident in February 1923, 150 warriors assaulted two cops and shot at 10 others in defence of their leader Toy One. Police prevailed and seized a small amount of cocaine. Montreal's Chinese were perennially frustrated, as the federal government made it nearly impossible to bring wives from China, with the Head Tax (1885-1923) requiring a massive cash payment to reunite families. Some got bored and built a tunnel network that linked 15 homes, filling them with stolen goods before in 1936. A massive gambling den at 71 La Gauchetière W. was busted a year later, as was another at 1023 Clark, which attracted $200-a-hand players. The Chinese Freemason Society's Chee Kung Tong gang settled its feuds in 1939 and peace reigned thereafter. Reverend Yvon Wong, a Princeton grad who came to Montreal at the age of 16, later led the battle against the head tax while wife Janet Wong founded the Canadian Wives Circle for Chinese Women, of which there weren't many in Montreal.

Lease living Montrealers have never been big on owning homes, as a large majority of residents have trekked to their landlord with rent cash in hand whenever a new calendar page  gets torn off. Only seven percent of Montrealers owned their homes after 1945 and owner-occupancy remains far lower than other Canadian cities. The dominant tenant demographic has kept things lively on July 1 when hundreds of thousands of uprooted Montrealers haul couches and fridges from apartment-to-apartment. But it has also meant that most Montrealers failed to accumulate financial equity, eroding a sense of citizenship and creating a nothing-to-lose spirit that has coloured the city, both for good and bad. More recently Montrealers have also become kings of solitude, as almost one-in-three residents inhabit their dwelling alone, one of the highest totals in North America. Montreal apartment living has one advantage however, as a relatively low percentage of tenants live in high-rise apartment buildings. Most prefer living in triplexes and sixplexes, which remain less common elsewhere in Canada where tenants have little choice but to opt for apartment towers. Big apartment tower developers largely shied away from Montreal, partially because the multitude of island municipalities complicated the building process.

Cops capture Park Transforming Lafontaine Park into a peaceful haven was no easy feat, as officials had first to conquer a tenacious old woman in order to claim the space in 1889. Logan's Farm, as the park was then known, was used as a military parade grounds when Montreal arranged to transform it into park, but officials first needed to remove the combative Mrs. Dansereau, who aimed to protect her lengthy ramshackle home that jutted right onto Sherbrooke Street. City officials Leprohan, Flynn and Doran knocked on her door while watching out for out for her shotgun-wielding friends. After a nervous standoff, the authorities finally carted her off in a cab and demolished her

home. In 1908, the federal government leased the park to the city for 99 years at the cost of $1 a year, with Ottawa reserving the right to take it back at any time. The deal led to considerable public apprehension about the future of the green space, as the feds considered building military barracks in the park in 1912 and 1951. Montreal later installed a zoo, leading to some unnatural animal deaths, such as in 1963 when a madman killed 17 birds from a shed, while an escaping kangaroo was killed by a passing motorist in 1972.

White light dreaming Buckminster Fuller came to Montreal in 1913 to tinker with machines after lousy marks got him expelled from Harvard. After leaving Montreal, Fuller's life

remained woeful and he considered drowning himself to give his family insurance cash. But things changed after he found himself suspended in a sparkling white sphere of light listening to a voice instructing him: "From now on you need never await temporal attestation to your thought. You think the truth." After hearing God's word, Fuller designed Montreal's famous Geodesic Dome, which proved a hit at Expo 67. The $9.3 million U.S. pavilion was covered with a thin acrylic skin and souped up with an Apollo space program theme, complete with a display of a simulated lunar landing. "Not strong on substance but strong on showmanship," wrote one critic. The dome attracted 5.3 million visitors in 1967 and remained a Montreal landmark even after its skin burned in an impressive 1976 blaze.

Olympic tropical housing Athletes need bed rest, so Mayor Jean Drapeau suggested visiting Olympians be lodged in the 66,000-ton France ocean liner for the 1976 games. Alas the ship would have been too tall to fit under the Quebec City bridge

upriver. Drapeau then hired a consortium of builders to create a knock-off of the *Marina Baie des Anges* in Nice, France, a structure suited for warm Mediterranean climes, complete with outdoor walkways, which force Montreal residents to put on coats to get to the stores downstairs. IOC President Lord Killanin called the Olympic Village "the height of Montreal's folly," after the projected $30 million cost tripled. One of the consortium, Joseph Zappia, had run a stalking horse mayoral campaign against Mayor Drapeau in 1970, attacking only Drapeau's opponents. He was rewarded with the partial contract before being convicted of taking kickbacks. The province later considered demolishing the 19-storey dual pyramid structures, which they claimed cost $75,000 a day to operate. But the apartments were all rented out in 1979 and soon turned a $3 million annual profit. Mafioso Frank Cotroni lived there, as did Mayor Pierre Bourque's father who leaped to his death from a balcony.

Fiery devastation A small blaze that started either at Brown's Tavern on the Main or nearby at Waugh's Bakery in 1852 spread so fast that it left one-in-five Montrealers homeless, 100 dead and 1,200 buildings ruined at a time when Montreal was a small town of just 45,000. Indeed the fire claimed almost every structure between St. Lawrence, Papineau, Dorchester and Notre Dame, as aquatic resources required to battle the flames were unavailable due to ongoing pipe repairs at the St. Louis Square aqueduct. The 24-hour fire could be seen from

Molson Brewery burns 1852

Burlington, Vermont and ruined the St. James Church, Molson's Brewery and Hays House, described as Canada's first shopping centre, which also housed Parliament after the riots of 1849. Hays House owner Moses J. Hays was later named Montreal's chief of police. Two years earlier, a fire had claimed 357 buildings, so authorities banned new wooden buildings, completed the McTavish Reservoir and hired a dedicated professional firefighting squad, ditching the system which saw freelance carters paid per bucket, which often spilled en route.

Nocturnal demolitions William Cornelius Van Horne's home fit the hard-drinking, cigar-smoking, mind-reading, all-night-poker-playing lifestyle he pursued while not

building the Canadian National Railway. Van Horne's 52-room 1869 Art Nouveau gem at Stanley and Sherbrooke was earmarked for demolition in 1973, a victim of inadequate anti-demolition rules and a $31,000 annual municipal tax bill that nobody was rushing to pay. When Montreal failed to greenlight its demolition, owner David Azrieli sent in a wrecking crew in the middle of a September night and later installed a plaque in his own honour at the corner of the drab office tower that was build on the site. Artwork in the home suffered a similar bad luck streak, as a 1933 fire claimed much one of the world's great collections, including works by Rubens, Rembrandt and Velasquez. What wasn't ruined was worth $20 million in 1970 but the inheritor, a woman married to Van Horne's grandson, sold the art without offering any to Canadian museums.

Boring underground No architectural element is as dear to Montreal's heart as the tunnel, as residents have gotten busy with shovels since the first settlers created safe spaces to deal with Indian attack anxiety. So good were Montrealers at digging that when the two teams met in the middle of the Mount Royal train tunnel, they were only off by one inch. Montreal's most-used tunnels remain the 70-kilometers of underground tubes that hook up 68 metro stations, as city planners opted to go underground rather than building cheaper monorails above. The oft-expanding, shopping-friendly 32-kilometer Underground City tunnel system links downtown malls such as Place Ville Marie, Central Station and The Eaton Centre, allowing countless people to go coatless during the cold weather, including scribe Don Bell who managed to go over a month indoors in a 1978 experiment. While other cities built skybridge-type overhead

structures to link buildings, Montreal's longtime mayor Jean Drapeau nixed all such overhead dreams, insisting all go underground. The Louis-Hippolyte Lafontaine Tunnel put another

Maria Monk

engineering feather in Montreal's cap, as the traffic tube spanning the St. Lawrence River 22-metres below low water level was the world's most ambitious prefabricated-anchoring style tunnel when completed in 1966. Some lesser-known tunnels include one in front of the Notre Dame Cathedral, which holds religious archival material, as well as another going south under Notre Dame St. from the basement of City Hall. Criminals dug Montreal, as Frank Cotroni's crew excavated from the basement of 5146 Trans Island to a nearby City and District Savings Bank. Cops allowed the work to go on for months in 1967 before making arrests. In 1992 Marcel Talon and his bank robbing crew dug a nine-metre foot path under St. Antoine by using the Craig Street sewer. The highly-elaborate one-year scheme fell apart when a tree collapsed above, requiring maintenance that exposed the tunneling. Talon never got his hands on the $200 million he sought from the Bank of Montreal but was never charged for the caper. Another tunnel stirred passions even though it probably did not exist. *The Awful Disclosures of Maria Monk* (1836) tells of a secret tunnel at the Hotel Dieu Hospital where priests and nuns would meet to have sex. Children born of such unions were killed, the author claimed, as were nuns who rebelled. The book made money for its publishers but many of the key descriptions were vigorously refuted.

Soviet Sex on Towers

Steamy sex at the spanking-new Diplomate apartment building at 1420 Towers sparked an espionage honey-pot spy scandal, as German Gerda Munsinger

inhabited apartment 512 while working as an escort. Her bed mates included federal Conservative cabinet ministers George Hees and Pierre Sévigny. Munsinger wished to remain in Canada, so she applied for citizenship and recruited the political bigwigs to sign her application papers in 1960. Authorities red-flagged the application, as it seemed almost impossible to get such high-level support on such a request. Soon the cat was out of the bag and the opposition was asking tricky questions of Prime Minister John Diefenbaker. It didn't help that Munsinger had a possible background as a Soviet spy and was also good friends with mobster Willie Obront. The media leaped on the scandal after it was brought up in Parliament. But Munsinger had already returned to Germany. Sévigny quit politics and Hees would fall into disfavour for several years, while Munsinger herself denied all suggestions that she was ever spy, although she found the rumours profitable as an early benefactor of chequebook journalism. She and her mysteries died in Munich in 1988.

Prison beneath the mayor The slammer beneath what's now city hall opened back in 1808 and its 300 cells fast filled with drunks, prostitutes and any vagrant unlucky enough to get rounded up. Builders gave lip service to progressive rehabilitation but critics rapidly condemned the poorly-heated,

windowless facility as inhumane. Chicken thief Joseph Lince was sentenced to six months in 1825. Waiter William Wardrobe from the Masonic Hall Restaurant on St. Paul was jailed after pilfering Sir George Hoste's silver snuff box. Offender Jacob O'Dougherty was

pilloried nearby for "passing a Spanish milled dollar," while rapists and other murderers were hanged in nearby Champs de Mars. Adolphus Dewey, who murdered his wife with an axe, was given keys to escape by a jailer's daughter in 1833. But Dewey declined and willingly shuffled to the scaffold. The prison closed in 1838 and was replaced by the *Pied du Courant* prison further east, which lasted from 1835 to 1912 and was replaced by Bordeaux Prison.

Burgled letdown The noble old house at 3459 St. Hubert, just above Sherbrooke, might not seem an object of intense desire but three levels of police were drooling to get inside in 1971

when it housed pair of fringe separatist-sympathizing organizations. Police planted bugs and tapped its phones and dreamed about getting their hands on the membership lists, with the aim of averting a repeat of the violence of October 1970. Cops got wind of an important letter coming to the house from separatist FLQ terrorist Jacques Cossette-Trudel, then

exiled in Cuba. That letter proved just too much to resist, so a team of cops broke in on the night of Oct. 6, 1972 and filled hockey bags with every document they could carry and dumped the booty in an officer's basement. Police attempted to misdirect suspicion to a rival separatist outfit but the victims vigorously suspected police following the burglary. The stolen papers proved to be unreadably-dull newsletters, the membership lists inconsequential, as many radicals had renounced violence in favour of the democratic option offered by the new Parti Quebecois. The letter from Cuba turned out be a string of laments about homesickness and the horrors of violence. The break-in was finally exposed after a rogue officer got caught in another illegal affair and many police careers were tarnished by the blunder.

Parade route hustlers Desperate small-scale, cut-throat entrepreneurs leaped on an opportunity to exploit a market for chairs along Sherbrooke Street for the wildly-popular St. Jean Baptiste parade, as they set up chairs well in advance each

year after World War II. Would-be chair magnates would man and protect their temporary seating for days and then rent them out when the parade kicked off. It didn't always pan out, as a certain Monsieur Gagné invested $200 in 1954 to pay off a resident for a spot in front of his house and also rented 500 chairs. His anticipated $300 profit from $1 per-backside-fee turned to dust after competitors simply displaced his chairs. Better-known czars of the estimated 7,000 parade route chairs included Bébé "Lisette" Vendetti, and Ti-Pit Sutton, whose full time job was as a waiter at the Café Mexico.

9

Transportation

Though we now move faster, much of the charm of getting there has been lost. Strap on the seat belt for a trip through the stranger moments of Montreal transportation history.

Mystery fly

A fearless masked Montrealer once defied death by strolling atop a DC-8 flying at a speed of at 250 miles per hour. The Human Fly, it turned out, was not a single person, but a rotating series of anonymous freelance daredevils hired by bored sausage-making brothers Joe and Dominique Ramacieri of Roma Foods. Rick Rajotte was the most accomplished of the Human Flys, as he calmly agreed to leap a motorcycle over 27 buses at sparsely-attended Gloria Gaynor concert at the Olympic Stadium on Friday Oct. 7, 1977. Motorcycle whiz Ky Michaelson affixed a pair of 1,500-lb thrust hydrogen peroxide rockets under the fuel tank of a Harley Davidson motorcycle,

creating a machine capable of traveling over 480 km/h. Rajotte ambled in late and gave the superbike a mere glance. He yawned when Michaelson warned him that the ramps were not properly angled. The Fly flew too high and crashed down on himself, breaking his ankle. The leap still beat Evel Knevel's 13-bus record. The Human Fly was never seen again.

Trolley to the top

Orphans rode for free on Montreal's most spectacular train ride after The Mountain Funicular Railway was installed on the eastern slope of Mount Royal to

encourage non-climbers and lazy folk to get to the top of the park. From 1884 the train climbed from the bottom of the hill and was later extended to Park Ave. The ride—if you weren't an orphan—cost a nickel and was considered a magical Montreal experience, as tree branches scratched gently at the side of the ascending craft as the view became more magnificent with each turn of the wheel. Interest eventually waned and the company that ran the contraption closed in 1918 after it could no longer afford maintenance and repairs.

No night driving West Island police unveiled one of the most innovative and ridiculous car theft prevention programs in 1993 when they handed out fluorescent window stickers to drivers who vowed never to drive between 11 p.m. and 5 a.m. If a police officer were to spot a car with a I-never-drive-at-night sticker on the road late at night, he would immediately know the car had been stolen. According to the plan, the cop would then pull the driver over and ask tough questions about why the decal is not being properly respected. The short-lived sticker program might have prevented thefts (unless the car thief scraped the sticker off at the first red light) but it also surely discouraged late-night drives. "Hey honey, I have an idea. Let's drive down to the Ste. Anne's marina!" "Great idea sweetcakes, except police will interrogate us because of that darn florescent decal in our windshield!"

Carjackers inspire cop car redesign Montreal police cruisers are now wisely equipped with barriers dividing front and back seats, but it took an incident that left five dead to

finally install the obstacles. The morbid saga began at sleepy Dagenais and Monty in Montreal North when carjackers Dennis Colic, 21, and Jacques Bélanger, 19, attempted to grab Giovanni Delli Colli's souped up Camaro in Oct. 1984. Cops rushed to the scene and placed one suspect in the same car as the carjacking victim, who expressed his irritation by leaping over the seat to attack the would-be thief. One of the thieves then grabbed an officer's gun and shot the cop and Delli Colli dead. The fugitives then carjacked another vehicle and holed up in an abandoned house in Woodstock, Ontario. Police shot one of the thieves dead, while accidentally shooting colleague Jack Ross. Colic, the survivor, hanged himself in prison in June 1986, raising the death toll to five. The barriers were installed in all police cars soon after.

Don Juan car thieves Early victims of car theft were discouraged from reporting their missing vehicles as Montreal police charged them $60—over $800 in today's cash—to file a stolen car report. As a result, many slick young men routinely appropriated cars belonging to friends or strangers in order to impress young women exiting stores downtown. Police denounced the seductive scofflaws who offered women free lifts. "Most of these people don't have a cent. They use their bosses' cars and make the girls believe they belong to them. The girls allow themselves to be tempted," complained Montreal police in 1919. Many young women were unimpressed with endless joy-ride offers, as the bachelors on the prowl constantly implored them to hop aboard after the stores closed each evening. Police lowered the stolen vehicle report fee to $1.50 in 1919 and car thefts decreased.

Aviatrix shuns voice of doom Verdun-born Muriel Hanning-Lee enjoyed taking to the skies but disaster lurked. Hanning-Lee was raised by her best-friend's family after her mother died and later moved to London where she worked as a

Hanning-Lee

stewardess after World War II. She found the work so exciting that she shared her experiences in her autobiography *Head in the Clouds*. One day Hanning-Lee was asked to work on an extra flight in order to train a newly-hired colleague. Hanning-Lee volunteered to go but had a nagging premonition of impending doom. "She was so convinced something was going to happen that she thought of getting a doctor's certificate stating unfitness to fly. She kept saying, 'I don't want to go on this flight,'" a friend later said. She overcame her apprehensions and boarded the Solent G-AKNU flying boat plane that set off from Southampton for Lisbon but the voice of doom proved correct as a propeller malfunctioned and the plane crashed into a chalk pit near the Isle of Wight killing Hanning-Lee and 42 others on November 15, 1957. Fourteen survived.

Taxis with legs Flagging a hack required the cooperation of furry four-legged pulling beasts for much of this city's timeline, as 1,800 equine taxis served Montrealers in 1900, a total

reduced to a mere 50 in 1933. At their peak, 45 horse cabs lined up at Philips Square, some adorned with plush buffalo rugs and shiny brass fittings. Drivers were mostly vigorous Irishmen who lifted weights and thrashed a punching bag in front of the posh Joyce Boarding House south of the square, with Tom Tierney recognized as the resident champion fighter. Not all was harmony among the horsemen, as in 1879 the thriving Morey cab service on de la Gauchetière just west of Bleury was attacked by jealous competitors, likely the McGarr clan, who killed a night watchman and torched the stables. Seventy terrified horses bolted to safety.

Busing nowhere All it took was pocket change to join a Saturday night magical mystery tour that rolled from downtown Montreal for four decades. The weekly Metropolitan Provincial

Inc. Bus to Nowhere was clearly marked NOWHERE in front and that proved destination enough for aimless passengers, who tended to be jovial seniors that would sing and make a festive ruckus while on the road to surprises. None could resist pestering the driver to tip them off to where they were headed. The driver, nattily clad in a tan-coloured suit, dubiously claimed that even he didn't know where he was headed. On one trip in 1973, driver Rudolph Laporte brought the passengers to Hotel Royal in Ste. Julienne, a one-hour drive north of Montreal where the passengers got off and watched a four-piece rock band and a stage show that included an acrobat, a stripper and a singer. About one-quarter declined to enter.

Licensed bicycles Pedaling without a license could land a rider with a fine, as a police flatfoot could write up a cyclist for pedaling *sans permis*. So every spring cyclists waited in lengthy license lineups, with some arriving extra early in an aim to score the coveted #1 plate. The licenses proved ineffective in deterring bike theft, as at least 4,500 bicycles were stolen in 1973. The license rose to $2.25 five years later but eventually the requirement was forgotten. Mayor Jean Doré proposed reinstating mandatory bike licenses in 1991, arguing that they would make it easier for cops to bust scofflaw riders. Even bicycle activist Bob Silverman argued for mandatory bicycle licences, saying they might reduce rampant bike theft. The license requirement never returned.

Royal blood on tracks Henry Locock's Canadian visit might have exposed an embarrassing British royal secret, which makes his mysterious death on the Montreal West railway tracks particularly tantalizing. Queen Victoria's sixth child, Princess Louise, secretly gave birth to little Henry out-of-wedlock when she was 19. Royal physician Frederick Locock was granted a stipend for pretending that he was Henry's father. Locock grew up and came to Canada to find his biological father, Walter Stirling, who was living in Kelowna, B.C. But Locock got so inebriated at the start of his train trip that he opened the wrong door, fell out onto the tracks and died on December 10, 1907. Such was the official story and the possibility of foul play was never investigated. Princess Louise never had another child. She married Canadian Governor General Lord Lorne, a promiscuous homosexual who never met a waiter he didn't accidentally brush up against. The province of Alberta is named after the train victim's mother, as is Lake Louise. At the time of Locock's death, Montreal West was largely undeveloped, as a large chunk of the area had been filled by the sprawling Blue Bonnets racetrack until about 15 years before.

Henry Locock

Water fountains for horsies

Drink up, said the sidewalk trough to the thirsty horse, back when large stone sidewalk vessels offered watery relief to beasts around Montreal

until 1958. Montreal's prime sidewalk trough sat at McGill and Craig (St. Antoine) from 1850 after temperance activist and *Montreal Witness* publisher John McDougall installed what he described as a "fountain of health" to quench equine thirsts, as steeds lingered while their farmer proprietors got hammered in nearby taverns. The trough was smashed by a police van in 1946 after it was struck by a drunk driver. The Molson family installed an ornate granite water trough, complete with brass plate, at Dorchester and de la Cathedrale but it was removed and stored in a yard on Grand Truck Street when a roadway was widened in the 1940s. Another venerable trough was taken from downtown Sherbrooke Street in 1957 and others were carted away the next year. "They serve no useful purpose now and are a nuisance to pedestrians motorists and snow removal crews," said city bureaucrat Frank Dowd. Though no horses sip from them, troughs still sit on Olmsted Road, Jacques Cartier Square and at Landsdowne and Ste. Catherine.

Valentine's shocker

The overnight train from Toronto contained a grisly surprise when it rolled into Windsor Station on Valentine's Day weekend 1949. The lifeless bodies of two tourists from Toronto, lawyer Earl Fauman, 31, and nurse

Kelly & Fauman

Martha Leona Kelly, 28, the wife of a top Toronto police officer, were found in a compartment with .38 calibre gunshot wounds to their heads. Both were married with children, but not to each other. A coroner said that both had been shot in their open mouths. Booze, pills and a couple of guns were found in the cabin.

Metro mapping

For generations planners plotted ambitious plans for a Montreal subway system in the same manner that today's transit geeks draw the perfect fantasy metro

map of the future. But the shovels only came out in 1962 and 68 stations now welcome traveler into transit tunnel. Many metro locations were chosen for unusual reasons. Côte St. Luc residents opposed a metro to their area, imagining criminals descending on their happy homes. The Vendôme metro was slated for the southeast corner of Sherbrooke and Decarie but nobody wanted to expropriate and demolish the classy apartment building at the site. Meanwhile logistics doomed a second proposed station in Old Montreal. Namur station was planned at Victoria and Jean Talon but Robert Campeau persuaded planners to place it closer to his Blue Bonnets Race track at Decarie. Transit boss Lawrence Hanigan even proposed a pedestrian tunnel from the station to the track under the Decarie Expressway.

Welsh span

Montreal's Victoria Bridge was a massive game-changer when it became the world's longest bridge and Montreal first span in 1859, finally allowing visitors to get to and from Montreal without crossing the oft-icy waters in a

steamboat. Robert Stephenson's incredibly durable bridge was designed as a knockoff of the Britannia Bridge, built a decade prior in Northern Wales and many nearby streets celebrated the heritage by being named after Welsh places, including Brittania, Menai and Conwy streets of the Goose Village area. All admire the sturdy bridge for its long-lasting durability but some have criticized it for falling short of the disarming charm offered by the considerably-shorter Welsh original.

The lost station Drummond and Dorchester served as a landing pad for budget tourists and wide-eyed bus-riding farmers' daughters rolling into the big city for the first time. The bus terminal opened after the 1866-built American Presbyterian Church was demolished in 1937 and the handily-placed transport hub sat a short stroll from such legendary Golden Square Mile establishments as Slitkin's and Slotkins, Chez Paree

and the Windsor Hotel. Power Corp had moved the station from its previous spot at overcrowded Phillips Square, ignoring a deed stipulation that forbade a bus station from occupying the land, leading to a 1960 legal kerfuffle. Big drama came to the station in 1958 when Greta Goede, the daughter of an SS agent, kidnapped Joel Reitman, the two-year-old toddler she was babysitting. Goede got $10,000 delivered to the station but did not come to pick it up. She was caught and sentenced to seven years. The station was razed and an office tower now occupies the site. All out-of-town bus traffic was shifted to Berri in 1971.

Shanghaied on the waterfront There was always that risk, in old time Montreal, of being knocked out and tossed onto a ship headed for the other side of the planet. Quebec City hardware merchant A.D. Fraser learned this hard way after coming to Montreal in 1876. Fraser asked around for the Montreal House Hotel and a guide brought him to an entirely different place on the waterfront full of hard-drinking sailors. Fraser had a drink while trying to figure how to reach his hotel. The drink was drugged and Fraser awoke aboard a ship bound for Capetown, South Africa. He arrived without luggage and cash but found work as a bookkeeper and earned enough to make his way back to Quebec City in September of 1877 via London. His wife and children were delighted by his return and presumably believed his story.

Phone poles in traffic Telephone poles occasionally

found themselves in the middle of Montreal traffic, leading astonished motorists to slam into the immovable barriers. Phone poles migrated into streets after crews failed to remove them when roads were widened.

One fine day in 1960 an otherwise carefree motorist went cruising down St. Catherine E. near Prefontaine in his 1957 Lincoln Premier and slammed into a pole planted eight feet from the sidewalk. Identical towering obstacles blocked nearby streets. Mayor Sarto Fournier blamed the Montreal Electrical Services Commission, calling the group "useless." The group has replaced phone poles with underground wires since 1910, now at a pace of seven streets per year. Montreal city council banned new poles in favour of underground wiring in 1905. The order was ignored.

Angels squabble Crime was supposedly so rampant in

the Metro system in the early 1980s that transit chief Lawrence Hanigan sought to hire 100 security guards to protect attendants,

claiming that villains had overwhelmed the 68-member Metro security force that oversaw the half-million daily riders. So New York City's Guardian Angels launched a Montreal branch in 1983, led by pacifist Jean Boisvert whose methods were derided as too gentle by the 20 volunteers. Volunteer Toussaint Klusmann, a bartender at the 1234 disco, was then locked up in an insane asylum for committing gross indecency. The Montreal Guardian Angels split, as the *Anges Gardiens* spinoff competed for new recruits. Both sides eventually gave up, retired and hung up their berets, T-shirts and fancy belts. Lisa Sliwa, wife of Guardian Angels' founder Curtis Sliwa, initiated a short-lived effort to relaunch the Montreal group a decade later.

Wandering into America It was long a cinch to sneak into the United States south of Montreal until terrorist spoilsports put an end to the fun. Until the 1970s, small border crossings employed an off-hours honour system that allowed travelers to cross even when no attendant was present. Baader-

Meinhof Red Army Faction member Kristina Berster entered Canada with poorly-faked Iranian passport and then walked into the United States via Noyan, Quebec in July 1978. U.S. border patrol only noticed her after an accomplice flashed his car lights to get her attention. "When I was in Paris, I was told that to get into the States all you had to do was walk through Vermont's northern border," she explained. Berster was sought for the murder of German banker Jurgen Ponto and the 1977 kidnapping of industrialist Hanns Schleyer.

Killing grassy sidewalks Delightful grass strips separated concrete sidewalk from asphalt roadways on many Montreal roads until green-hating politicians had them eradicated. The verdant blades of grass were doomed in 1961 when city administrator Lucien Saulnier ordered the linear lawns paved over. Saulnier said that paving over the grass would

Grassy St. Joseph Blvd

sanitize homes, as lawns turned muddy and kids got dirty traipsing over them.Those filthy little tykes would then track mud into their mother's spotless homes, causing toxic family drama, as domestic bliss was contaminated by feculent youngsters. Darn those sidewalk-adjacent lawn strips! Other Montreal-area municipalities paved over their grass strips, as once-verdant streets like Willibrod in Verdun now feature homes flanked first by pavement, then asphalt where the grass once grew and then paved roads. A similar cemented fate awaited grassy medians, as featured on once-picturesque boulevards like St. Joseph.

Chopperjacking introvert

Rory Shane and his girlfriend Rachel Dubiel (who a witnesses later described as "very ugly") rented a helicopter for a sightseeing tour of Montreal in 1979 but soon Shayne's gun was out and pointed at the pilot's head.

Shayne & Dubiel

Shayne, a soft-spoken German-born diabolical introvert, forced the pilot to land at a bank at the Place Vertu mall where the aeronautically-inclined bandits made off with $11,000 before whirling off into the skies. The thieves, alas, were betrayed by their fingerprints. Shayne scored another outlandish first by smuggling a tiny gun into his court hearing, likely by transporting it in his anal cavity. The gun discharged but no harm was done.

Bungling bus bombers

Richard "Joker" Bertrand, 27, and Gilbert Groleau, 25, anonymously warned crime reporter Claude Poirier of an impending bloodbath before they drove to

Bertrand & Groleau

the Berri bus terminal on January 21, 1976. The bearded duo parked their borrowed green 1970 station wagon near the bus station to transport a bunch of highly-explosive Danish-made Schaffler detonator caps inside, with the intention of killing as many people as possible in protest against prison conditions. However the bomb exploded in the car, leaving the would-be bombers as the only victims. Police rolled the five-foot-tall Groleau in snow to extinguish the fire that had ravaged his lengthy hair but he later succumbed in hospital. Bertrand was killed instantly. Police found a note threatening a follow-up bombing "10 times worse." Bertrand had spent time in prison psych wards while Groleau was a convicted rapist. Prisoners at St. Vincent de Paul and Archambault had been boycotting prison activities in protest of cruel treatment but their committee claimed no knowledge of the attack.

Car theft dooms trapper

TV Early-day trapper Pierre Radisson's forest adventures would have been better appreciated had a car not been stolen in Montreal 247 years after

John Lucarotti

his death. The CBC paid John Lucarotti $300 per episode to write 30 hours of Radisson's adventures. He celebrated by attending a Christmas party at the Renaissance Studios on Cote des Neiges Blvd. in December 1956 only to find his car stolen with his invaluable scripts gone. All of his work—which he surely did—was lost. He rewrote the series from memory and when it was finally shot on Perot Island, the budget had quadrupled to $26,000 per episode. Critics were unimpressed, with one writing that the Native Indian characters looked like white men "who dunked their heads into a bucket of multi-coloured paint then donned ill-fitting and badly decorated bathing caps." The CBC lost $1 million on the flop. Lucarotti, a self-described "ardent-naturalized Canadian" moved to England and died in 1994.

Japanese terrorists spy airport

Staffers at the Dorval Airport Hilton Hotel might have wondered why Japanese guest Kozo Okamoto enjoyed their hospitality for an entire

Okamoto

winter, from November 1971 to March 1972. They got a shocking answer two months later when Okamoto led one of the world's most vicious-ever airport attacks, which saw 24 people gunned down dead and another 80 injured at what's Ben Gurion Airport in Tel Aviv. Okamoto and two fellow travelers from the Japanese Red Army terrorist group blasted innocent people with machine guns they had hidden in violin cases. Okamoto survived and served 13 years in prison but his two partners were gunned down at the scene. The group had a convoluted arrangement to commit crimes for Arab terrorist groups, who were expected to return the favour for their cause, whatever that might have been. The terrorists used Dorval (now Trudeau) Airport to practice.

Jockey courage Jockey Jimmy Darou lost the use of his legs but found his purpose after a 1933 racing accident, as his support for others bound to wheelchairs proved so inspiring that

Eleanor Roosevelt sent him a new wheelchair and LIFE magazine wrote a feature article on him.

The Montreal Sportsmen's Association organized a benefit entertainment show to raise money for Darou's long-term care and he used the proceeds to lease the gas station in Montreal West in April 1937. He went on to breed horses, call races at Blue Bonnets and opened a second gas station near the track in 1960, where jockeys were his best customers. Darou also helped buy radios for shut-ins before he died in 1975.

Jimmy Darou

Rustbox city Decaying, abandoned rustboxes once filled Montreal streets, as motorists would remove plates, file off IDs and ditch unwanted cars on quiet streets. The process saved

time and the $20 required to scrap a car officially at the license bureau and streets became burial grounds for rusty, dysfunctional Pontiacs and Buicks, as authorities lacked manpower required to track down owners. City workers groaned that the abandoned vehicles disrupted their street cleaning and snow clearing operations, as 8,000 abandoned cars were orphaned in 1971, up from just 200 in 1957. The city tried selling the wrecks at a Papineau Street pound for $15 each. Other motorists discarded unwanted beaters by driving them into the Lachine Canal. The license bureau started refunding unused car registration fees and scrapyards offered enough to make recycling worthwhile, putting an end to the vehicular litter.

Airport grounded Prime Minister Pierre Trudeau took aim at Quebec separatism by remodeling Montreal into a leading international hub, a scheme that entailed building the world's largest jumbo jetport in a spot so remote that nobody would complain of noise made by the noisy, new Concorde. Mirabel Airport was built 55-kilometres from downtown on a colossal piece of land two-thirds the size of Montreal island. Mirabel aimed to be the world's most efficient airport when it opened in October 1975, as it was to be linked by superhighways and high-

speed rail. Provincial-federal squabbling hindered those plans and travelers fussed about the pricey cab fare. Boeing's new 747 soon killed the Concorde, so noise at Dorval Airport became a minor issue. Mirabel was built to handle 50 million annual passengers but only got to three million and became the western world's most inefficient airport, with $50 million in annual losses. Mirabel had one employee for every two passengers compared to Chicago's O'Hare which had 1:20. Disasters included the Air India Flight 182, which saw terrorists bomb a Boeing 747 en route from Mirabel to London, killing 329 people in 1985. The $500 million white elephant ($2.2 billion today) was reduced to holiday charters and closed October 21, 2004.

Blackmail bridge Barren Nun's Island was worthless in the early 1950s, as no bridge connected it to the mainland and the soil was seen as too muddy to build upon, as great sheets

of ice floated down the St. Lawrence and crashed over the land. The Catholic church repeatedly attempted to sell the property but it always reverted to their ownership, as no buyer could keep up payments. Colin Gravenor purchased it in 1956 for $5,000 down, without a prayer of making the second installment of $100,000 due in 90 days. Gravenor couldn't find a buyer, so he flooded Prime Minister Louis St. Laurent with fake letters from fictional concerned citizens, all urging the bridge be built through Nun's Island. The proposal placed the bridge at a wide part of the river but Gravenor argued that cheaper land expropriations would make up for the higher cost. Days before he would be forced to forfeit the island, Gravenor received news that the Champlain Bridge would be built through his property, complete with ice bridge blocking floes and road ramps to the isle. Gravenor sold the land for about $2 million. Some claim Gravenor, who wrote for *Midnight* tabloid scandal sheet, might have influenced the PM's decision by bringing his attention to compromising photos he had in his possession.

Parking prisoners Montreal declared war on parking ticket scofflaws in 1983 with the new Denver Boot wheel-locking and public shaming device. Some rebels pried off the

locks off with crowbars, with one modifying it into an ashtray that he brazenly gifted to a police station. Others changed their license plates to escape detection and another had the bylaw overturned, as immobilized drivers had not been given their day in court. The city relaunched the boot the next year but shelved it between 2008 and 2011 as unprofitable. They are now used sporadically for extreme cases. Jail time for unpaid tickets was a common fate until 2004 and inmates included translator David Smith who tallied $12,500 in 128 parking tickets in 1988 and was sentenced to 30 months in federal prison without going before a judge. A woman who refused to pay a $10 ticket for parking in a handicapped zone in 1989 was also jailed, even though her husband was handicapped. Sickly Manon Chouinard was restrained to a bed at Ste. Justine's Hospital in 1996 after she failed to pay $2,200 in parking tickets. Jail was not so bad, claimed 60-year-old Jim, who said he enjoyed eight restful weekend days at Bordeaux Prison after refusing to pay parking tickets.

Streetcar slashing Panic gripped Montreal in January 1954 as a mysterious knife-wielding villain slashed the calves of women climbing onto streetcars. Four riders were cut at St. Catherine and the Main on January 22 and four days later Mimi

Dufour, 30, needed 18 stitches after being sliced at Pine and Park. The "flat nosed savage on a slashing rampage" was assumed to be a pervert. Armies of plainclothes police cops failed to locate the knife-wielding maniac and victims were simultaneously attacked at different places, leading to concerns about copycat slashers. Schools closed early to allow girls to return home before dark for fear of Montreal scariest villain since a lunatic threatened kids with a syringe in 1938. A laughing attacker sliced May Meikle, 21, downtown at Metcalfe and Mariette Gareau, 17, Marie Meiberreiter, 31, and Laurette Menard, 21, also joined the list of victims. Several men made false confessions but police made no arrests and estimated that at least half of the cuts were self-inflicted. Complaints stopped after 10 days.

Robots park cars Super cool parking technology allowed 1950s motorists to drive onto platforms and simply leave, as machines lifted the cars into indoor

Old Montreal lot 1956-2000

spaces. The Turnbull Bowser Skyscraper Parking System was considered a slam-dunk for investors of the publicly-traded Pigeon Hole Parking company, backed by three Town of Mount Royal residents. Montreal's first such lot survived 44 years after opening in 1956 with 280 spaces at St. Jean and Notre Dame. Four more robot car nests were built over five years from 1958, including one at 2020 Mansfield

(1958-1984) where Joseph Monaghan was crushed by an elevator in 1959. Mountain Street Pigeon Hole Parking (1958-1970), Sun Automatic Parking (1960-1991) and McGill Auto Park (1963-1989) followed. Lawyer Jean-Paul Parent proposed a 550-space pigeon parking lot in Old Montreal in 1963 as part of his plan to demolish 16 buildings. The futuristic lots were doomed by salt corrosion, while owners realized their buildings could be replaced by more profitable structures. Montreal's last such lot was torn down in 2000.

Urban toll grabs Traveling around Montreal long required coughing up coins at street tolls, a much-reviled rite of urban passage that aggravated all, as every municipal council chinwag featured solemn promises to eradicate the fee at all cost.

The Toll Gate by Krieghoff, 1861

From 1840 the Turnpike Trust placed collectors in small wooden shacks that sometimes required bodyguards to discourage robbers and chase toll-runners. Drivers were fined for employing detours, as were landowners who created them. The booths shifted frequently, as municipalities purchased more roads. Tolls could be found on Notre Dame at Frontenac (later moved to Valois, then Viau), Landsdowne at St. Catherine, Greene and Sherbrooke, on the Main just south of Duluth, at Rosemont and Des Carrières, and in Montreal West at Elmhurst and on Avon Road (then called Blue Bonnets Hill). The tolls discouraged residents from straying outside their districts, as delivery drivers were forced to bear much of the cost of the road maintenance, which were "kept by a couple of cheap men and a horse and cart." By 1890 booths still gobbled coins on St Lawrence, Mount Royal Ave., Lower Lachine Rd., Côte des Neiges Rd. and Papineau. In 1905 tolls were found on Côte des Neiges near Ridgewood, Cote St. Antoine near Marlowe, Decarie and De Maisonneuve, Sherbrooke and Decarie and on The Boulevard. Quebec finally outlawed street tolls in 1922.

Motoring firsts George Rothwell was nailed with Montreal's first speeding ticket, earned by driving down Beaver Hall Hill at 40 km/h, over four times the 1904 limit. A judge fined

him $10 for "automobile scorching," as speeding was called. "Don't be too pious. By neglecting your duty on Sunday you have endangered lives on a Monday," Judge Weir cryptically told driver Rothwell. U. H. Dandurand became the first licensed Montreal motorist in 1899 but car licenses didn't exist, so he took to the road under the "bicycle, tricycle and similar vehicle clause." Only four cars cruised Montreal streets until 1902. Seven years later Blue Bonnets race track hosted car races, which saw two drivers killed that year. Long-distance winter driving remained impossible until at least 1936, as competitors raced to be the first to drive from Montreal to Quebec City after the spring thaw. Montreal's first pedestrian traffic fatality died on Aug 11, 1906, as Antoine Toutant was hit by Herwald Atkinson on St. Catherine Street. E. Montreal's first traffic light was lit November 1927 outside the Craig (St. Antoine) Street streetcar terminus.

Highway's jammed with pious heroes on a last-chance prayer drive

Travel was slowed in early-day Quebec by piety, as calèche drivers felt compelled to stop at every roadside cross to pray. Farmers would plant the crosses—which sometimes stood six metres high and included crucifixion-related detail—near roadways as spontaneous expressions of faith, much to the frustration of one British officer

whose driver stopped at every such cross to pray for five minutes in 1776, leaving his passengers almost frostbitten. The crosses often marked borders and served as landmarks but were usually placed to give farmers a chat with Jesus where churches were distant. The crosses fell out of fashion when transportation improvements made it easier to get to church but during World War I farmers planted them in hopes that their sons would be spared from conscription, none fearing that the crosses might tip off authorities to the presence of draft dodgers. About 200 wayside crosses still stood around Montreal in the 1920s but nationalists encouraged their return and there are now about 15 times that total in the province.

Errors in equinicide Police officer Victor Côté was directing traffic at Dorchester and St. Lawrence on April 14, 1931 when a little Polish girl summoned him to shoot an injured horse in a nearby backyard. Stableman J. Leavitt's stallion had a

broken a leg and killing it was deemed the humane option. A crowd formed to watch the grisly act, as a second officer kept the viewers at a safe distance. Côté shot the horse but it did not fall. Just as he fired a second time the horse went down and the second bullet ricocheted off a wall and struck a bystander in the neck, killing him. Witnesses called the family to tell of their son being killed, but the boy answered and reported to feeling just fine. Another man was later confirmed as the victim. The accident wasn't unprecedented, as a man named Gagnon was awarded $2,500 after losing his eye to a stray police bullet caused by an officer shooting a small dog at Frontenac and Rouen in 1929. Montreal police later equipped officers with a highly-specialized British-made tool designed specifically to slaughter animals without collateral risk to passersby. Public animal killings continued at least until 1957 when Westmount mayor Colonel Tucker confessed that his workers routinely shot pigeons after several other less murderous approaches failed.

Trailer saves taxi-driving souls

Catholic taxi drivers eager for an earful of prayer could motor right up onto the grass at the Georges-Étienne Cartier Monument in the 1950s to listen to sermons organized by the *Bon Dieu en Taxi*. Tubby World War II veteran Paul Aquin preached from a trailer souped up with a 24-hour snack bar, radio and TV. Aquin, who once spent four days helping haul a huge cedar cross across the island in a 1961, lost some taxi-driver support by preaching against labour unions and the church also eventually soured on him and axed his funding. Aquin then toiled for the provincial government far from the city he loved. He was imprisoned for a year in 1973 after killing two people while drunk driving near Rimouski. He returned and worked at a detox clinic where he was reprimanded for allowing boxer Alex Hilton to leave the facility. Hundreds attended Aquin's 2009 funeral, including his grief-stricken pal, Canadiens great Jean Béliveau, who passed out at the ceremony.

It took a toll

A dangerous curve on the Jacques Cartier Bridge (originally Harbour Bridge) was born in 1939 after soap magnate Hector Barsalou slipped away from attempts to force him to sell his factory at 1600 Delorimier. But the resultant Craig

Curve was not the crookedest thing on the bridge. Toll booth attendants long practiced the disappearing coin trick, pilfering untold millions in coin payments. The theft was rife until machines replaced human collectors in 1959, resulting in an immediate 30 percent rise in revenues. Attendants had been giving half-price specials to truckers and pocketing the payments, absconding with mountains of coins even though supervisors searched their pockets at the end of shift. Twenty-six toll booth attendants were charged and a handful fined $1,000, a pittance considering the loot they had bagged over the years. One attendant was imprisoned for six months and another was so irate at being pushed off the gravy train that he broke into a booth and grabbed $400. The scandal sparked political bickering in Ottawa and a report noted that fraud had been reported to federal authorities 25 years prior. The province had a chuckle at the feds' expense, as they had been urging the tolls be removed since 1943. The tolls were finally taken down in 1962.

Monolithic monstrosity Endless white-knuckled bumper-to-bumper frustration occurred daily at Pine and Park, where 7,000 vehicles passed per hour, making it Montreal's

busiest intersection in the early 1950s. Planners resolved the congestion by demolishing over two dozen sturdy old homes and creating an overpass reminiscent of Stalinist East Berlin. Work was completed in 1961, as traffic lights were removed and so was born the costly new structure that begged motorists to slam down the gas pedal to bust through what was once a slow-go zone. The resulting mountain-adjacent Pine-Park Interchange was so comically hideous that it became iconic for its ugly mockery of the surrounding beauty offered by the

mountain. The highway-like structure formed a sort of Berlin Wall between the McGill Ghetto and the Plateau district, complete with a graffiti-welcoming wall along a tunneled pedestrian underpass. A chorus pined for its demolition in the 1990s while

others secretly wondered whether the gods would approve of messing with such imperfection. The structure was demolished and replaced by a more verdant $25 million intersection in 2007.

Tunnel drama The tunnel on Ontario near Moreau has long offered stony, gloomy passage but for a few brief minutes in 1924 it hosted a payroll heist that left two dead, a city shocked and led three thieves, including a local heartthrob, to the gallows. Handsome Louis Morel could outrun and out-wrestle all comers and he further impressed when he was fired from his police inspector job for trying to start a union. He was reinstated but dismissed permanently in 1920 for having some dodgy underworld friends, including Mafia boss Tony Frank. Morel then led a gang in a meticulously-planned $142,000 heist that required setting up metal chords to entrap a Bank of Hochelaga car that was transporting payday cash, just weeks before the advent of armored cars. A bank courier and a bandit died in the tunnel shootout and police found an address in the dead man's pocket. Cops proceeded to Coursol Ave. where they arrested more of the thieves. An initial trial flopped and so gunman Ciro Nieri was offered immunity in return for testifying against his crew, a first in Canada. A jury took 12 minutes to find the gang guilty in the retrial and five were sentenced to hang. Morel forgave his betrayer and was the only one to confess to the misdeed. He pleaded for clemency for one of his accomplices, whose hanging was commuted to life in prison. Hangman Arthur Ellis whistled a jazz tune as he hanged Morel, Frank and another accomplice. Nieri was killed in underworld slaying soon after. Mayor Médéric Martin was voted out and his replacement Charles Duquette could do little to probe police involvement in Morel's caper, as all power lay with the Chairman of the Executive Committee. The resulting Coderre Commission denounced police bureaucracy but its recommendations were ignored by a hostile provincial government until 1928 when Executive Committee Chairman Brodeur died and sweeping changes finally implemented.

Morel & Frank

INDEX

PHOTO CREDITS